INTERNATIONALIZATION

DEVELOPING SOFTWARE FOR GLOBAL MARKETS

TUOC V. LUONG
JAMES S. H. LOK
DAVID J. TAYLOR
KEVIN DRISCOLL

JOHN WILEY & SONS, INC.
NEW YORK ✦ CHICHESTER ✦ BRISBANE ✦ TORONTO ✦ SINGAPORE

Publisher: Katherine Schowalter
Senior Editor: Diane D. Cerra
Assistant Managing Editor: Angela Murphy
Text Design & Composition: North Market Street Graphics, Dave Erb

Library of Congress Cataloging-in-Publication Data

Internationalization : developing software for global markets / Tuoc V. Luong . . . [et al.]
p. cm.
Includes bibliographical references.
ISBN 0-471-07661-9 (pbk. : alk. paper)
1. Computer software—Development. 2. International trade.
I. Luong, Tuoc V.
QA76.76.D47I599 1995
005.1—dc20 95-10551

Printed in the United States of America
10 9 8 7 6 5 4 3 2 1

About the Authors

TUOC V. LUONG is Vice President of Client/Server and International Development at Borland International. He is responsible for the development of the Borland Delphi, Reportsmith and Interbase product lines. He is also responsible for internationalization and localization of all Borland products, including Paradox, Quattro Pro, dBASE for Windows, ObjectVision, C++, Pascal, and Delphi. Mr. Luong was involved in internationalization from the early days of Uniforum's internationalization */usr/group*. He has been a long-time contributor to standards groups such as Uniforum's Internationalization Technical Subcommittee and Unix International Internationalization Working Group, and currently represents Borland on the Unicode Consortium. Prior to his association with Borland, Mr. Luong was Director of Advanced Technology for Pyramid Technology, directed Asian Development at Oracle Corporation, and founded the International Development Group at Informix Software.

JAMES S. H. LOK founded Borland's European Localization group over six years ago, and continues to manage this group today. He has managed localization into more than fourteen languages of products such as Paradox, Quattro, dBASE, C and Pascal compilers, Sprint, Reflex, SideKick, and ObjectVision. Mr. Lok created Borland's original internationalization strategy, designed and implemented Borland's standardized Software Translation Kit, and has developed several innovative processes for delivering localized products.

About the Authors

DAVID J. TAYLOR brings more than twelve years of software development and quality assurance methodology design and automation to his current position as International Program Manager for Microsoft. As Manager of International Quality Assurance for Borland International, he was responsible for all test planning and execution for the dBASE for Windows Asian localizations, and worked extensively on managing QA for many European localization and enabling efforts. He served as Vice President of Software Development for Sold Software, Inc., a leading developer of specialized office automation software for the real estate industry.

KEVIN DRISCOLL has more than seventeen years of experience in developing user-education materials for the small-systems software user, including research, design, and development of technical documentation, on-line help systems and CBTs, classroom courseware, and interactive multimedia and video presentations. He founded the Publications and Training departments at Gupta Inc., and worked for three years in Internationalization at Borland, managing the localizations of the C++ and dBASE for Windows product lines. Currently, he is working as Program Manager for Borland's Delphi product line.

Contents

Contents

Foreword

The international revolution is changing the software industry forever, and *Internationalization: Developing Software for Global Markets* is the book you'll need to change with it. Finally, in one place: Everything you need to know about why, when, where, and how to localize your product has been collected by some of the best people working in international development today.

The rewards of internationalization and localization are high: You'll have access to markets dozens of times larger than just the United States. But the process of getting there has traditionally been a haphazard minefield of varying problems. In this book, Tuoc Luong, who revolutionized international software development at Oracle, Informix, and now Borland, works with his management team to show you all the aspects of what it really takes to create great international software. They cut through the jargon and confusion you hear from vendors and magazine articles to give you just the real facts you need to get your internationalization and localization jobs done right, the first time.

If you are even *thinking* about whether to localize your software product, this is the book for you—it shows you the tradeoffs to help you decide. If you've already started the process, this is also the book for you—it gives you the concepts straight, and tells you the pitfalls to avoid. I think you'll be very pleased with this book regardless of whether you've never done a localization, or you've done a hundred.

PHILIPPE KAHN
Chairman of the Board
Borland International

What Is Internationalization?

Any product can be localized. It's a matter of how long the process will take and how much effort must be expended. The challenge is twofold: to localize applications as quickly as possible with a minimum of resources and costs, and to enable an application to sell worldwide without localization.

Half or more of most large American software companies' revenue is generated outside the United States due to the companies' worldwide marketing strategy. These software products, however, are often biased toward users who speak English and use U.S. conventions. To be competitive in the international marketplace, the software must communicate with end-users in their native language with local conventions. Successful companies make the transition from designing American-centric software to internationalized software that supports multiple languages and conventions.

Current Localization

Currently, most companies provide native language support by replacing the U.S. bias with the local country bias. The result is a localized version that meets the requirements of a particular market. However, such versions do not meet the requirements of other markets. For each country, the process must be repeated and yet another version of the software must be developed. The static binding of language and local conventions to the software creates numerous versions of the product: French product, Japanese product, and so on. This is very costly to develop, maintain, support, and localize.

Recently, a new technology has emerged and is named appropriately, *internationalization.* Internationalization allows the dynamic binding of language and local conventions to the software. The result is one software program capable of supporting multiple languages and conventions.

Internationalization Concepts

People often confuse internationalization with localization. It is important to make a distinction between the two. Internationalization provides the framework and structure in which localization takes place more easily and more efficiently. Localization is the process of targeting the product for a local market by translating the product and adding local, specific features where applicable.

A simple analogy can be made with automobiles. Cars in the United States have the steering wheel on the left side, while cars in the U.K. and Japan have the steering wheel on the right side. Each of these options is a localized solution requiring multiple production lines. However, if there were a way to create a chassis that allows a steering wheel to slide to the left or right and lock in place, that's an internationalized solution: one production line to deliver products for multiple markets. This may not be possible with a physical entity like an automobile; however, it's possible—and recommended—with software.

What This Means to Software

For software companies, the goal of internationalization is to have software that can run anywhere in the world without having the source code changed or recompiled for different languages and local conventions. This requires the software to be independent of language, code pages, and local conventions. Only at runtime will the software determine which language and local conventions to use and the code page with which to interpret the data. As with the

automobile analogy of "one production line to deliver products for multiple markets," in software, we have one source code base or, ideally, one version of the software for multiple markets.

Most companies start out with one product on one platform. As revenues grow, the company may port the product to multiple platforms, as well as add new products. The development, maintenance, and support complexity is then two dimensional: a *product-line* axis and *platform* axis. New features or bug fixes are done not only on a particular product, but also apply to that same product on multiple platforms.

For larger international software companies, the development, maintenance, and support complexity becomes *three* dimensional: In addition to multiple products on multiple platforms, these companies also have targeted multiple international markets in their worldwide marketing strategy. When a company fixes a bug or adds a new feature, the company has to make sure that the bug fix or new feature is available on multiple platforms, as well as in multiple language versions. The three-dimensional development scenario can be expensive in both resources and time (see Fig. 1.1). How can a company reduce the complexity of its development environment?

Object-oriented technology allows *reusable* software *components,* which will shrink and decrease the complexity of the product axis. Engineering *portable code* will shrink and decrease the complexity of the platform axis. Developing *internationalized code* will shrink and decrease the complexity of the language and market axis.

Many companies understand object-oriented technology and are moving toward sharing components, and class libraries. Fewer companies understand portability. And even fewer companies deal with the issues of the language and market axis. To fully address the language and market axis, these companies are developing and using internationalization technology. They are developing software for the international marketplace, not just for the U.S. market.

Why Is Internationalization Important?

Internationalization is important for the following reasons:

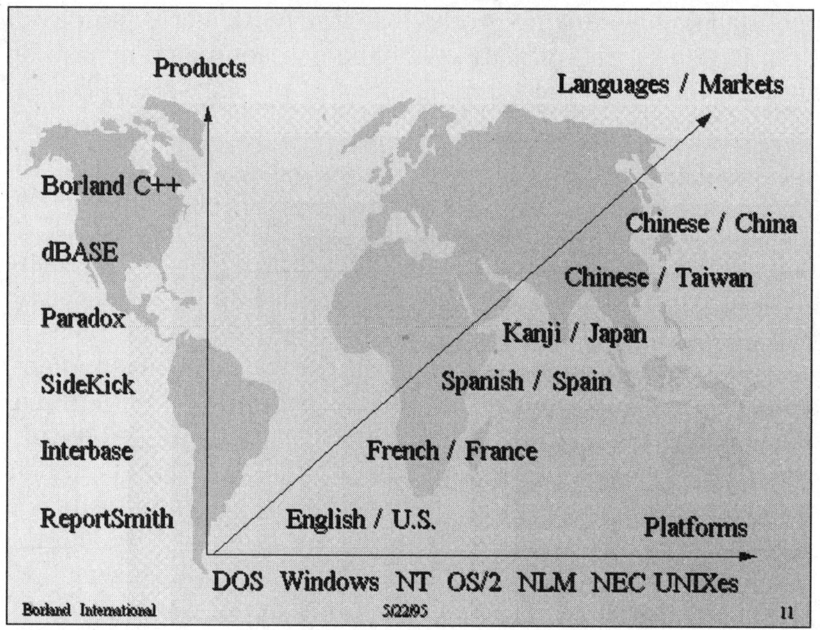

Figure 1.1 Three dimensional complexity of software development.

- ✦ Enables U.S. product to be sold worldwide.
- ✦ More efficient development of quality localized software product. It's much easier to create a German product if the English product already works with German data.
- ✦ Faster time to market for localized software product. Once the product is released in the United States, all the international requirements are met. No additional enabling development is needed and thus no in-line version of the U.S. release is necessary. Localization can even be started in parallel with the U.S. development cycles.
- ✦ Consumes fewer resources, time, and money for localization. Adding international support after the U.S. product is released requires an in-line version. An in-line version requires a recertification of the U.S. functionality all over again in addition to the international features. This means

you cannot leverage off of the original version's quality assurance (QA) effort as much. This means more resources, time, and money are spent to deliver the localized version of the software.

- Single-sourcing of code is possible and thus maintenance is easier and less expensive. If the international requirements are done up front, no in-line version or branching of the source code is necessary. Maintaining a single source code is much cheaper in terms of bug fixing and adding new features.

Internationalization/Localization Levels

A software product can be enabled and localized at various different levels.

English Product Only

One option, of course, is not to enable or localize the software product at all. The result is that the software is an English-language product only. The product can sell in the United States and possibly in other English-speaking countries like the U.K., Australia, Singapore, and so on. The important word is *possibly*: Certain types of software (often vertical packages like accounting software) cannot be sold in non-U.S., English-speaking countries because they are so dependent on conventions used only in the United States.

English Product Handling European Data

At this level, the product is not localized. Both the on-screen user-interface and the printed documentation are in English. However, the product is enabled to handle most single-byte character sets used in European countries. Additionally, the software is enabled to handle the cultural conventions used in the European countries.

An example is the English version of Borland's database product, such as dBASE for Windows. Although the on-screen user-

interface and documentation are in English, dBASE for Windows can process most European data using Borland's Language Driver technology. Each table in dBASE for Windows is tagged with the current Language Driver ID at creation time. The Language Driver provides the information necessary to process and collate text for that particular language. Additionally, the product can handle multiple date, time, and monetary formats above and beyond the U.S. formats.

Figure 1.2 shows English dBASE for Windows running a German dBASE for Windows form. In other words, a German user would have no problem using the English dBASE for Windows to develop a German application. The English dBASE for Windows can process German data both in the dBASE table and as text labels on the dBASE forms.

Figure 1.2 English dBWIN running German dBASE form.

The result is that the English version of dBASE for Windows can sell in many of the European countries because it can process European data. Of course, a localized version will sell even better.

English Product Handling Far-Eastern Data

Enabling software to process text used in Far-Eastern countries like Japan, China, Taiwan, and Korea is more complicated and requires more expertise than it would be for European text. It requires changing the logic of the U.S. product and could require re-architecting the U.S. product. Enabling for the Far East may require architecting the software for hardware independence as well. In Japan, the most popular PC hardware is the NEC hardware, which has the Intel processor but is not compatible with U.S. PCs. You will find more detailed information in the chapters on enabling and localizing for Far-Eastern countries.

Figure 1.3 shows an English dBASE for Windows browsing a table containing Kanji data.

English Product Handling Bidirectional Data

Similar to the Far East, enabling software to handle data from the Middle East requires special logic and architecture. Middle-eastern texts are bidirectional. Hebrew or Arabic text goes from right to left, but western text or digit will go from left to right. It's common to see a mixture of text used in the Middle East. (Middle-Eastern internationalization is not covered in this book.)

Full or Partial Translation of English User-Interface and Documentation

In addition to enabling the software to handle different languages, there is also the need to translate the on-screen user-interface (menus, dialogs, help, error, and status messages) and printed documentation.

Translation is often the most expensive component of any localization project. If budget is limited and the marketplace is not sufficiently large to warrant a full translation, partial translation can

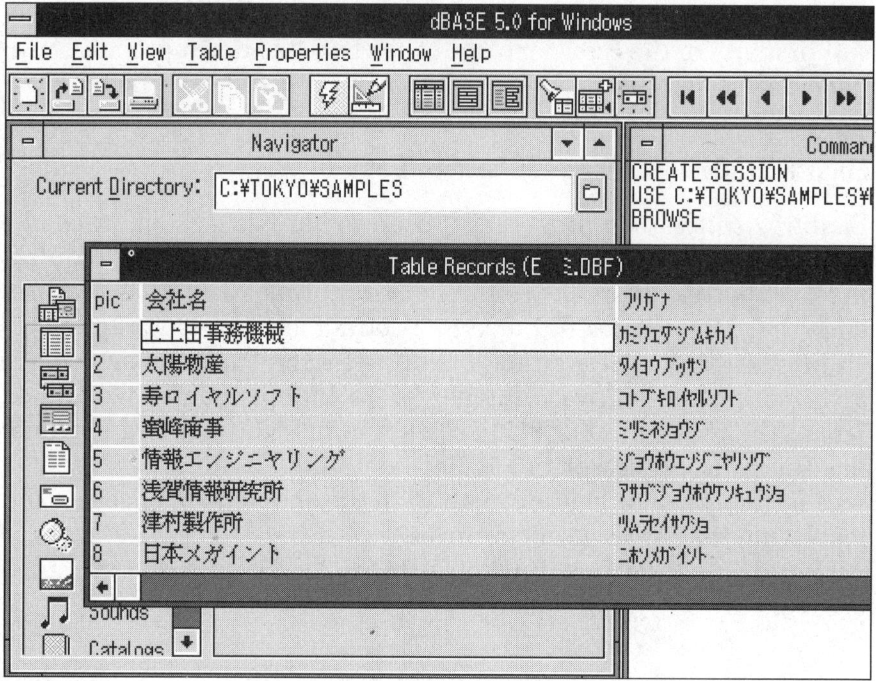

Figure 1.3 English dBWIN accessing table with Kanji data.

be done. Below are some of the components that a company may choose to translate or not translate in a partial translation of the software product:

- User-interface
- On-line help
- Tutorials (CBTs)
- Sample programs
- Printed documentation

Partial translations are usually done with products that are developer oriented. For example, in France, Italy, and Spain, only the documentation is translated for Borland C++. The reasoning is that C/C++ programmers are to some extent English proficient. In

some marketplaces, it may even represent a status symbol that the programmer is using the English software programming environment. In other markets, such as Germany, Borland has found that even developer-oriented software products need to be localized. Both Borland C++ and Borland Pascal products are fully localized in Germany because the market is larger and demands full localizations.

Most end-user-oriented products require full translation of the user-interface (UI) and documentation. Application-type products are end-user oriented. If the application is being used by an end-user such as a secretary or data entry operator in a foreign country, it's unlikely that he or she will understand English well. Full translation is necessary including all the components mentioned above. The ideal situation is for the end-user never to suspect that the product was developed in another country.

Full Localization Plus Local Market Features

The ideal product for a local market is not only fully localized, but also has local market-specific features. The European markets are similar to the U.S. marketplace. Other than support for language and cultural conventions, the U.S. product features are often sufficient for the European marketplace as well. The Asian markets tend to require additional features to be competitive. For example, Borland shipped a Kanji version of dBASE for Windows that includes many specific features, beyond those of the U.S. product, that are important to computer users in Japan. Some of these include:

- Kiri import (a popular local database product in Japan)
- Import/export of Lotus 123J formats
- Auto-furigana (automatic phonetic entry)
- In-line IME (input method editor) conversion
- dBASE language enhancements specific to Asia, including IME control functions
- Japanese word wrapping in dBASE editor
- Japanese sorting and indexing

The point here is that your competitors in the United States may not be your competitors (or your only competitors) in foreign markets. There may be popular products in your category that were developed locally. You need to be competitive with those products as well, which may require you to implement local-market-specific features beyond those in your original product. For example, in Japan, there is a popular DOS database product called Kiri with over 100,000 installed users. It's important that your product be able to import the Kiri data format.

Different Companies/Different Options

Depending on the size of your company and the size of your market outside of the United States, your company may choose to localize a product at a particular level. What's important is to focus on the return on investment (ROI) whether you are doing partial localization or full localization. It's important to capture the full costs of localizations and count only the incremental revenue associated with the localized product.

Even when the ROI is not attractive, your company may still decide to localize the product for a particular market. They may consider a particular market strategically important in the long run, and thus view localization for that market as a strategic investment. Later chapters cover the ROI issue for localized products in more detail.

CHAPTER 2

Components of Internationalization

Internationalization poses many challenges. Many people make the assumption that one need only extract and translate the text of the software to provide *native language support.* Although extracting and translating text is in itself a complicated and expensive endeavor, it is only one of several components of internationalization. Most of the issues associated with internationalization fall under the following areas:

- User-interfaces/on-screen and printed documentation
- Character classification
- Character transliteration
- Numerical/monetary formats
- Date/time formats
- Collation or sorting
- Regular expressions
- Encoding schemes
- Text directionality
- Character versus byte processing
- Input method editors (IMEs)

The key to internationalized software is not to hard-code any of the above components in the source code. All this information should be kept *external* to the source code. The software should be able to use this external information to communicate with users in their own language and local conventions at runtime.

User-Interface

The most obvious part of an international environment is the text that end-users see. This includes error messages, help text, menus, prompts, and graphics. All of the text should appear in the user's native language. This text should be resourced outside of the source code. Consideration must be given to the growth of and spacing between items, since translation often expands text. Expansions can occur both horizontally and vertically, because Asian fonts can be both horizontally and vertically larger than their western counterparts (see Fig. 2.1). The result is that the translated text may not fit the space originally provided.

Special consideration should be given to computer-based training (CBT) components. CBTs should be translatable like other online text. Ideally, CBTs should also be customizable in terms of the logic and sequence of tutorials. Different cultures may approach tutorials in different ways and the CBT components should be easily customizable in the both the text translation as well as the structure of the tutorials.

Printed documentation is another critical component of the product. Documentation should be internationalized as much as the software components. Translation is much easier when the documentation does not have U.S.-specific idioms or metaphors. Equally important are the tools that the Technical Publication

Western Font	Far-Eastern Font
abcdefg	ａｂｃｄｅｆｇ
ABCDEFG	ＡＢＣＤＥＦＧ
	ニホンゴ日本語

Figure 2.1 Western and Far East font comparison.

department uses. If the tools are not readily available worldwide, then conversion(s) to the proper tool is necessary before translation is even possible. All these considerations make the translation process easier and, more importantly, less expensive.

Graphical interface should have the same consideration as text. Icons should be culturally neutral, if possible, or a mechanism for easy replacement of icons should be in place. Any text in icons should be resourced separately from the graphic image itself. Some icons that are perfectly acceptable in the United States may be offensive in other parts of the world. Some icons may make perfect sense or invoke the right metaphor in the United States but may not make sense at all in other marketplaces around the world.

The icon in Figure 2.2 is from a popular spreadsheet software package in the United States. The icon containing an American baseball coach is appropriate for the United States or Japan, but would not be appropriate where American baseball is unknown and "coach" may refer to a transit bus.

An important part of the user-interface that's often overlooked in terms of internationalism is the packaging of the product box itself. The box forms the potential customer's first impression of your product. Color schemes that may draw the customer to the shelves in United States retail stores may not be appealing to potential customers in other parts of the world. Contents on the box that are perfectly acceptable in the United States may be illegal in other parts of the world. For example, competitive comparisons of features are illegal in Germany. If your U.S. box has a table comparing your product features with those of a competitor, the table must be removed from the German box. Careful planning up front will save time, and more importantly, be less expensive and more effective in reaching the customer.

Figure 2.2 Icon represents a coach in a popular spreadsheet.

Classification

Different languages classify characters differently. English classifies only 52 characters as "alphabetic": [A–Z] and [a–z]. Any other characters are not considered alphabetic characters. Unfortunately, most software applications are hard-coded with the English character classifications. This means that a database application that restricts identifier names to U.S. alphanumerics would not accept an accented character in an identifier. This would not suit a user whose native language includes accented characters. The foreign user would not be able to create database, table, or column names containing accented characters. Imagine a French user wanting to create a school database. The word for school in French is *école.* The application may reject it with an *invalid identifier* error, since *é* is not considered an alphanumeric. For example, the following structured query language (SQL) statement would fail if the database management system (DBMS) does not accept accented characters as part of an identifier:

```
Create Database École; {Will fail due to illegal character}
```

This is a limitation in the DBMS. European users have come to accept such limitations since only a few of their characters will be restricted (and only if the advantages of using the particular DBMS outweigh the limitations). Asia is another story. In Asian languages, such as Chinese or Japanese, almost all of the characters used are phonetic and ideographic, not alphabetic. Not allowing phonetic and ideographic characters in Asia is unacceptable. The classifications (isalpha, islower, isupper, etc.) must be language definable. In addition, there needs to be a mechanism to define additional classifications not present in the English language (for example, isdiacritical, isdbcs, isphonetic, isideogram).

```
SET TALK OFF
INPUT "Please input your name in double quotations:" TO sName
IF ISDBCS(sNAME) = .T.
  ? "KANJI NAME ENTERED. NAME :"
  ?? sNAME
ELSE
```

```
  sNAME = BTOW(sNAME)
  ? "NON-KANJI NAME ENTERED. NAME :"
  ?? sNAME
ENDIF
```

The previous example is a dBASE for Windows code segment that checks to see if the input name is Kanji or not. If it's not Kanji, then the input name is converted to the double-byte equivalent prior to displaying. The example is, of course, contrived but it illustrates the usage.

Transliterations

On most systems, the C programming language provides the macros toupper(c) and tolower(c) to perform case conversions from lower to upper and vice versa. However, these macros are often biased toward the English language and ASCII code page. If you look at a typical implementation of the toupper(c) and tolower(c) macros on most systems, you would see the following:

```
#define    toupper(c)  ((c) - 'a' + 'A')
#define    tolower(c)  ((c) - 'A' + 'a')
```

This method of case conversion works only for the English language and more specifically the English language as represented by the American Standard Code for Information Interchange (ASCII) code page. In ASCII, lowercase alphabetic characters have numerically contiguous values. This is true for uppercase characters as well. In addition, both lower and uppercase characters have the same relative ordering. This is not necessarily true for European or Asian code pages. How can a developer get the uppercase of the character *é*? Calling toupper('é') will not work on most systems.

The table must be read in at runtime and must be user definable. In addition, the table must be able to handle Asian languages as well, which means it cannot be a simple array of 256 characters. Asian character sets can include double-byte versions of the western alphabet. Transliterations between the single-byte western character to a double-byte version may be desired. The above example shows the usage of a byte to widechar function *btow()*.

Numerical Formats

Numerical formats differ from one country to another. The representation of numbers varies with respect to the symbol indicating the radix character (separating the integer from the fractional portion of the number; in the United States this is the "decimal point") and the digit-grouping symbol. For example, the United States and Germany both represent numbers using decimals and commas, but the symbols are interchanged (5,434.25 versus 5.434,25). The radix and digit-grouping characters are not restricted to just "." and ",". For example, countries like France may use a blank character as the digit-grouping symbol.

Country	Numerical Format
United States	5,434.25
Germany	5.434,25
France	5 434,25

Monetary Formats

Monetary formats also vary from one country to another. The radix and digit-grouping symbols are usually the same as those used in the numerical format. In addition, the currency symbol and its position relative to the monetary value changes from one country to another. The currency symbol for the United States is the dollar sign "$" and it precedes the amount, as in $5. In France, the currency symbol is "FF" and it follows the amount, as in 5 FF. In countries such as Portugal, the currency symbol is placed in the middle of the amount separating the currency's whole and fractional units.

To further complicate things, the local currency symbol differs from the international currency symbol associated with a particular country. For example, the currency symbol used locally in the United States is "$". However, internationally, the U.S. dollar currency symbol is "USD".

Date and Time Formats

Most Western countries use the Julian calendar, while Middle-Eastern countries use a lunar calendar, based on cycles of the moon.

Asian countries often use multiple date formats. Japan uses both the Julian calendar format and a format based on the number of years the current emperor has reigned. Taiwan and China use a date format based on the number of years since the start of the current era.

Even if you limit the discussion to the Julian calendar, the date formats differ from one country to another. Below are different outputs of date formats for the same date:

Country	Date Format
United States	Wed Aug 15 10:25:14 PDT 1990
Italy	mer, 15 ago 1990 10.25.14
Germany	Mi., 10. Aug 1990 10:25:14 PDT

Collations

Sorting in most applications means sorting in the codepoint order, which is in the ASCII code page order. The ASCII sorting order is not correct for foreign languages, nor is it sufficient for the American English dictionary ordering. Following are some characters and their ASCII numerical values:

Char	A	B	C	...	Z	...	a	b	c	...	z	...
Value	65	66	67	...	90	...	97	98	99	...	122	...

Note that with the ASCII numerical ordering, all uppercase alphabetic letters sort before any lowercase alphabetic letters. This means that the letter *a* sorts after the letter *B,* which is incorrect in the American English dictionary order.

ASCII Sort	Dictionary Sort
BOBBY	angela
Beth	Beth
angela	BOBBY
david	david

The sorting concept permeates many systems. For example, the File Manager in Windows displays the filenames in a directory sorted. This is a tremendous help in locating a specific file in a crowded directory. However, it is important to realize that the sorting order that most of us are accustomed to is just that, a *custom.* And, as such, it is only one of many customs, each equally natural to its users.

The sorting conventions of foreign languages are in general more complex than the sorting convention Americans are accustomed to. Non-English alphabetic sorting includes:

- 1-to-2-character mappings (*ß* sorts as *ss* in German)
- 2-to-1-character mappings (*ch* sorts between *c* and *d* in Spanish)
- Don't-care characters (the hyphen and em-dash)
- Primary sort, secondary sort, and so forth

The collation properties mentioned previously apply to alphabetic languages. Asian languages and conventions have not been addressed. Asian ideographic characters represent concepts. The western notion of sorting is not sufficient for ideographic languages such as Chinese and Japanese. If you have the "haha" (mother) character represented by 0x95EA and the "chichi" (father) character represented by 0x9583, how do you determine which character is first? Does "mother" sort before or after "father"? This is a strange question if taken from a western cultural point of view. However, Asian languages can be sorted by many methods. For example, Kanji text can be sorted by its phonetic representation, by the number of radicals (atomic parts) that makes up the Kanji character, and/or the number of strokes that makes up the Kanji character.

Regular Expressions

Often overlooked but associated with collation are regular expressions. Regular expressions are patterns used for searching text in data. Pattern matching is used in many applications. Once again, the pattern matching in most applications is biased toward English and the ASCII code page. For example, most users mean "all lowercase letters" when they specify "[a–z]." However, with alphabets that do not end with *z*, "[a–z]," meaning all lowercase letters, does not apply to that alphabet.

In some languages, there are collating elements that are made up of more than a single character (e.g., *ch* in Spanish collates after *c* but before *d*). How do you specify a regular expression that represents *a, b, c* or *ch*? The regular expression [a–ch] does not work ([a–ch] means *a, b, c* or *h*). Additional regular expression syntax is needed. An international regular expression syntax was created by X/Open for this and other purposes. Now, one can use the regular expression [a–.ch.], where the multicharacter collating element is surrounded by periods.

Regular expressions need to be extended further for the multibyte character sets used in Asia. For multibyte character sets, pattern matching must now be done on a character basis regardless of the character size in bytes. Metacharacters like "?" must match any single-byte or multibyte character. When searching for "\", the software must be able to find the single-byte character "\" and not necessarily the second byte of the double-byte "Hyou" character (0x955C), which happens to contain the same byte value as the single-byte character "\" (0x5C).

Encoding Schemes

One of the most important and most difficult components of internationalization is dealing with multiple encoding schemes or code pages. An encoding scheme illustrates the one-to-one mapping between a character and the computer's bit representations. The most common code page is ASCII; unfortunately, it does not support much more than the English language.

Most American developers are so used to the ASCII code page that they often overlook the fact that there are many other code pages besides ASCII. Because of this, developers tend to write code with ASCII-specific assumptions. This can lead to misinterpretation or, in the worst case, alteration of non-ASCII data. More specifically, ASCII is a 7-bit code page capable of representing 128 characters. This is sufficient for the English character set. Armed with this knowledge, developers use the extra eighth bit to store additional information. The problem arises when the software has to deal with data coming from 8-bit or multibyte code pages. The software looks at only the lower 7 bits of each byte in reading the

data. What is worse, some applications strip the eighth bit when sending or writing out each byte of data.

Even with an 8-bit code page, you can represent only up to 256 characters. Far-Eastern languages that use ideographic characters require a character set containing thousands of characters. One byte is not sufficient. You must use at least two bytes to represent the characters in these languages. The double-byte character set (DBCS) was created to handle the far-eastern languages. DBCS encoding schemes use 16 bits to represent each character. In theory, this means that each DBCS code page can represent up to 65,536 characters. However, in practice, this is not true.

Most DBCS encoding schemes try to be totally compatible with the ASCII code page since ASCII data is so prevalent throughout the industry. DBCS code pages maintain compatibility with ASCII by ensuring that the first byte of the double-byte character is always equal to or above 0x80. This allows algorithms to determine immediately whether or not the next byte represents a single-byte character, by simply checking the value of the first byte. This compatibility limits the number of characters that a DBCS code page includes. Actually, DBCS is a misnomer. The DBCS used in the Far East is not truly *double-byte* as the name implies. It should more realistically be called multibyte character set (MBCS), since it is a mixture of single-byte and double-byte characters. For example, in Japan, the Kanji characters are double-byte, but the Latin characters used for western words are single-byte as are some of the Kana characters.

Unicode is a true double-byte code page because every character in Unicode is encoded with two bytes. For example, Latin characters, such as the letter *a,* are represented by two bytes in Unicode (0x0061). Unicode is totally compatible with the basic multilingual plane (BMP) of the ISO 10646 character set standard. Chapters 4 and 13 will discuss Unicode in more detail. You can also consult publications available from the Unicode Consortium and ISO.

Character versus Byte

The need to support multibyte code pages creates many problems that did not exist before. The scope of the problem in providing multibyte support can be summed up as character versus byte pro-

cessing. Contrary to most developer's belief, they produce code that is byte oriented rather than character oriented. This is because for most developers, a byte and a character are interchangeable, because in ASCII every character is represented by one byte. This does not hold true in the international arena. Incrementing your character pointer by one (ptr++) may or may not get you to the next character in the string. The same is true for screen display in terms of character width.

The concept of character versus byte seems simple enough. However, text processing permeates applications software. To satisfy one requirement of processing text based on characters versus bytes requires the modification of a lot of code. In addition, associated with multibyte characters are new problems and considerations that do not exist with single-byte characters:

- Truncation and splitting of characters
- Wrapping and splitting of characters
- Window borders and splitting of characters
- Regular expressions and pattern matching by characters, not bytes
- Memory size versus display size
- Variable size cursor movements and editing, insertion, and deletion based on characters

Text Directionality

Most Latin-based scripts are left-to-right oriented. Hebrew and Arabic texts are bidirectional. Hebrew and Arabic characters go from right to left. However, numbers and Latin characters intermixed with Arab text, are still written from left to right. For Asian languages, the ability to edit, display, and print vertical text is also expected. Text directionality raises many issues, including scanning issues for user-interface:

- Left-right/top-down
- Right-left and left-right/top-down
- Top-down/right-left

Directionality is not limited to display issues only. If software is scanning or parsing for an open bracket, is it "[" or is it "]"? The answer depends on the direction in which you are scanning or parsing.

Far-Eastern Input Methods

Far-Eastern character sets like Kanji include thousands of characters. Obviously, a keyboard cannot provide keycaps for all the characters. Asian operating systems as well as many third-party companies provide software-driven input method editors (IMEs). The software-driven IME provides the user with the capability to enter thousands of different characters into an application. Most of these IMEs are based on phonetic conversion.

For example, Japanese keyboards do not have keycaps for Kanji characters. They only have keycaps for numeric, Kana, and English characters (Romaji). As such, there are basically two ways to enter Kanji characters into an application. One way is the tedious task of entering hexadecimal representations of Kanji symbols (similar to the Alt-xxx method of most PC keyboards). The second and more popular method is by using an IME with Kana-Kanji (Japanese phonetic conversion) converter. The process is as follows:

The user has a choice of entering the Kana or Romaji keys (phonetic spelling of Kanji characters). If Romaji, there is a parser that converts it to Japanese phonetic spelling (Kana). The Kana is then converted into a Kanji character using a Kana-Kanji dictionary lookup. The Kana-Kanji conversion may produce many Kanji homophones from which the user has to select the one he or she wants. The sophistication of the Kana-Kanji conversion will determine the amount of selection that the user will have to do.

Figure 2.3 shows the Kanji version of dBASE for Windows integrated with the IME. The IME window is shown popping up where the cursor is positioned. This may not always be the case depending on how an application is integrated with the IME.

Additional Areas

There are additional platform and application specific internationalization issues. This chapter covered the generic issues that are

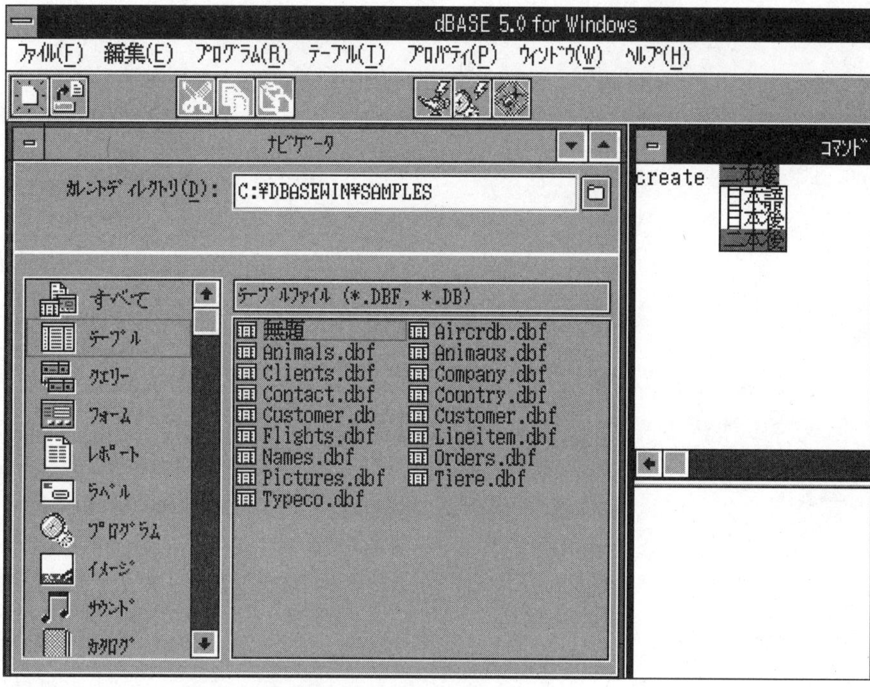

Figure 2.3 Kanji dBASE for Windows.

common to all applications and platforms. An example of an application specific issue is an accounting software package. The accounting software needs to consider variable accounting practices in different countries like value-added tax and pre-dated versus post-dated checks. This is in addition to the generic international issues like dates, time formats and so on. Application specific issues are too broad to be covered in this book.

CHAPTER 3

Corporate Support for Internationalization

The single most important requirement to achieve truly internationalized software and thus efficient localization is support from upper management in the corporation. Support from upper management has to come in many different forms. Obvious support is to provide resources and budget to focus on internationalization and localization of software products. But although this is a necessary requirement, by itself it's not sufficient.

Education

Support from upper management should not be limited to resources when requested; it must be at a deeper level. The corporate culture must be a global culture where day-to-day activities and operations are performed in a global manner. Everyone from junior staff up to the CEO must think and act globally on a daily basis. It should be second nature to every employee. Education is the way to achieve this mindset.

Education needs to occur at all levels, from the entry-level staff on up to top management. We need to educate all the development engineers to think globally when designing and coding. We need to educate the managers to think through the international implications of business and legal decisions. Awareness that international issues are important is a start; however, awareness is often at the surface level only. A company needs to push the global mentality deeper, to a more fundamental level.

Education of the engineers can be achieved through three avenues: communication, the International Functional Requirement Document (IFRD), and the International Guide for Programmers and Writers.

Communication

Communication between the core and international engineers must be free and ongoing. They must function together as one team. The international engineers must function and be accepted as part of the software product development team. The international engineers must be involved from the very beginning of the software design process and not just pulled in as an afterthought. Just as Research and Development (R&D), Quality Assurance (QA), and Publications work together as a virtual team on a single product, the international engineers must be part of the virtual product development team to create a global product.

Communication from management to the core engineers on international revenue ramifications plays an important role in reinforcing and educating the engineers in thinking and designing internationalized software. It's a strong motivation factor when an engineer realizes that half of the revenue for his or her product may be coming from outside the United States. This communication must be ongoing and part of the corporate culture.

International Functional Requirement Document

The IFRD defines "what a product must be able to do" to be accepted in worldwide markets. The IFRD is a checklist for programmers and writers to see if their work is properly enabled for localization or not. An example of Borland's European IFRD is included as Appendix D in the back of this book. The document is useful both as a functional specification and as an educational tool.

The IFRD can be used as a checklist for all engineers and techwriters to follow. It's important that the checklist be enforced by the Development and Publications managers. How can it be enforced? One way is to make it part of the job requirement of every engineer and techwriter to follow the IFRD guideline. IFRD compliance can be part of an engineer's, a techwriter's, and a manager's formal review. These workers are reviewed based, among other things, on technical skills, timely delivery, and quality of their design and code. Companies should add "how localizable is the code or documentation" to the list of criteria on a performance review for programmers and writers.

The IFRD should be appended in all third-party contracts. It's common for software companies to license or sometimes acquire third-party software products or components. The IFRD can be used as part of the contract to ensure compliance for the global marketplace.

International Guide for Programmers and Writers

The IFRD defines what a product must be able to do to be accepted in worldwide markets. The International Guide for Programmers and Writers illustrates how a programmer or writer can go about achieving the requirements in the IFRD.

The international handbook should not be limited as a general internationalization concept book. Rather, it should be very hands-on with specific examples on how to program or write for the global marketplace. For a programmer, it should include detailed usage of the proprietary or platform-specific international application programming interfaces (APIs).

Management Education

The internal education on international awareness needs to be widespread and not limited to just engineers and their managers. Top management has to be committed to achieve success in the international marketplace. International awareness and commitment need to be more than just at the surface level. Management must work and function on a global basis daily and not just when international issues are raised. In fact, management itself should be the first to raise the international issues.

When negotiating with third parties on licensing, it's important that management understands the ramifications of the contract worldwide. It can be very costly if contracts are signed without a clear awareness and understanding of international implications. An example can be licensing a third-party component to be included as part of your product. It's important to check the availability of localized versions of the third-party component. Part of the contract should include the deliveries of localized versions when possible, and if not, then access to the source code or resource files so that localization can still be done. For the Asian marketplace, the contract might need to include all source code in order to localize and port to different hardware, such as the NEC hardware in Japan, for PC applications.

When acquiring technology or a company, due diligence must be given on a global basis as well. When acquiring technology, it's important to make sure that you have all the source code that's necessary to compile from scratch and produce the product. All source code is not always available. For example, if the acquired technology includes third-party components, then you need to check if the source code is available or just the binaries are available. You need to follow the chain of technology all the way through to make sure that you have source code to all the components.

When acquiring a company, it's important to make sure you understand the company's presence in the international marketplace. Among the questions and issues to resolve are:

- Where does the company have subsidiaries and where are its distributors?
- Are the subsidiaries wholly owned or joint ventures with a local company or companies?
- Do any of the distributors have exclusive rights in a particular country and, if so, for how long?

- ✦ How is the company or its product viewed internationally? (Just because a company or product is popular in the United States does not guarantee international acceptance or vice versa.)

Management is the initial point for many critical external business developments. It's important that management is educated to make the mental shift necessary to be successful in a global marketplace.

Design versus Retrofit

Education is a continuous process. Few companies start out immediately recognizing the need for internationalization. It's only when companies grow and expand into the international marketplace that the need for international education is recognized. It's at this point that management appoints or hires people to focus entirely on international issues and deliver localized versions of the software.

From a software perspective, it's always better to design up front for the international marketplace. Internationalization is much simpler and less expensive if designed in from the beginning. When international issues arise or become critical, it's often with existing products. With existing products, you have to deal with the retro-enabling of the software for efficient localization as well as with backward-compatibility issues, because the product is already out in the marketplace.

At one stage in Borland's history, the company was organized by business units. Each business unit had its own development group that was responsible for delivery of its product worldwide. One of the business units took the approach of developing solely for the U.S. release first. They felt it was important to get the U.S. release out as quickly as possible; then they would focus on retrofitting and localizing the software for the international marketplace. (Contrary to popular belief, international enabling from the beginning seldom if at all delays the U.S. release of the product.) In this example, the product was not designed properly for localization, with the result that the localization effort was very expensive in both money and time. The time to market of the localized versions was too long after the U.S. release of the product so that international revenue for the product was only about 20 percent of the total product revenue. Borland products generally generate about 50 percent of their revenue from outside the United States. This product was the exception because it was not enabled properly for localization.

We are not suggesting that this will happen each time for all products that focus only on U.S. markets. However, the potential for such a disaster is there unless the development, design, and implementation are done with the global market in mind. Shortly after this, Borland centralized their international development team worldwide under one organization.

Organizational Structures

There are several ways to organize the development teams to do the international enabling and localization work:

- One centralized development team is responsible for both the U.S. and localized versions of the software worldwide.
- The core development team is responsible for the U.S. release as well as the internationalization enabling work necessary for localization. Another centralized localization team is responsible for all the localized versions of the software.
- The core development team is responsible for the U.S. release as well as the internationalization enabling work for localization. Each subsidiary office or region is responsible for the localization work to produce the localized version(s) for their marketplace. They are also responsible for working with distributors or outside services to do the localization work for markets where the company does not have a physical presence.
- The core development team is responsible for the U.S. release. A centralized international development team is

responsible for the internationalization enabling and localization of the software on a worldwide basis, including dealing with distributors for markets where the company has no presence.

There are advantages and disadvantages in each of the organizational structures described above. Some structures fit small-sized companies better, and some structures fit large-sized companies better. There are a lot of variables for why a certain structure is a better fit for a particular company. However, we will discuss how Borland is organized and the benefits we see in such an organizational structure.

Borland is organized with a core development team that is responsible for the U.S. release of the software. A separate development team, which is centralized, focuses on the internationalization enabling and localization of the software. Of course, there's a lot of cooperation between both development groups and the core team does a lot of the internationalization enabling work. However, it's ultimately the international development team that's responsible for making sure that the software is enabled for localization. After all, it's the international development team that pays the price if the software is not properly enabled (resulting in a more difficult, time consuming, and expensive localization of the software).

International development is centralized under one organization. However, the team is distributed throughout the world. The majority of the team is located at headquarters. There are also development teams in Tokyo and Singapore as well as translation people in different countries throughout Europe. All of these teams are centralized under the Vice President of International Development.

There are several benefits from this organizational structure:

- ✦ International development is represented even at the upper-management (vice president) level. International development is properly represented in upper-management discussions of all subjects (strategy, resource allocations, acquisitions, third-party licensing, cost control).

- All international development costs are captured in one centralized budget. This makes it easier to assess the true cost of localization and thus the return on investment (ROI) of localization for any particular language market.
- Resources are all fully focused on the enabling and delivering of the localized versions. If international resources are part of the core development team, there's a natural tendency to pull those resources to help deliver the U.S. version and thus ignore the enabling issues or put them at a lower priority (especially under the tremendous pressure of shipping in the shrinkwrap software industry).
- Internationalization and localization technologies are standardized and shared among the localization efforts of all the company product lines. This benefits the company in many ways. For example, there can be a single software translation kit among all the product lines. If the translation vendors that a company deals with do not have to learn a new translation environment each time they translate different products, this means less time and money spent on localization projects.
- A centralized international development team will be able to share similar enabling or localization problems and solutions among different products.
- The structure gives the international development team a sense of identity and creates a stronger centralized force in educating for a more global approach to product design and development. If the international development team were not centralized under one organization, international awareness and education would not be as strong or widespread throughout the company. Various smaller, distributed international voices do not carry as strong a weight as one single focused voice that has support from the entire international development team worldwide.
- It gives the international engineers or managers more career opportunities without their having to leave the international development area and focus. If international development was distributed instead of central-

ized, it would be difficult to attract and keep talented people for a sustained period of time.

For different companies, different structures may be more appropriate. Borland went through several different ways of organizing the international development effort and found the centralized worldwide organizational structure to be the best one for them.

Hardware/Software Needs

Besides human resources, special hardware and software are needed and can be quite expensive. Hardware can range from foreign keyboards to expensive NEC PCs or other OEM PCs for the Japanese marketplace. You may also need additional specialized peripherals, such as printers and monitors with different resolutions, that are popular in localized markets outside of the United States.

For software, you will need localized versions of the operating systems, network software, and third-party software. For example, in testing the Kanji dBASE for Windows version, Borland had to test it against MS Windows 3.1J on both DOS/V and NEC systems, Netware/J, LAN Manager/J, and Sybase/J. In addition, there are localized versions of developer tools and productivity tools that may be needed on the localized platform and OS. This software can be very expensive, in addition to the hardware.

Simultaneous shipment of U.S. and localized software will require network systems to facilitate quicker and easier transmission of translation work and disk images for manufacturing in the local regions. Often the R&D and QA work are done at headquarters in the United States, while the translation is done in the local country. Access to a Wide Area Network (WAN) or equivalent means of fast file transfer is indispensable. Time is money when dealing with simultaneous shipment of localized products and the U.S. version.

These hardware, software, and network systems are incremental to the normal capital equipment budget needed for the U.S. release of the software. Upper management support is necessary to budget these incremental costs so that simultaneous shipment of the U.S. and localized versions is possible.

Small versus Big Company Strategies

Your company's investment in hardware, software, and network systems will obviously depend on its size and the size of the international marketplace for your company's products. The size of your company may also determine the investment and type of localization you take. You may choose to simply enable the U.S. software to sell in other language markets but not do any localization work. You may choose to do only partial localization as opposed to full localization. You may choose to focus your localization in only the European markets because it's easier and cheaper than the Asian markets.

A small- to medium-sized company may decide to focus only on the four largest language versions: English, German, French, and Japanese. (English is included here to reemphasize the fact that even an English version needs to be enabled properly to sell well in English-speaking countries outside of the United States. Enabling the English version properly will help to avoid the retrofitting problem described earlier in this chapter.) As the company and its international revenue grows, it may choose to expand into other markets that are smaller but have great potential, such as Italian, Spanish, Chinese, and Korean.

CHAPTER 4

Internationalization and Development

Enabling Technology

In the past few years, internationalization technologies have substantially matured. There are now many sources to obtain internationalization technology from. Many companies such as Borland have internal technology to handle the enabling of their software. (Borland's internal technology will be discussed in detail later in this chapter.) There are also a few independent software vendors (ISVs) selling their own version of internationalization technology. Global software is becoming more and more of an issue for everyone. System vendors are now starting to include internationalization technology as a sellable component of the operating system.

Many UNIX system vendors are standardizing on the set of internationalization APIs as defined by POSIX and/or X/Open. Microsoft is adding more and more internationalization APIs in its Windows 95 and Windows NT operating systems. Apple has had great internationalization APIs and development environment with its script manager from the beginning. We won't discuss the details of these operating system services; you can get various books from the operating system vendors as well as some third-party books.

Internationalization versus Localization

It's important to understand that internationalization technology will help enable the software for efficient localization. However, internationalization technology will not yield a localized product. Chapter 1 discussed briefly the difference between internationalization and localization. We will now elaborate on these concepts.

Any software product can be localized. It's a matter of how long the process will take and how costly it is. The challenge is to localize applications as quickly as possible with a minimum of resources and costs. One way to localize a product is to replace all U.S./English-specific code with that of the local country's language. This technique, at first glance, may seem to be the fastest and most efficient way to localize. The reality is that this technique has proven to be the slowest and most error-prone way of localizing a software product. The technique yields a localized product that is probably sufficient for one particular market. The entire process has to be repeated for each market your company would like to enter, which is very inefficient. It's error prone because it relies on a hit-and-miss method rather than a systematic method to localize. You will be chasing a continually moving target because the developer has not learned anything. The developer will continue to develop software with hard-coded U.S./English bias. You will never be able to keep up with all the developers in the company by merely replacing the U.S./English bias with, say, France/French bias—not to mention all the other countries' languages.

A better solution is to work with the developers to internationalize their software. At the same time, educate them to use the internationalization technology to enable future versions of their software. Remember the old proverb: "Give someone a fish and you will feed him for a day. Teach someone how to fish and you will feed him forever."

This is where internationalization technology comes into play. Rather than replacing the U.S./English-biased data, the developer should be taught to extract all the U.S./English-biased data outside of the code into a central location. The data is then read in at run-

time when needed. We are using the generic term *data* here to mean all the components that may change from one local market to another (the main internationalization components were discussed in Chapter 2).

Internationalization Technology

Borland's internationalization technology uses the POSIX locale model. However, Borland's international API extends usability beyond the POSIX specification. Borland's technology includes a Borland Locale Compiler (BLC) (Figure 4.1) and a set of international APIs. The BLC takes two source files (character map and locale definition) as input and generates a "locale library" containing one or more locales. A *locale* consists of the international data (mentioned previously) for a particular language and market that

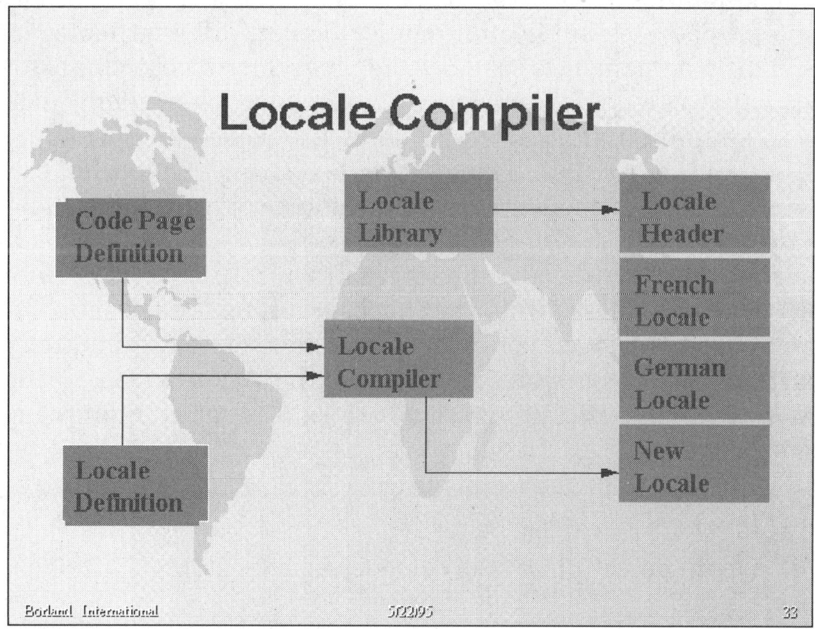

Figure 4.1 Borland Locale Compiler architecture.

Borland sells to. The locale library is a binary data file that is accessible from an application through the internationalization APIs.

The BLC takes two input files to separate the character-encoding mapping information from the locale definition information. This way, multiple locale definitions can be applied to the same character-encoding mapping. For example, both the French and German locale definitions can be applied to the same character map file representing ISO 8859/1 character encoding.

The international API loads the data from a particular locale into memory and operates from it. With the API, a program can switch locales on the fly or work with multiple locales at the same time. The API allows a developer to create applications independent of language and local conventions. This is internationalization. The details of the locale can be left to the experts in the native country to define outside of the source code. This is localization.

The API supports multiple clients and maintains multiple locales for each client. This makes provision for applications and other APIs and libraries to manage objects of different languages. For example, a database application could display different tables or fields in different languages at the same time. Once an object is associated with a locale, knowledge of language-dependent data becomes simplified and culturally correct. Locales are opened by name, which is a U.S. ASCII single-byte text string. All locales' categories loaded into memory are shareable between clients (and threads).

The concept of how to use the internationalization APIs is quite simple. The examples in this chapter use Borland's internationalization syntax. However, concept and sequence of calls are pretty similar regardless of whether it's Borland, the Windows NT, or the UNIX APIs. The application basically goes through the following sequence of calls:

- BL_Init()
- BL_OpenLocale(IphLocale, category, Ipszlocale)
- Blx_xxxx call(s)
- BLT_StrCollate(hLocale, IpszStr1, IpszStr2) as an example of a BLx_xxxx call

- ✦ BLx_xxxx call(s)
- ✦ BL_CloseLocale(IphLocale)

BL_Init() initializes, registers, and verifies API usability for the client. This call must be used by all clients of the API. It ensures a correct and maintainable individual environment for the client.

BL_OpenLocale() opens the *Ipszlocale* for use by the API for the specified *Category.* A locale handle is returned in *hLocale.* This function accesses narrow, multibyte, and wide locales. *Category* is a value consisting of one or more of the predefined supported category constants OR'd together. Basically, BL_OpenLocale() loads the locale data into memory for future BIx_xxxx() calls to operate from.

BLT_StrCollate() collates the two strings *IpszStr1* and *IpszStr2* based on the locale handle *hLocale.* The locale handle *hLocale* gives BLT_StrCollate() access to the locale data in memory as loaded from the previous BL_OpenLocale() call. BLT_StrCollate() is defined at compile time to be BLN_StrCollate(), BLM_StrCollate(), or BLW_StrCollate() depending on whether you are dealing with narrow, multibyte, or wide-character strings. Details on narrow, multibyte, and wide-character types will be discussed in the next section.

BL_CloseLocale() closes the locale specified by IphLocale and deallocates all memory for the locale.

The code segment in the next section is taken directly from the source code of dBASE for Windows, which was internationalized using Borland's internal technology. The German version of dBASE for Windows shipped on the same day as the U.S. version. Borland shipped six European languages within three months of the U.S. release. The Kanji release (which included many new features not included in the U.S. release) was shipped within three and a half months of the U.S. release, followed a month later by both the Korean and Traditional Chinese versions. The Simplified Chinese version was released a month after the Traditional Chinese version. All this was accomplished with a brand-new product and code base. This required a tremendous amount of teamwork between the teams at headquarters, Tokyo, and Singapore. Borland's internationalization technology helped significantly in maintaining a single code base worldwide and leveraging everyone's work.

Narrow, Multibyte, and Wide Characters

Borland's internationalization technology is based on the notion of three different types of characters: narrow, multibyte, and wide. There is a *type* character that is set at compile time to be one of the three: narrow, multibyte, or wide. A narrow-character definition means that every character is encoded by a single byte. A multibyte-character definition means that a character can be encoded by one or more bytes. A wide-character definition means that every character is encoded by two bytes.

The API set is reflective of the character types. Each API function has a BL (Borland Locale) prefix that may be followed by either a T, N, M, or W.

- T indicates that it is a *type*-character version
- N indicates that it is a *narrow*-character version
- M indicates that it is a *multibyte*-character version
- W indicates that it is a *wide*-character version

Providing different types of character-handling functions allows clients to run in different character-handling modes. Clients can handle either narrow, multibyte, wide characters, or all three simultaneously. Using compile time definitions, the generic character *type* can be set and fixed. However, all character-type APIs are available.

The advantage here is that client applications can be built to work in wide-character mode as well as be recompiled to work in narrow-character mode. This method is utilized to ensure that narrow-character-only processing can still be performed in cases where being wide-character only is unnecessary or has memory and performance issues. Here is an example taken from the dBASE for Windows source code illustrating the usage of the different APIs depending on the type of characters: narrow, multibyte, or wide. Note that a BL_Init() and BL_OpenLocale() would have been called prior to this section of code being called and that BL_CloseLocale() will be called at some point afterward.

```
//----------------------------------------------
//       IntlStrCollate
//----------------------------------------------
// Collates according to the language driver
// case sensitive order (cs_order table)
//----------------------------------------------
extern "C" int IntlStrCollate(const tchar * pStr1, const tchar * pStr2)
{
   if (GLOBALLDOBJECT && BLTYPE(GLOBALLDOBJECT))
   {
      switch ( BLTYPE(GLOBALLDOBJECT) )
      {
      case BL_NARROW:
         if ((GLOBALLDOBJECT)->DriverID == 0x1B)
            return tstrcmp (pStr1, pStr2);
         else
            return BLN_StrCollate( BLHANDLE(GLOBALLDOBJECT), (nchar *)
pStr1, (nchar *)pStr2);
      case BL_MULTI:
         if ((GLOBALLDOBJECT)->DriverID == 0x13 ||
               ((GLOBALLDOBJECT)->DriverID == 0x19 && SET_ON_OFF
(Ld19As13)))
            return tstrcmp(pStr1, pStr2);
         else
            return BLM_StrCollate( BLHANDLE(GLOBALLDOBJECT), (nchar *)
pStr1, (nchar *)pStr2);
      case BL_WIDE:
         return BLW_StrCollate( BLHANDLE(GLOBALLDOBJECT), (wchar *)
pStr1, (wchar *)pStr2);
      case BL_WIDE_FROM_NARROW:
        {
         if ((GLOBALLDOBJECT)->DriverID == 0x1B)
            return tstrcmp(pStr1, pStr2);
         else
          {
            return BLN_StrCollate( BLHANDLE(GLOBALLDOBJECT), CSTRING
(pStr1), CSTRING(pStr2));
          }
        }
      case BL_WIDE_FROM_MULTI:
        {
         if ((GLOBALLDOBJECT)->DriverID == 0x13 ||
               ((GLOBALLDOBJECT)->DriverID == 0x19 && SET_ON_OFF
(Ld19As13)))
            return tstrcmp(pStr1, pStr2);
         else
          {
            return BLM_StrCollate( BLHANDLE(GLOBALLDOBJECT), CSTRING
```

```
(pStr1), CSTRING(pStr2));
            }
        }
      } ;
    }
    return tstrcmp(pStr1, pStr2) ;
}
```

Wide Characters and Unicode

We will discuss in more detail the concept of wide characters in this section. According to ANSI C, the size of a wide character (wchar_t) is implementation defined (please see the ANSI C standard for more detail). Borland treats a wide character (wchar_t) as a 16-bit entity. Wide characters are useful because double-byte ideographic characters are treated in the same way as single-byte Latin characters.

As mentioned previously, far-eastern languages are represented by multibyte character sets (MBCS). In MBCS, a character can be one or more bytes. For example, Shift-JIS (Japanese Industry Standard) is a popular encoding scheme used in most Japanese PC systems. In Shift-JIS, a character can be one or two bytes. This requires special handling in processing Shift-JIS characters. Something as simple as moving to the next character in a string requires special handling. The programmer must check to see if the next byte is a single-byte character, or is actually the first byte of a double-byte character. Moving back one character in a string is even more cumbersome, since a second byte of a double-byte character may in fact fall in the range of the ASCII characters. (This is discussed in more detail in Chapter 13.)

The wide-character data type allows an application to treat ideographic characters the same way ASCII characters are treated. If an application treats every character internally as a wide character, then moving forward and backward in a string is no problem, since every character is fixed width. The application simply has to convert all characters coming into the application into wide characters, and back to their original form when exiting the application boundaries. The disadvantage, of course, is that the application uses more

memory since every character is double byte. There may or may not be performance issues related to continuous conversions to and from wide characters at the application boundaries.

Recently, the Unicode character encoding has been getting widespread coverage in the software trade magazines. Unicode is a true double-byte character-encoding scheme. Every character in Unicode is 16 bits regardless of what language the character is part of. As an example, the letters *A, B,* and *C* are encoded as 16 bits each, 0x0041, 0x0042, 0x0043, just like ideographic characters (e.g., Kanji characters) or any other symbols in Unicode. This means that software can treat each Unicode character equally in terms of size; no passing ahead and other special processing for different characters of different languages. This means incrementing to the next character or decrementing to the previous character works exactly like it did with ASCII characters. This means that randomly indexing into arrays can be done without fear of landing at the second byte of a double-byte character (e.g., indexing into an array of char containing SJIS characters). Unicode can be viewed as a multilingual ASCII. In fact, Unicode was modeled after the ASCII code set. You can get more information on the Unicode encoding scheme from Volumes 1 and 2 of *The Unicode Standard,* available from the Unicode Consortium.

This leads to the question: Why not use Unicode as the encoding scheme for wide characters? In fact, this was what Borland intended to do during the Asian version of the dBASE for Windows project. We had planned for dBASE for Windows to process everything internally as 16-bit wide characters and our wide-character representation was going to be Unicode. At the application boundaries, dBASE for Windows would convert to and from Unicode from and to the native code set of the keyboard input, display output, printer, and file system (Figure 4.2).

However, Borland chose not to use Unicode as the representation for wide characters. We discovered a round-trip conversion problem using Unicode (discussed in detail in Chapter 13). In the end, we chose to have the Asian version of dBASE for Windows process generic wide characters internally, where the bit pattern of the wide-character representation was not fixed. The only guarantee is that a wide character is 16 bits in size.

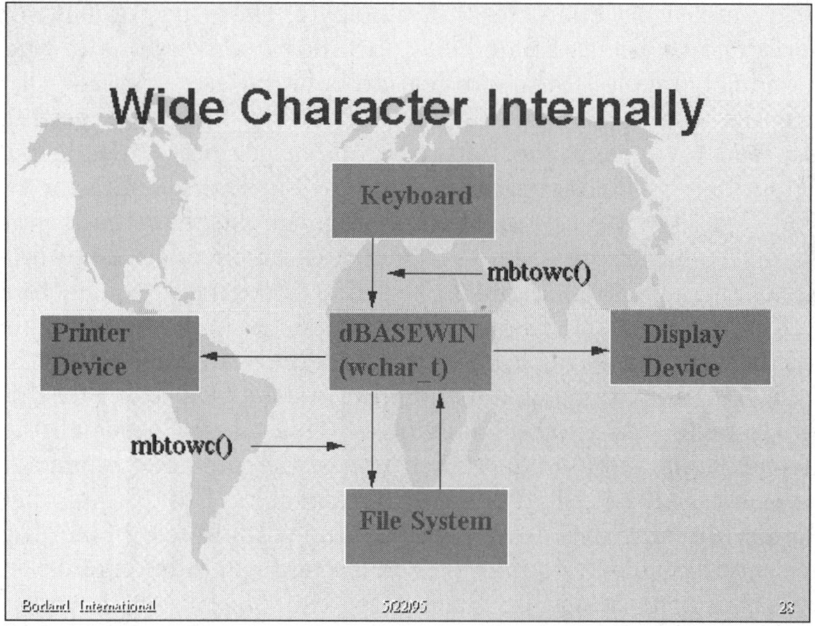

Figure 4.2 Example of wide character processing.

Influencing the Core Development Team

The IFRD and Internationalization Programmer's Guide mentioned previously are excellent tools to influence the core development team to properly internationalize their code. These will make the U.S. release of the product sellable around the world, as well as enable the software for efficient localization. The programmer's guide should be tailored to the company's products and platforms. Some platforms will provide a lot of internationalization API services. If so, the programmer's guide should talk about how to use the operating system's internationalization services.

If a platform does not provide any internationalization services, then the company must either develop internal internationalization technology of its own, or license it from a third party. The company may choose to develop its own internal internationalization technology whether or not the platforms provide it. This is because of the following reasons:

- ✦ Multiple platforms may support different levels of internationalization services. Some platforms may not support any. If cross-platform support is important, a company may choose to develop its own internationalization technology and port it to different systems, thus guaranteeing consistent behavior.
- ✦ If an application needs to process and sort data in its own peculiar way (for whatever reason), then it makes sense to develop its own character processing and data APIs. For example, dBASE for Windows has to sort and process characters in the same way that dBASE DOS did before. Windows 3.x or Windows 95 internationalization collation APIs will not be able to sort the way dBASE does in each of the target international markets.
- ✦ An application may have to work with third-party applications and networks that may process data in their own unique ways. For example, in a client/server environment, dBASE for Windows has to be able to mimic the way an Oracle SQL server collates text data to ensure compatibility. Having control over the internal internationalization APIs provides the flexibility to change things on the fly.

The best way to influence core developers is to provide them the tools and documentation on how to enable their code. The IFRD and Internationalization Programmer's Guide will help in this endeavor.

CHAPTER 5

Internationalization and Documentation

Many software developers are surprised by the large role played by documentation in both internationalization and localization. After all, the application, its functionality, and its user interface are the most obvious and seemingly most difficult areas to localize. They're also the areas developers are most interested in.

However, in most software projects the volume of documentation is huge compared to that of the user interface. Often the costs of the documentation translation alone are several times the costs of the software translation. Also, since completion of the printed documentation is often the critical path of any software development project, document translation is usually the last part of any localization project to be completed.

Careful planning and thorough enabling can keep costs low and allow for quick time to market. In fact, careful documentation enabling and well-managed documentation localization can allow first-language localizations to ship on the same day as the U.S./English product.

When we talk about documentation, we mean both the *printed materials,* such as manuals, quick reference cards, keyboard templates, and so on, and the various types of *on-line information,* such as sophisticated help systems that interact with the program, CBTs (computer-based tutorials), readme files, text files listing known bugs, and manual correction files.

Most of us immediately think about translation when we consider these documents, and in this book we discuss document localization in subsequent chapters. But proper enabling of the documents in two areas is critical to success, and that is the subject of this chapter.

Just as in software enabling, document enabling falls into two categories: *international enabling,* and *localization enabling.*

✦ *International enabling for documentation* is the process of creating documents that are suitable for international distribution *without localization.* In these cases, the English-language product will be distributed in different counties and enabling steps must be taken to make sure the documentation is not too specifically American. In practice, this involves working with the document writers to make sure that they write appropriately for international audiences. This is especially critical when either the product or its documentation is not to be translated.

Important areas here are avoiding too-specific American idioms and clichés, and avoiding examples that aren't universally appropriate, such as baseball analogies or examples of W-4 tax forms. Also critical is clear writing and avoidance of jargon.

✦ *Localization enabling for documentation* requires working with the document writers in deciding the document production process. The document cycle should be planned to make sure the cycle of creating and revising documents allows for ease of translation and updates. Specifically, the document creation technologies must be considered to ensure that the tools they are using are appropriate for international translators, and that the technologies support the specific update needs of localizers. For example, using a word processor or desktop publishing tool that is not available in Europe or Asia creates unnecessary steps for the localization team.

The other area important to localization enabling is clear writing. This is related to the clear writing required for an international English product, but also includes writing for ease of translation.

Each of these areas is discussed in detail in the following sections.

International Enabling: Writing for an International Audience

In previous chapters we talked about enabling the software so that it is internationally useful even when it is not translated. Most of the same principles apply to enabling documentation that will not

be translated. No company or developer can afford to localize into every language on earth, and few can afford to localize into every language they want to sell into. Therefore, at some point most developers decide to sell their product into a market for which their product is not yet localized.

But even if you decide not to localize, you still need to consider that the international audience is *not* the U.S. audience, and target your documentation appropriately. Even if you are selling only into a marketplace where much of the customer base has proficiency in English, such as Germany, writing that remains Americanized will be confusing to your reader and detrimental to your product.

Clear Writing

First, the language used must be clear and easily understood by nonnative English speakers. This means you must:

- ✦ Keep sentences short.
- ✦ Use as few clauses as possible.
- ✦ Maintain active voice wherever possible.
- ✦ Maintain present tense wherever possible.
- ✦ Avoid synonyms.
- ✦ Keep vocabulary, especially technical jargon, to a minimum.
- ✦ Develop a standard glossary of technical terms—with definitions—so that your writers use each term specifically and consistently.

Using active voice is a particularly difficult issue for technical writing in general, for writing to an international audience, and for translation. Passive voice is used in most technical documentation: "The Open File dialog is displayed by selecting the Open button." Most writers and editors would agree that the following active-voice rewrite is superior: "Press the Open button to display the Open File dialog."

For the past decade or so, there has been a consistent effort in American technical writing to eliminate passive voice in favor of the clearer active voice. For Americans, active voice is less formal, more direct, and easier to understand. But due to cultural considerations, some European countries, and Japan, prefer to stay with passive voice, usually because rewriting for active voice often results in using the second-person *you* form. This is often called a friendly or even "chummy" style, and while most Americans prefer it, outside America many people prefer the more formal and old-fashioned passive-voice style where the user is never identified or referred to directly as "you."

For example, the passive-voice sentence, "If command-line options are preferred, refer to Chapter 7," would most likely be rewritten in America as, "If you prefer command-line options, refer to Chapter 7."

The second sentence, in active voice, is preferable for American audiences and easier to translate. However, since some Europeans and Asians prefer to retain formality, the decision of which to use is not always an easy one. Therefore, if you are not localizing or are localizing into a very few languages, then you should use active voice. If you are localizing into several languages, you may want to consider not using active voice so much in order to decrease translation confusion and costs.

All the above points are always important for clear technical writing, but for an international audience, they become *critical.* Most people involved in technical writing at any level are well aware of the importance of clarity and understanding even within the American marketplace, so it is easy to see that this is all the more critical for nonnative English speakers.

Cultural References

The product must be free of culturally specific references. Specifically, you need to make sure that all of your features, samples, references, graphics, and metaphors are named and modeled on concepts that will be familiar to non-Americans.

Features

Some Windows products refer to their computer-based tutorials (CBTs) and advanced user interfaces as "Tutors," "Coaches," "Wiz-

ards," or "Experts." You must be careful in considering such terms, because even though your international users understand English, they may not understand your reference. "Expert" has a specific meaning that anyone familiar with English will understand, but in many English-speaking countries a "Coach" is a carriage or bus, and the connotation of that word as an instructor is completely foreign.

Samples

If you want to show your user a sample form, don't show them one based on the American W-4 tax form; use something more universal such as a health history form. If you want to show a sample game application, don't use baseball, which is unknown outside the United States, Canada, and Japan; use something such as soccer, which is played the world over—but is called "football."

Be especially careful here in using addresses. Address fields in Europe are very different from those in America, and from those in Japan. However, in this case there is no universal substitute. You may want to try including both an American and a Canadian address example to show versatility.

Another problem here is paper size. The software may consider paper size as a function of the operating system (as does Windows), but your documentation may refer specifically to American sizes only.

References

Be careful not to refer your non-American user to books, on-line services, bulletin board services (BBSs), and periodicals that are only published in the United States. Also, be careful with references to power sources, television scan rates, video tape formats, and other technical specifics that are different outside America.

Also, be careful when using American cultural references. For example, you may not want to quote President Truman in a manual that will be sold in Japan without translation.

Graphics

You need to be even more careful about graphics selection than about any other issue. An icon of an open book may look like the book is open at the beginning to Americans, but that same icon will confuse users who read from back to front. Likewise, be careful of text icons that obviously show left-right paragraph divisions, or even horizontal lines; many cultures write vertically, and some that write horizontally write right-to-left instead of left-to-right. Graphics that represent certain kinds of buildings, such as schools, office buildings, factories, and of course churches, might also not apply well internationally.

Even animal graphics can cause confusion. For example, in some countries a pig symbolizes filth, but in China a pig is a symbol of wealth.

Be most careful when using graphics that portray human figures. Some cultures are very sensitive about portrayals of men, women, children, and the various races. One of us worked on a project where an icon of a genie was proposed—an icon of a man's head wearing a turban and sporting a drooping mustache. Is this appropriate in a product that will be sold untranslated in the Middle East? Perhaps so or perhaps not, but why take the chance of offending? In this case the genie icon was discarded.

In another case, an error message box is displayed with a orange-colored hand facing palm out. Later we were informed that an orange hand is the symbol of a freedom-fighting group in Northern Ireland and that some of our customers were concerned about it.

Here you may also have to make value judgments. You may have decided to use a graphic of a woman to introduce each chapter, or even a video of her in a multimedia presentation. Then you find that one of your biggest markets is a country where women in the workplace are discouraged. Do you change your decision? Is it a small issue of tailoring the product to the marketplace, or is it a capitulation to forces of oppression? Fortunately, such judgments are not the subject of this book, but you should be prepared in advance to make such decisions.

Localization Enabling: Writing for Translation

Writing documents that are to be translated poses a tough problem for any writer: Can the text be lively, interesting, and enjoyable to

read and at the same time easy to translate? Most of the time this is too much to ask of any writer, especially the typical harried technical writer working against a stiff deadline where he or she is lucky merely to get the material complete and accurate, much less interesting and easy to translate at the same time.

The most that can be expected in most software development situations is to give the writers a list of guidelines for writing for translation and work with them as time permits and during review cycles to help them keep to the most important of the principles.

First, all of the principles described in the previous section must be followed. Most of the issues that apply to writing English for international audiences also apply to writing for translation: Clear writing and cultural references are especially important. However, in writing for translation there is an important difference: You are writing for the ease of the translator, not necessarily for the ease of the reader. When writing English for an international audience, you must consider the cultural and clear-writing issues or your product is bound to fail. But when writing for translation, you have the relative luxury of knowing that native translators should be able to catch your mistakes. So, in a sense, writing for translation doesn't need to be quite as careful.

Of course, there is a tradeoff here as well: If you don't take care to address clarity and cultural issues, then your translation will take longer and cost more. Therefore, it's wise to address these issues diligently in the original writing, regardless of whether it will be used directly by international users or will be translated.

Most of the time we have to ask the writers to try to do both at the same time, on top of all their other concerns. Both require writing clearly and simply. The important difference is this: Writing for translation can be "cleaned up" during translation, but writing English for an international audience cannot. Unclear writing takes longer and costs more to translate, but can still be corrected—this costs you only money. However, writing that won't be translated doesn't have a second chance—and if it uses culturally misleading or even offensive metaphors it can hurt acceptance of your product. This costs you *more* than money—you can lose the trust and goodwill of your customers.

Summary of Principles of Writing for Translation

- Keep sentences short.
- Keep vocabulary small.
- Limit technical terms.
- Define all technical terms the first time they are used in each chapter.

Localization Enabling: The Documentation Cycle

Whether you know it or not, every company has a documentation cycle. And every documentation cycle is actually a part of both the internationalization and the enabling work in any project.

The documentation cycle is highly dependent on the user-interface (UI) development process. In the simplest model, the product is designed, then implemented, and then the documentation is designed and written after the UI is complete. However, this simple cycle is neither desired nor usual. Most products cannot wait for documentation to be written once the UI is complete—time-to-market pressures dictate that the documentation must be ready to ship as soon as the executables are ready. Even more important is the need to design the documentation as part of the product in tandem with the user-interface so that the product and documentation work well together.

Therefore, most documentation development follows the product development cycle closely. The following chart shows how documentation and development milestones are intended to work together during Borland projects.

Milestone	Development Task	Documentation Task
Beta 1	First release of product; core functionality is present; product is usually not stable. Specification should be complete by now.	Portions of reference documentation after one review cycle; often nothing is available at this point. Documentation Plan is complete.

Beta 2 (Optional)	Additional functionality is present; better stability. User-interface should be frozen.	Portions of each book and help system are done. All books, help systems, and CBTs are fully designed.
Beta 3	All user-interface features should be fully implemented; all features present but not all are working properly or completely.	On-line help and CBTs are first-draft complete; at least one technical review has been completed and all comments incorporated. Books are completed and go to print soon after this milestone.
Gamma	Product is complete, tested, and ready to ship; this should be the first release candidate.	Help and CBT are complete and fully tested, and all critical bugs have been fixed.
Release to Manufacturing	Product is fully tested and all critical bugs have been fixed.	Any last-minute additions to the readme files are done.

Let's examine more closely the specific milestones of documentation development, and show how they relate to localization.

Planning and Preliminary Design

In this phase the development manager puts together the Project Plan, or specification. Usually this document is intended to describe the features, functionality, proposed schedules, and implementation risks for the project. Often, but not always, this document also contains marketing information, such as competitive analysis, marketplace evaluations and potential revenues, and project justifications.

Ideally, this document also contains sections on testing, or quality assurance (QA), documentation, and internationalization, as well as others. The development manager usually looks to the QA

Manager, Publications Manager, and Localization Manager for input on these sections. Each of these managers should also prepare a separate, more detailed Project Plan for each of these areas.

The Documentation Project Plan should include:

- ✦ Definition of the intended users.
- ✦ Statement of that user's documentation needs.
- ✦ Detailed description of each book in the proposed documentation set, including estimated page count, number of illustrations planned (by type), and the name of the assigned writer or manager responsible for this book. Ideally, the assigned editor, production worker, and principal programmer assigned for information provision and technical review should also be added for each book.
- ✦ Detailed description of each help system in the proposed documentation set, including estimated size in number of topics and sometimes size in bytes (uncompressed), number of illustrations planned (by type), and the name of the assigned writer responsible for this book. As with the book description, additional personnel should be identified if possible.
- ✦ Detailed description of the CBT system and each tutorial proposed for the product, and the writer or programmer responsible for each tutorial. Depending on the CBT methodology being used, size and content information may or may not be detailed.
- ✦ Detailed proposed schedule. This is usually provided as output from a project scheduling software package, and is usually divided so that each book, help system, and CBT has its own section. Usually, milestone dates such as for research and writing, technical reviews, editorial passes, and delivery are included for each item. A detailed statement of the assumptions for the schedule should be provided here as well.
- ✦ International considerations, including the number of illustrations that are screenshots (and therefore must be reshot after the product is localized), the dates when first

translatable material will be available, and the criteria for that milestone (see *Eighty Percent Complete and Translation Start* section).

The Documentation Project Plan is an important tool for planning the localization. If your Documentation Manager is aware enough of international and localization issues, then you will benefit from his or her consideration of issues throughout the project, starting with the Documentation Plan. If your Documentation Manager is not internationally aware, you can work with him or her to ensure that localization needs are considered.

User Interface Design and Implementation

In this phase of the product cycle, the technical writers learn the product, define the users, and design the documentation part of the product: books, on-line help, and possibly CBTs. At this point the writers also start writing the actual text, starting with documenting the parts of the user interface that are already completed. As more parts of the product become complete, the writers continue filling out the outline of the designed manuals and help systems, and eventually enough material is available to begin the technical review cycles.

Technical Review

Usually by the time the product itself has reached a late beta stage, the first drafts of documentation have been written for every section planned in the documentation plan. At this point, the technical review cycles begin. Printed copies of the manuals are provided to critical team members and other writers, and a schedule is distributed and agreed to for every member of the review team to read the material and mark changes. Sometimes, specific individuals are assigned specific sections only to review, in order to preserve their time. Usually help systems are printed out and copied for technical review, so that comments can be written directly on the pages, which is easier for the writer during integration of comments.

Technical review periods usually last no more than absolutely necessary. The shorter the review period, the better, as reviewers tend to put off the review until the last minute (literally, the last day, or even hour, in many situations). A rule of thumb is to give team members no more than 100 pages per week to review; however, this is routinely violated due to aggressive schedules and late changes to the product that require last-minute changes in the documentation.

The writer collects the reviews at the end of the review period, and then incorporates the review comments and corrections into the original draft, producing a second draft. Optimally, at least two review cycles are desired; sometimes three cycles—with different individuals reviewing different sections—are used to ensure best quality. However, often a single review cycle is all that can be managed with many projects. No matter how pressed a product's schedule is, eliminating the review entirely should never be considered as an option, since technical accuracy and completeness will almost certainly be poor.

Documentation Localization

Technical review usually means that the first complete drafts of the manuals and help systems are done—and often people want to start translation immediately at that time. Many people assume that technical review produces a few clear technical corrections that can be easily mapped to a work that has already started translation—but in fact this is almost never the case. Technical reviews often produce complete rewrites of entire chapters, reorganizations of entire books, and removal or addition of significant sections. For this reason, translation should not be started at technical review if at all possible.

Eighty Percent Complete and Translation Start

However, sometimes translation cannot wait—as when translating for *simultaneous shipment* (see the discussions on simultaneous shipment in Chapter 8 for more detail). When the localized product

has to ship at the same time as the U.S. product, documentation translation cannot wait until the U.S. docs are done, as there is not enough time to translate and print before the U.S. product ships. In these cases, translation is started at an earlier milestone—often, at technical review.

We have used the phrase *eighty percent complete* to describe the translation start milestone. Ideally, this means that the documentation is at least 80 percent complete. Very often, the 80 percent date is essentially a technical review date, even though technical review is not the definition of this milestone. In practice, the deliveries at this milestone are not actually 80 percent complete, but the files have reached a point where the writer and the localization project manager have agreed that they are complete enough to start translation. This is often a very subjective evaluation.

Documentation Translation in the Simultaneous Shipment Model

For simultaneous shipment, documentation translation usually proceeds as follows: at 80 percent, documents are handed off to translators (translation start milestone). While the translators work to localize these products, the technical writers add the final changes until the final books are complete—often referred to as the *100 percent complete* or *to-print* milestone. The to-print documents are provided to the translators to make the final changes to their documents, which are now completely translated (or nearly so) at the 80 percent level. Ideally these changes can be made very quickly and the translated documents sent to a printer who has agreed to print the documentation on an accelerated schedule in order to ship the translated product at the same time as the U.S. product.

Problems with the Simultaneous Model

In practice, the simultaneous model poses several problems, all of which are related to the nature of software development: change.

The problem starts with the fact that the software product keeps changing even after the technical review period. In fact, in many cases the software product keeps changing even after the manuals have gone to print, which poses even worse problems.

When the technical writers and the localization project manager together make the determination that a document is 80 percent, that document usually is nearly complete—compared to the current, known state of the software product. What usually happens next is that the product changes significantly after this date, meaning that the material already handed off as 80 percent complete is more like 50 percent complete compared to the eventually released product. So, far more than 20 percent changes are made in the documentation after the 80 percent handoff. Very often, the document changes more than 50 percent between the 80 percent handoff and the final, to-print handoff. Of course, this means greatly increased costs for the translation, and much of what has already been translated must be reworked and retranslated before it can be considered final.

In general, these problems cannot be avoided except in an environment of highly structured software development. The best alternative is to avoid simultaneous shipment at all costs unless it has been unquestionably established that the increased revenue from simultaneous shipment will more than pay for the vastly increased costs of documentation translation required for the simultaneous shipment. This can boil down to a series of specific questions: If we wait six weeks for the translated version, how much revenue will we lose in that country compared to a simultaneous release? Does that increased revenue contain enough profit to pay for the extra costs of simultaneous shipment?

Much of the time you probably won't have enough information to make these determinations with any accuracy. However, the potential revenue gains of simultaneous shipment can be significant—as can the additional costs. The decision must be carefully considered and consciously made.

CHAPTER 6

International Enabling Quality Assurance

When we test the international enabling aspects of a program, our job is to assess the extent to which it is as functional in other cultures as it is in its native culture. Depending on the level of internationalization in the product, it could involve any or all of several areas:

- Checking that the program handles accented characters properly throughout
- Verifying that strings are sorted appropriately for every country we wish to support
- Testing support for different date, time, numeric, and currency formats
- Making sure that your program is capable of properly displaying translated messages
- Checking the availability of alternative measurements, paper sizes, and so on
- Testing compatibility with a reasonable set of hardware and software from other countries
- Checking all icons, bitmaps, and so on to be sure that they are all internationally sensitive

While this chapter focuses on European enabling, additional testing is needed if your product needs to be enabled for Asian markets (please refer to Chapter 13).

Much of this work is related to other core quality assurance (QA) tasks. We develop a quality plan and test outlines that discuss the enabling testing that we will be doing, write test suites, do ad-hoc testing to verify international functionality, isolate and report bugs, then negotiate the importance and impact of those bugs with the project managers and with research and development (R&D) engineers to be sure that they are fixed at the appropriate time.

Note that most of our experience is with shrinkwrapped PC software, and much of this chapter reflects that experience. We don't aim for bug-free products; our goal is produce high-quality software that is delivered in a reasonable time, with minimal risk and with a reasonable number of resources. To accomplish this in the international arena, we focus on black-box testing and we aim to control risks by getting broad coverage early in the core development cycle. If your organization has a different set of goals, such as producing mission-critical software, you will need to modify the QA concepts outlined in this book accordingly.

QA Documentation

Whether core engineers or those on an international QA team handle the enabling QA, there is a need for a clear definition of the work involved in ensuring proper international enabling, the level of quality expected, the responsibilities of each group, and the expected workload. This is the International Quality Plan. It should provide enough information so that the QA, R&D, and project managers involved will know how international enabling issues will be tested and who is responsible for each aspect of them.

In addition, each engineer writes a detailed description of the testing in the area for which he or she is responsible. These are the Test Outlines. These outlines have several purposes:

- ✦ They can be used to bring new engineers up to speed as quickly as possible. If one of the engineers leaves unexpectedly, someone new should be able to get an overview of the project from the Quality Plan plus detailed information on his or her test area from the outlines.

- If we are not using automated testing tools, the test outline should act as a guide for each pass of the testing.
- If we are automating our testing, the test outlines should provide the basis for the test suites we write.
- The test outlines should provide a good overview of the testing coverage done by each QA engineer for review by the manager. The QA manager can use these to suggest holes in the outlines, to make sure that there is no overlap between two or more of the outlines, and to make sure that no areas of the product are missed.

Engineers are often reluctant to write test plans and test outlines because of time constraints and because many prefer to implement test suites than write documentation. However, it's important to remember that the planning process is a necessary element of quality assurance whether or not the planning is documented. The documentation of that planning is a small part of the process.

The International Quality Plan

There are many workable formats for such a plan, but it should contain at least the following elements:

Overview of the Product

- What is the product; what does it do; who is the target audience?
- What will be the level of international enabling in the product?

Overview of the Plan

- What are the reasons for writing the test plan?
- What is the target audience for the plan?

- ✦ List other pertinent documents.
- ✦ Where is the retrieval and archival information for the document stored; when and why was it last updated?

Purpose/Scope of the Testing

- ✦ State that you will be testing for international enabling issues and are not responsible for other areas.
- ✦ Give general types of international functionality that will be tested.

Exclusions

- ✦ What are some specific areas of the product that are outside the scope of your testing responsibilities (and might be construed otherwise)?
- ✦ Who or which group is responsible for each area?

A Description of the Testing Approach

- ✦ How will the enabling testing be carried out?
- ✦ How will the work be shared?
- ✦ What form of automation will be used?
- ✦ What tools will be used?

Responsibility for Enabling QA

- ✦ Who is testing the international enabling aspects of the product? Which aspects will be covered by core engineers? Which will be covered by engineers specifically assigned to cover international enabling? Which will be covered by people in foreign subsidiaries?
- ✦ What is the relationship between the international QA engineers and the core QA engineers?

- What is the relationship between core and international R&D engineers?

Information on External Testing

Are you planning on using beta sites or bug hunts to supplement your enabling testing?

An Overview of Resources Required for the Project

- How many QA engineers will be required, and what hardware and software will they require?
- What special hardware and software will be required, say, for compatibility testing or for storing and backing up test suites? Will you need localized versions of operating systems or localized versions of competitive products?

A High-Level View of the Areas to Be Tested

- Will you divide the testing by functionality of the product or by international functionality?
- How is each area delimited? What is the general approach for testing an area?

General Schedule for the Project

- Provide a high-level functional decomposition of the project (described in the next section), with broad estimates of the length of time required for each phase and for each aspect of the testing.

Quality Expectations

What level of quality do you expect to achieve for each milestone, including final release?

Test Outlines

When a QA engineer is assigned an area to test, she or he generally writes a test outline to describe in more detail the process for testing. It consists of the approach to the testing, the source of testing materials (such as whether the test suites are based on related test suites from other groups), a list of every item that will be tested and how it will be tested, and a detailed estimate of how long it will take to write test suites and how long it will take to run them and analyze the results.

It's critical that the test outline clearly defines two things: the *test domain,* the list of items that are to be tested, and the set of *test cases* that will be applied to each item in the domain.

The test domain is derived by doing a *functional decomposition.* Every functional aspect of the test area is listed, then each of those is successively divided into more and more detail until each item on the list is a single, testable element. For instance, if the test area is the File | Open dialog in a Windows product (a test area is generally broader than this), the functional decomposition would include the filename field (which can be further divided into filename and file extension, depending on preference), the file list, the directory name field, the directory list, the drive selection field, and the file type selection field. In addition, it should include navigation in the dialog (by mouse, pickletters, and the tab key), the Okay, Cancel, and Help buttons. Notice that this is multidimensional; each of the editable fields must be tested with each of the buttons.

We must apply test cases to each one of these items. For internationalization QA, the test cases for the filename will include a variety of names that contain accented characters with and without extensions that contain accented characters, entering directory names that contain accented characters, and so on. Here are some examples of test cases:

```
fíléñámë.èxt
FÍLÉÑÁMË.ÈXT
ß
ß.ß
Ðæøç
c: \dïrêçt.örÿ\fíléñámë.èxt
```

We'd want such a list for each element of our test area. The test cases for the file list are likely to be the files that we've created with the filename field.

When testing similar aspects of a product, it may happen that you can use the same test cases to test several domains. Internationalization QA is often well suited to this matrix type of testing. For instance, most programs have many filename fields, and other areas of many programs (such as function calls in a macro language) must access files also. International filenames need to be handled properly throughout the product, and the same test cases can generally be used to test filenames in each area.

Testing the Internationalization Components

You will need to decide on the level of testing based on your product's specifications. Here are some ideas for testing internationalization components.

Appropriate Use of String Collation Functions

Most programs do sorting in some form or other, whether it's a list of filenames in a dialog, or a list of names in an address book, or whatever. There are two distinct types of tests for sorting or collation: that the product sorts using the appropriate collation rules, and that the collation rules are correct.

When programmers aren't aware of international concerns, they use standard C functions for string manipulation. As we've seen in previous chapters, these functions produce incorrect results for most languages. In other words, the sort doesn't follow appropriate collation rules. We'll look at testing collation rules in the next section.

In testing that the appropriate rules are used, we need to verify that the product is using locale-sensitive collation functions and that the correct locale is used. (Locales are discussed in Chapter 4.) The test domain consists of each area in the product where strings might be sorted including file lists, data indexes, and alphabetized lists of names.

To test each element of the testing domain, it's important to ask, "If the program isn't using the correct collation rules, what would the behavior be?" We don't actually want to test the functionality or the correctness of the sort, since that's the job of the operating system (or of a task that must be tested separately). Generally, it's sufficient to test several cases. For example, the German locale in Windows sorts the sharp-s character *ß* right after *ss*. If a program is run under these conditions (and uses the correct collation function), it should sort as follows:

1. masse
2. maße
3. master

If we tried this test under U.S. settings, or if the program wasn't using Windows' standard collation, we would have the following:

1. masse
2. master
3. maße

Similarly, accented vowels such as *â* or *é* will sort among other letters *a* or *e* under French Windows settings, so we should end up with:

1. beauté
2. bête
3. beurre

U.S. collations would put the word *bête* at the end of the list because they wouldn't recognize that *ê* should be sorted with other *e*'s.

String Collation Rules

Under some operating systems, such as Windows and Macintosh, most programs use function calls to the operating system for locale-sensitive string manipulation. If this is what your product does,

you can assume that it isn't necessary to test the actual collation rules. Other programs need to define their own collation rules. If your program defines its own collation rules, please refer to Chapter 7 for information on testing.

Character Classifications

Some programs have a macro language or a programming language with character classification functions such as *isalpha(), isalphanumeric(), isupper(),* and *islower()*. If your product has such functions, they can be tested in a manner similar to collation: Choose test cases that prove that the correct calls are being made. For example, in the case of isalpha() and islower(), the letter *â* should return false under U.S. settings and true under French settings. Using C functions from the standard runtime library, these functions would return false no matter what the locale was set to.

Character Transliterations

There are several areas where transliterated characters must be checked:

- ✦ As with the character classification functions in a macro language or programming language, we need to check transliteration functions such as *toupper()* and *tolower()*. Under German settings, the letter *á* should uppercase to *Á*, but in the United States, it will uppercase to itself (*á*) because this isn't an alphabetic character under U.S. rules. In France, accented characters generally uppercase to their nonaccented equivalents, so *á* becomes *A*.
- ✦ Everywhere our product displays a set of strings in upper- or lowercase, we need to check that the programmer has used the appropriate function. For instance, in a list of words that appear in uppercase, verify that the German word, *Bäume,* appears as *BÄUME* when displayed using the German locale and as *BäUME* using the U.S. locale. Remember to check case-insensitive searches, data filters, and so forth.

- In the case of Windows 3.1 programs, we need to handle both the Windows code page (ANSI) for displaying strings and the DOS code page (OEM) for file handling and other string handling. Every string displayed by the program has the potential to be displayed incorrectly, particularly strings that can be shared with other programs. (While this coverage is necessary for Windows programs, it is also very likely to uncover international enabling bugs in other products running on other platforms as well.)

  To cover such a broad test area requires several strategies. The messaging tests (in the next section) should cover the static pieces of the user-interface (UI). In addition you must check all edit and static controls, list boxes and combo boxes in dialogs, all editors, and everywhere else that your program displays text or the users enter text.

  You can check these strings by entering several key characters and checking that they are displayed correctly. Then save the window or dialog and reopen it to be sure that the characters are still displayed correctly. Among your test cases, include a test case for each of the following:

  - One character that doesn't exist in the OEM code page. The character *Ø,* ANSI code point 216, doesn't exist in DOS code page 437.
  - One character that exists in both code pages but at different code points. Most accented characters match this description, including *ß,* which is at code point 223 in Windows and 225 in code page 437.

One area to pay particular attention to is file handling. You will need to save and open files with filenames that contain 8-bit characters, and you will need to save and open files in directory names that contain 8-bit characters. In our experience, accented characters in file and directory names is one of the buggiest areas. Make sure you test all aspects of your program, including File | Save

and File | Save as, saving files from a macro or programming language, installing to a directory that contains accented characters, and so on.

There are some areas that might be easy to overlook. DDE (Dynamic Data Exchange, a Windows protocol for exchanging data with other programs) can cause problems with accented characters, since some programs will expect the data in OEM format and others will expect the data in ANSI format. Similarly, copying and pasting to and from other programs (including a DOS program) must be tested with 8-bit characters. OLE (Object Linking and Embedding in Windows) must also be checked.

- ✦ Another area that can have transliteration problems is pickletters and incremental searches. When the user enters an accented character, the behavior should be the same as with a 7-bit character.

- ✦ If your program exchanges data with another program, you need to verify that accented characters are passed back and forth appropriately. This is particularly the case if you are passing data to or from another platform, since the code pages may not match and character conversion will be required. An example of this might be a PC database product accessing SQL data from a UNIX server. We will need to know what code page the data is stored in, and we will need to know how to convert those characters to a code page we can display.

  To test this case, we could build a database on the SQL server that consists of fields for code point and character description. We would have one record for each code point 0 through 255. We would then access the data from the PC and verify that the characters display properly. (Note that there will be some characters that exist on one platform and not on the other. Your program will need to handle these cases in a manner that's reasonable for the application.) You would then want to build a similar database on the PC and upload it to the SQL server and verify that it displays appropriately there.

- Generally, anywhere a user can enter a character it needs to be checked that 8-bit characters can be entered and handled properly. This includes named areas, styles, glossaries, filters, views, field names, filenames, search and replace, edit controls, and so forth.

Messaging

There are several types of internationalization problems that programmers can introduce into the UI:

- Hard-coded strings. As discussed earlier, the costs of translation go up significantly if there are hard-coded strings in the executable; the earlier these strings are discovered and resourced, the better.
- Display fields that are too short. If the programmer allows just enough room for the English string, longer translated strings won't be completely displayed.
- In Windows programs, OEM/ANSI problems. While resources are normally ANSI and no transliteration is necessary to display them, it occasionally happens that strings are inadvertently converted.

Probably the easiest way to check for these problems is to build and test a dummy translation of the UI using a Pig Latinizer program or other means of automatic translation. Our Pig Latinizer uses database tables created by the Software Translation Kit (see Chapter 11) and replaces all displayable text. As in Pig Latin, the first letter of each word is moved to the end of the word and the syllable *ay* is appended. In addition, vowels are replaced with accented equivalents.

By having a QA engineer test the Pig Latin version of the product, we can find hard-coded strings, areas where there isn't enough room to display long strings, and OEM/ANSI problems in the UI. The coverage need only be surface-level; we need to be sure that all strings are in Pig Latin, that there is room for the complete string, and that all the characters display properly.

Formatted Fields

Everywhere a formatted field is displayed, the user may want the value to appear in a format other than what we are used to in the United States. Formatted fields can be dates, times, numbers, or currency values. For each field, there are three things we need to test for:

- ✦ The field must be capable of displaying all required formats.
- ✦ The default format for the field must be appropriate.
- ✦ The value in the field must be correct, no matter the locale or the localized version under which it is displayed.

You will need to start with a list of every formatted field in your program. Remember to include fields in reports and forms and those displayed as a result of a macro or function call. Select a subset of each type, and test all possible formats.

For dates, these include month/day/year, day/month/year, and year/month/day formats using "/", "-", "." and other possible separators. Test with and without leading zeroes and with and without the century. Test that the month can be spelled out, abbreviated, or numeric. Remember to check the ability to specify the first day of the week, and check the position of the day of the week if required by your program. See the date formats in Appendix A for test cases.

For time fields, you will need to test 12- and 24-hour formats, different separators, and so on. Depending on the needs of your program, you may need to test additional formats. Try the set of the test cases in the time format section of Appendix A.

You can approach numeric and currency fields in the same way. You can create a list of test cases by referring to the currency section of Appendix A and to Chapter 7.

After you've tested several of the display points of each type of field exhaustively, you will need to decide if you need to test all the other display points as thoroughly or if you can limit the testing to a few test cases. The answer will depend on the success of the initial testing, the extent of internationalization in the program, your confidence level in your R&D engineers, and so forth.

You will also need to verify that the default format settings are appropriate, based either on the formats specified by the operating system or on the language of the program. For instance, if the user sets his or her Windows country settings to Swedish, your Windows program should default to a date format of year/month/day. You may want to specify one set of defaults for your French versions and a different set for your Italian versions. If this is the case, you will need to verify that the correct defaults are set in each localized version (including the core version).

One problem to watch out for in this area concerns numbers and dates as used in macro languages and programming languages. If date values are entered and stored based on locale, the value will be incorrect if we change locales. For instance, if our program uses a date of "01/02/95" in the United States, this will become 1 February 1995 if we run the program in England. We discuss various solutions to this in Chapter 4, but it's important to verify that the solution your program uses works properly, either by providing the ability to specify the format in the program or by storing the date as an absolute value, independent of locale. You could run into similar problems if users are allowed to use a comma or a period to specify decimal digits.

Depending on your program and your operating system, the program should be aware of changes to the locale as they occur and modify the display accordingly. For instance, if a user displays numbers in a Windows spreadsheet and concurrently opens the control panel to change the numeric format, the spreadsheet should be aware of the change and redisplay.

While most formatted fields should change formats when the locale changes, your program probably shouldn't change the format of currency values that have already been entered. If we enter a value of "£100," we certainly don't want the value to shrink to "L.100" when we switch to an Italian locale; we probably still have 100 pounds, not 100 lire.

Separators

If a comma is used as a decimal point, we can no longer use it as a separator in comma-delimited files or to separate arguments passed

to macro calls. We need to test all import and export functions to verify that they can handle numbers in any format and can use a separator that's appropriate for the selected number format. Similarly, if our macro or programming language allows numbers to be expressed using local formats (as in spreadsheets), we need to test the parser to make sure that it can parse numbers of various formats and that it understands the corresponding argument separator.

Other Formatting Issues

If your program displays rulers or grids, the user should have the option of either metric or English measurement systems, and you need to verify that this works properly.

In addition, the program should know how to handle paper sizes that are used outside the United States. At the least, you should have A4 and B4 paper available for testing purposes and do a set of printing tests using these paper sizes.

Compatibility Testing

While it may not be practical to do complete compatibility testing on non-U.S. hardware and software, there are a couple of areas in which you will find the most serious problems. Fixing such problems will make your U.S. software usable in other countries, and will resolve the problems in the core product, not in localized versions.

Keyboard Testing

In other countries, keyboards have different layouts. Generally, the biggest problems are caused by dead-key and ALT-GR key combinations. These are the keystrokes required to enter certain characters. You must test a set of these characters to be sure that your application allows them to be entered.

On all IBM-enhanced European keyboards, the right ALT key is called the ALT-GR key. The left ALT key works the same as on U.S. keyboards. As on U.S. keyboards, where the SHIFT key allows us to type different characters, the ALT-GR key allows you to access a third set of characters. These additional characters are generally printed on the front of the keys. For instance, to type square brackets on a French keyboard, you need to press the right ALT key.

To type certain accented characters on some European keyboards, you must first type the accent, then the character itself. This is called a dead-key combination, because the accent doesn't appear until the next character is typed.

Localized Operating Systems

While most internationalization problems are discovered by testing under non-U.S. locales, it is a good idea to have at least a couple of people testing under European versions of the operating system you are using. This may turn up some problems, such as when we display messages from the operating system, reliance on code page information, and so on.

Depending on your needs, you may also wish to test your product under the Chinese version of the operating system. While English products are generally not accepted in the Japanese market, they might be in other Asian countries, even if they are not well-enabled for multibyte character sets. If your program allows the user to simply enter double-byte characters (see Chapter 13), you may be able to gain access to this market with minimum effort.

Other Considerations

If your program has a macro language with translated function calls, your users still may want to run the programs they write under localized versions other than the one in which they wrote it. For instance, a German who develops spreadsheet products might want to sell them in France. If this functionality is required, it will need to be implemented in the core version, although you can probably only test it using localized versions. In fact, this functionality is useful for testing localized versions, since it means that the macro testing that is done for the core product can be used to test localized versions.

If your product is shipped with fonts, you will need fonts for each code page that you will be supporting. You will need to test that all characters in each font display appropriately.

Bug Reporting

Since internationalization bugs are simply one type of functionality bug, it makes sense to report them in the same way as core bugs are reported. In other words, they should be reported to the same database as core bugs, and the should be handled just like any other functionality bug. The alternative is to have a separate database for internationalization bugs if they are expected to be fixed by a different group of engineers. The problem is that this limits the awareness of internationalization issues to a select set of people. In addition, it tends to diminish the importance of internationalization bugs since they are not as visible as other kinds, and it tends to distort bug statistics, since not all the bugs are reported in the same place.

On the other hand, it's often useful to have a flag in the bug database to mark the internationalization bugs as such in order to generate reports on the state of internationalization.

As with other types of bugs, it's important to categorize bugs appropriately so that management and R&D can more easily determine:

- The effect of the bug on the end-user if the bug occurs
- How many end-users we can expect to run into the bug, and how often they will run into it
- When (and if) the bug should be fixed
- Which engineer should fix the bug

While you will need to determine your own categorizations, these are the ones we typically use:

- *Product area:* This is the broad functional area of the product in which the product occurs. There may be a dozen or so possible choices depending on the type of product you have. For example, a database product might have product areas for data handling, editing, commands, and functions, plus areas for particular components of the product.

Internationalization wouldn't be a product area. An internationalization bug would fall into another product area. For instance, if a component of the product doesn't display accented characters properly, the bug is entered as a bug of that component.

- *Keywords:* These are further refinements of the product area that specify the particular area in which the bug occurs. In the commands and functions area, you might use each command or function as a keyword. In an editor component you might use have keywords for string manipulation, cursor movement, formatting, and so on.
- *Category:* This is an indication of the effect of the bug on the user. We use the values of:

A. Crash bug or data loss—The bug will crash the program or corrupt the user's data. As far as internationalization bugs go, there are probably not a large number of common Category A bugs, but an example might be a crash that occurs when the program mishandles a separator character other than a comma, or a bug in the sort routine that doesn't handle keys that contain accented characters and throws away those records.

B. Bug without a workaround—The user won't reasonably be able to accomplish anything because of the bug. There are many possibilities for Category B internationalization bugs, including ones in which the program isn't able to save to a filename that contains accented characters, portions of the product where the user can't enter accented characters, and so on.

C. Bug with a workaround—The user will be able to accomplish what he or she is trying to do, but will have problems in the process. These are probably the most common bugs. An example of an internationalization Category C bug would be a pickletter that doesn't allow the use of accented characters, since the user can probably choose the item with the accented pickletter by using the mouse or other keystrokes.

D. Cosmetic bug—The bug doesn't cause a functional problem, but it looks bad. Hard-coded strings fall in this category, as well as dialog boxes that are too small to fit localized text and accented characters that behave properly but appear on the screen as the wrong character.
E. Suggestion—The program works as it was designed, but fixing the bug might make it work better for the end-user. This category can be used for flaws in the spec or for new ideas to improve the product.

✦ *Priority:* This is an indication of how quickly the bug should be fixed. While the options vary from product to product, these are the ones we prefer:

1. Fix as soon as possible—This is usually a test-blocking bug (one that prevents us from testing an area), or one that makes the product difficult to use.
2. Fix before the next release—This is a bug that will have a serious effect on users, but is not particularly getting in the way of testing. It should be fixed before we ship the next beta test version.
3. Fix before ship—This might be a bug that affects relatively few users, or it might be one that has a small impact on many. It's one that we aren't too embarrassed about shipping in our beta releases.
4. On hold/defer—This is a bug that we aren't planning to fix in the current version, usually because the bug isn't important enough to risk destabilizing the product and causing the schedule to slip.

Clearly, categorizing bugs properly requires careful consideration and fine judgment. QA engineers need to think of how and when each bug will surface and, when it does surface, how the end-users will be impacted. They will also need to take into account the goals of the product and of each milestone release. This is an important aspect of the job.

There are other categorizations that can be used for other purposes, such as the group that first reported the bug (QA, R&D, beta testers, bug hunters), and how the bug was found (through test automation, ad-hoc testing, or other means).

Test Suite Automation

While ad-hoc testing has its place, it's difficult to get consistent, comprehensive coverage unless a large number of test cases are automated. For international enabling testing using a matrix model of testing, this is particularly true. The idea is to write a small number of test cases for a test area, and then apply those test cases across the area's test domain.

For example, if we wanted to test how well accented characters can be entered throughout the product, we might write a subroutine that "types" a number of characters, then retrieves the characters that appeared and compares them with those that were entered. We would also have a driver test script. After starting the application, the driver would move in turn to each of the fields and windows to be tested and call the subroutine on each one.

In addition, test suites written for other purposes can often be leveraged for enabling testing. The core QA group may have many useful test scripts that can be modified to test enabling issues.

Models for Enabling QA

There are several models under which the enabling testing can be accomplished. While each has advantages, the most appropriate one for you depends on the makeup of your group.

The International QA Team Does the Enabling Testing

In this model, there is a separate international QA team that is responsible for all the testing outlined in this chapter. They write their own test suites (sometimes based on core test suites) and are accountable for the extent to which the product can be used by peo-

ple in other countries and (along with the R&D engineers) the ease with which the product can be localized. In addition, the international QA team tests the localized versions of the product.

In this model, it's important that the international QA team be a part of the signoff of the product for all external releases of the core product including field tests. This signifies that they are aware of the international enabling capabilities and bugs and are comfortable with releasing the product.

The advantages of this model include:

- ✦ The international QA engineers have a charter to focus on enabling. When time starts to run out in a tight development schedule and the pressure is on, they will continue to focus on enabling and not get sucked into other tasks.
- ✦ The international QA engineers are the same ones testing the localized versions. They know the problems they'll run into based on experience, and they know the cost of missing bugs. They are especially motivated to find enabling bugs, since they know that the onus of fixing an enabling bug will fall on them when they do their work on the localized versions of the product. We find that international engineers who move to the core team bring an awareness of international issues with them, but they tend to lose their focus on the international issues as they focus more on core functionality.

The Core QA Team Does the Enabling Testing

In this model, each core QA engineer does enabling testing for his or her area. As each engineer tests or writes test suites, he or she includes test cases to cover all the international issues. While this has the advantage of spreading the awareness of international issues and giving the engineers full ownership for their areas, there are several problems with this approach:

- ✦ There is rarely enough time in development cycles for the QA engineers to cover their areas completely, and the

international aspects are often the first items to be compromised in terms of coverage.

- ✦ As engineers work on their testing there is a strong tendency to focus on the core functionality and forget to test the international functionality.

Core QA and International QA Work Together

This is a compromise that provides some of the advantages of each of the other two models. In this model, international QA engineers are still responsible for the enabling testing. At the beginning of the development cycle, the international engineers provide training and detailed instructions on all the international aspects of the product that they would like the core engineers to cover. During the testing phases or test suite development phases, the international QA engineers would review the test cases to verify that there is sufficient international coverage and work with the core QA engineer to fill in any holes. Any international areas not covered by core engineers and any areas that received insufficient coverage would be picked up by international engineers. The success of this model depends on a very high level of communication among all the engineers.

- ✦ It is critical that the responsibilities of the core and international QA engineers are spelled out very precisely. The core engineers need to be told specifically what international areas they should cover, how much coverage they should do, how they should do it, and what an international enabling bug might look like. The international engineers need to know what areas they should cover, what their responsibilities are with respect to working with the core engineers, and how best to work with the core engineers.
- ✦ The international engineers need to look at the coverage done by the core engineers with a critical but nonjudgmental eye. If the review of the coverage is incomplete, it is likely that some bugs will be missed. If there are prob-

lems with the coverage and the international engineer doesn't handle them tactfully, tempers can flare and a lot of time can be lost in nonproductive activities.

Even worse, if the international engineer notices other types of problems with the coverage, he or she may be in a quandary. It may not be quite appropriate for the engineer to comment on these problems, but it can't be right to ignore them either. In these cases, if the engineers have a good working relationship, they may be able to discuss the problems in an open, honest manner. Otherwise, it may be best for the international engineer to raise the issue with his or her manager and let the manager address the problem.

External Test Cycles

Beta Tests

In beta tests, prerelease versions of the software are sent to sites outside the company. The beta testers use the product for their everyday tasks and report the problems they run into. The people involved in these beta tests (or field tests) are generally large or influential customers who have a vested interest in the quality of the software you release. They should sign nondisclosure agreements before participating, and often receive a free package of the shipping version of the product in appreciation for their service.

Beta tests offer many benefits to the customer and to the software developer. The customer gets an early view of the product, an opportunity to learn about the next revision of the product before its release, and an opportunity to influence the quality of the product and to let the developer know what the primary concerns are. The software developer gets help testing the product for little cost, and gets a sense of how the product will be received in the marketplace and when it will be ready to ship.

For internationalized software, versions should be sent to qualified customer sites overseas as well as in the country of development. While it may be difficult to arrange for such sites, it is important to make sure that people using different cultural conventions have the opportunity to test the product. They can often find many kinds of international enabling bugs. To find beta testers, you may be able to enlist the help of a subsidiary or sales office or a local distributor in other countries.

It's important to remember that a fairly small percentage of beta testers will actively participate. In a well-administered beta test, we would expect to have perhaps 10 percent who actively use the product and report significant bugs and 50 percent who dabble in the product and report a few bugs. In order to get the highest-quality feedback from beta sites, the beta tests need to be managed tightly. There are several things you can do to help improve the number and types of bugs you get back from your beta investment.

- Qualify your beta testers in advance for their level of interest in the quality of the product, time they're willing to spend on testing, knowledge of the product, and so forth. Make sure that they're aware of the importance of reporting bugs early.
- Include a set of specific questions that the customer must respond to in order to continue participation in the beta test program. These questions might be about the stability of new or relatively untested areas in your product, the usefulness of new features or ones that you are considering adding, the quality of the documentation, and so on.
- Follow up with them regularly to verify that they've been able to install the software, that they haven't found blocking bugs, and that they're working with the software. This is also a good time to ask questions about a particular feature that needs more investigation.
- Make sure you have a good line of communication with the customer. In countries outside the United States, you may want to communicate through your local office, but stay in close contact with your people in the office and make sure that they follow up with the beta testers.

It's important to identify (to your beta testers) what you expect to get out of the beta test, and it's important to identify what they can expect to get out of it. You should reasonably expect your beta testers to commit a certain amount of time per day or week (depending on the type and size of the product) to testing. You should expect the beta testers to maintain the level of confidentially you have defined. You should expect your beta testers to be familiar with your application (or at least ones similar to it) and know what features they want in such an application.

Your beta testers should be able to expect a product that's of the appropriate quality level, and they should expect to be informed of the problems they should watch out for and how to work around those problems. They should expect a certain level of responsiveness when they call to report problems or to ask questions. And they should expect that the bugs they report will be raised and addressed appropriately (although not necessarily fixed).

Bug Hunts

Compared to beta tests, a bug hunt is often a more focused, effective way of generating a lot of bug reports. It typically consists of inviting up to about 20 people to pound on the program for an evening or a day. We often award monetary or other types of prizes for each bug found.

The bug hunt should be held in a single room with enough staff available to work with each of the bug hunters to learn the product, identify the areas that are likely to be the buggiest, and help isolate bugs. Probably three or four engineers for 20 testers is sufficient. There should be several extra machines available for testing core bugs, verifying bugs, and searching the bug database for duplicates.

The bug hunters can be drawn from any of several groups of people. Our most successful bug hunts generally comprise QA and R&D engineers working on other products, although for localized versions we have used engineers working on the core product. We've also had successful bug hunts by bringing together our best beta testers or by using members of a local users' group.

It's important to make the rules of the bug hunt clear up front. For instance:

- ✦ There will be no payment for bugs that have already been reported, or bugs that can't be reproduced. The bug hunter is responsible for isolating the bug and identifying a clear set of steps to reproduce the bug (although the QA engineers should help with this as much as possible).
- ✦ State the amount you intend to pay for each type of bug. For an internal bug hunt, you might offer $100 for crash bugs, $50 for serious functional bugs (those for which there is no workaround), $25 for less-serious functional bugs (those for which there is a workaround), and $10 for cosmetic bugs. For bug hunts involving customers, you might award points that can be applied toward products, or you might offer vouchers that can be used to purchase gifts in an auction after the bug hunt has concluded.
- ✦ Specify who will be the ultimate arbiter of bug payouts. In our case, this is usually the QA manager.

Skill Set of International QA Engineers

Given this discussion of what international QA entails, what should we look for when we hire an international QA engineer? We find that the skill set pretty much corresponds to that required for a good UI tester:

- ✦ A programming background, which helps in developing test suites and in understanding the process of developing software.
- ✦ Knowledge of test automation tools.
- ✦ A good background in testing user interfaces.
- ✦ Analytical skills for isolating bugs and reporting them accurately.

- Diplomatic and communication skills for negotiating bug fixes with R&D engineers and for defining test areas with core QA engineers.
- While we don't require international enabling QA experience (because it's usually difficult to find), it's certainly a big plus.
- Sensitivity to and interest in international issues.

CHAPTER 7

Defining a Locale

We use locale definitions in our software so that it can handle character information and display numbers, monetary values, dates, and times in an internationally sensitive manner. The locale definition is the description our programs use of the customary formats, character set, character transliterations, and sort orders shared by people speaking the same language or living in the same region. For instance, we might have a locale for French-speaking people in France, and a different locale for French-speaking people in Canada. The character sets for the two are probably the same or similar and the collations would be similar but the monetary format would be different, where one uses the symbol for the French franc and the other uses the symbol for the Canadian dollar.

We use locales so that our programs are locale independent. We don't want our core developers writing sort algorithms for different countries; we want them to call a collation routine that knows the current locale and how to sort for that locale.

Many operating systems contain locale information in some form. DOS, for instance, contains a means of switching code pages along with simple locale-dependent collation rules. Windows NT contains extensive locale information. No matter what level of locale support your platform provides, there may be reasons that you'd want to provide your own locale definitions:

- ✦ To provide consistent cross-platform support. You might want your program to use only one set of APIs for handling locale information in versions that run on DOS, Windows, UNIX, and the Macintosh.

- To support preexisting sorting rules. If your customers have data tables that are sorted in a particular order for different countries, you might need to provide sorting tables or sorting rules so that they don't have to reindex their data when they receive an updated version.
- To provide complete locale support under an operating system that offers only limited or no support. If your program runs in DOS or UNIX, you may require more locale support than is available from the operating system.

Providing your own locale support requires:

- A set of international APIs for switching from one locale to another and for retrieving locale information
- A locale definition for each locale you would want to support
- A locale compiler to make the locale information accessible to your program

We'll look at defining locales in this chapter. We've discussed the APIs and the locale compiler in previous chapters. You may be able to find these tools in the public domain on various platforms.

As you will find, locale and charmap definitions can be large and unwieldy. We use databases to store and manipulate information in each section of the locales and to create new locale definitions.

Locale Format

While there may be other formats for specifying the elements of a locale, a common format is that specified by POSIX, the Portable Operating System Interface. This is an industry-standard definition language that allows characters and formats to be defined using 7-bit ASCII characters so that they are transportable across platforms. While a rigorous definition of POSIX is beyond the scope of this book, reading this chapter and looking at the sample of a

French Canadian locale in Appendix E should provide you with enough information to develop your own locales.

In order to make the locale codeset independent, we use symbolic names for characters. So rather than calling the letter *A* code-point 0x41, we call it <LATIN_CAPITAL_LETTER_A>. When the locale is compiled, it is bound to a character map (charmap) of the required code page. The charmap for code page 437 specifies that <LATIN_CAPITAL_LETTER_A> represents code-point 0x41. Most other charmaps will specify the same code-point, but for Unicode on a PC machine it will be 0x4100 (since the Intel architecture is byte-swapped), and for Unicode on certain other machines it will be 0x0041.

For a DOS program in France, you would probably want two locales—one with the locale definition bound to code page 437 and one bound to 850.

POSIX specifies that the name of the locale should be based on the target language and country, using the two-character ISO code for each (see Bibliography). A locale definition for French Canada would be fr_CA. For Spain, we might have a locale definition called es_ES.LC (Español in España).

Let's take a closer look at the elements of locale. Please refer to the sample French Canadian locale in Appendix E as you read along.

Sample Locale

The locale begins with several lines of comments that contain the character "#" in the first column. The locale compiler ignores these lines and it ignores blank lines. While these comments identify only the file and the version, you should also make a habit of identifying the creator of the locale and maintaining a revision history as well.

The locale_name and locale_desc are used by the locale's client applications and by the end users to identify which locale to use. We then have several large sections: LC_CTYPE, LC_TIME, LC_MONETARY, LC_NUMERIC, LC_MESSAGES, LC_COLLATE.

Each of these sections is terminated by a statement of the form END LC_CTYPE, END LC_TIME, and so on.

LC_CTYPE

The LC_CTYPE section describes character types and character transliteration. Each line of the character type section specifies which character type to define and the list of characters that fall in that particular category separated by semicolons. The "\" character is the line continuation character so that a chartype section doesn't have to be on a single physical line. The sample locale contains these chartypes:

- **lower:** The lowercase letters
- **upper:** The uppercase letters
- **cntrl:** Control characters
- **space:** Any characters that can be used as whitespace
- **blank:** Blank characters, usually just the space and the horizontal tab characters
- **digit:** The characters that represent digits
- **xdigit:** The characters that represent hexadecimal digits

Your program may also require some additional chartypes such as:

- **Hiragana:** The Japanese Hiragana characters
- **Katakana:** The Japanese Katakana characters

and possibly others. There are several categories we probably don't want to include:

- **alpha, alphanum, print, graph:** The functions *isxxx()* that would be represented by these tables are a combination of existing tables. You can use the macro construct in C to emulate this rather than create a new chartype:

```
#define isalpha(x) isupper(x) || islower(x);
#define isalphanum(x) isalpha(x) || isdigit(x);
```

```
#define isprint(x) isalnum(x) || ispunct(x) || isspace(x);
#define isgraph(x) isalnum(x) || ispunct(x);
```

- **Kanji:** Rather than create a large chartype table of Kanji characters, it's probably more efficient to use a macro construct to determine if a character is a Kanji character. Refer to the Asian development chapter for this macro.

The transliteration section follows the chartype section. These are tables that show how to transliterate from one character to another. For instance, the toupper table shows that toupper("a") should be "A". Each transliteration function is represented on a line starting with the function name (toupper), followed by pairs of characters. The first character in a pair is the character input to the function and the second is the result. Pairs are separated by semicolons and characters are separated by commas. Again, the backslash character "\" is used as the line continuation character. If a character is not specified in the table, the function returns the character itself. So toupper("A") returns "A", and toupper("^") returns "^".

While we include tables for toupper and tolower in the sample locale, a Japanese locale would also include tables for tohira and tokata. You may require other transliteration tables besides these.

LC_TIME

While this section may be difficult to read, it is simply a list of the names of the days of the week or names of the months plus formatting information for date and time strings. Each line represents a single type of entry, with each name separated by a semicolon. As in the chartype section, we use "\" as a line continuation, and we specify the characters symbolically to maintain code page independence.

In the formatting entries, you will see some symbols in the form of a percent sign followed by a character. These symbols represent elements of date and time strings and are to be filled in by the formatting function. Each entry is represented by a symbol, as indicated in the following descriptions:

- **abday:** The abbreviated names of the days of the week. The corresponding symbol is "%a".

- **day:** The names of the days of the week. The corresponding symbol is "%A".
- **abmon:** The abbreviated names of the month. The corresponding symbol is "%b".
- **mon:** The names of the month. The corresponding symbol is "%B".
- **am_pm:** The characters used to specify A.M. and P.M. in time strings. The corresponding symbol is "%p".
- **d_t_fmt:** The format of the long date string. The corresponding symbol is "%c".
- **d_fmt:** The format of the short date string. The corresponding symbol is "%x".
- **t_fmt:** The format of the time string as a 24-hour value. The corresponding symbol is "%X".
- **t_fmt_ampm:** The format of the time string using a 12-hour clock. If this string is empty, the t_fmt string is used instead. The corresponding symbol is "%r".
- **alt_digits:** The list of numbers when used as ordinal values—0th, 1st, 2nd, and so on. The corresponding symbol is "%0".

While not used in this locale, we could include the following entries for Asian locales:

- **era:** The list of emperor eras. The corresponding symbol is "%E".
- **era_year:** The format of the year in emperor era format. The corresponding symbol is "%EY".
- **era_d_fmt:** The format of the time string as a 24-hour value. The corresponding symbol is "%X".

LC_NUMERIC

The Numeric section describes how numbers should be formatted. It consists of the following entries:

- **decimal_point:** The character used as a decimal point. While we use a period in the United States, the French Canadians and many others use a comma.
- **thousands_sep:** The character used to separate groups of digits. While we use a comma in the United States, the French Canadians and others use a period, and some countries use a space.
- **grouping:** The grouping of digits. The value "3" indicates that the thousands separator should occur every third digit starting from the decimal and moving to the left.
- **exponential_sign:** The character used to show the exponent of numbers in scientific notation.

LC_MONETARY

The Monetary section describes how currency values should be formatted. It consists of the following entries:

- **currency_symbol:** The dollar sign in Canada, the pound sign in Britain, and so on.
- **int_curr_symbol:** The international currency symbol. This is the monetary symbol used outside the country, or it's used to indicate which currency is being used among several currencies. Canada uses the letters *CAD*. In the United States, we use *USD*.
- **mon_decimal_point:** The decimal point character used for monetary values.
- **mon_thousands_sep:** The character used to separate thousands.
- **mon_grouping:** The grouping of monetary digits.
- **positive_sign:** The character used to show positive monetary values.
- **negative_sign:** The character used to show negative monetary values.

- **frac_digits:** The number of fractional digits to show in monetary values.
- **int_frac_digits:** The number of fractional digits to show in international monetary values.
- **p_cs_precedes:** For positive currency values, a 1 if the currency symbol precedes the value or a 0 otherwise.
- **p_sep_by_space:** For positive currency values, a "1" if a space separates the currency symbol from the value or a "0" otherwise.
- **n_cs_precedes:** For negative currency values, a "1" if the currency symbol precedes the value or a "0" otherwise.
- **n_sep_by_space:** For negative currency values, a "1" if a space separates the currency symbol from the value or a "0" otherwise.
- **p_sign_posn:** For positive currency values, a value representing the position of the positive_sign positioning as follows:

  0 if the value and the currency symbol should be enclosed in parentheses
  1 if the positive_sign string should come before the value and the currency symbol
  2 if the positive_sign string should come after the value and the currency symbol
  3 if the positive_sign string should come before the currency symbol
  4 if the positive_sign string should come after the currency symbol

- **n_sign_posn:** For negative currency values, a value representing the position of the negative_sign positioning. Follows the format of p_sign_posn.

LC_MESSAGES

This section contains single-character expressions for *yes* and *no* responses. Programs can use these to accept responses from yes/no

questions. In our products, we prefer to use strings stored as resources rather than the strings in this section, but we include it in our locales for completeness. It consists of two lines starting with *yesexpr* and *noexpr* followed by a list of characters that are acceptable yes or no responses to a question.

LC_COLLATE

The collation section specifies how to order characters. It is formatted as follows:

```
LC_COLLATE
<List of collating-elements>
<List of collating-symbols>
order_start <flags>
<Ordered list of collating-symbols>
<Ordered list of characters and collating-elements>
order_end
END LC_COLLATE
```

We'll discuss each of these sections in turn.

We'll be taking a close look at the sample French Canadian collation to figure out how it works. This is a four-level sort, which means that if our sort algorithm compares two equal strings, it will examine the strings four times before it determines that they are equal. A difference in unequal strings could occur in any of those four passes. We can name the levels as follows:

1. *Letter differences:* At this level, we determine if we have two different letters. The letter *A* is different than the letter *B,* but at this level, the letter *A* is equal to *a* or *Ä*.
2. *Diacritic differences:* If the characters are the same at each point in the strings, then we check the accent marks. The letter *A* is still equal to *a,* but at this level, we determine that it is different than Ä.
3. *Case differences:* Finally, we make the distinction between *A* and *a.*
4. *Control character differences:* If strings are equivalent except that one contains control characters, the difference will be found at this level. This is based on the assump-

tion that control characters are not interesting in collations, so all other differences take precedence.

Let's take a look at a few examples:

```
Bête, Beurre
```

At a primary level, the sorting algorithm sees:

```
BETE, BEURRE
```

and determines that the first word should sort in front of the second, since *T* is less than *U.* The diacritic difference in the letters *e* is less significant than the primary difference of *T* versus *U.* Compare this to:

```
BÊTE, Bête
```

At a primary level the sorting algorithm sees:

```
BETE, BETE
```

Since these are the same, it goes to the second level. At the second level, we use collating symbols (as described in detail later) to determine if there are diacritic differences in the two strings:

```
<NO_DIACRITIC><CIRCUMFLEX><NO_DIACRITIC><NO_DIACRITIC>,
<NO_DIACRITIC><CIRCUMFLEX><NO_DIACRITIC><NO_DIACRITIC>
```

Everything is still equal, so we go to the third level. This time we'll use collating symbols to determine if there are case differences:

```
<UPPER><UPPER><UPPER><UPPER>,
<UPPER><LOWER><LOWER><LOWER>
```

Finally, we have a difference. As we'll see, our French Canadian collation defines <LOWER> as less than <UPPER>, so the second string sorts before the first.

The collating symbols used in the second and third levels act sort of like a character that has been introduced for the sake of collation and are used to specify weight criteria. As indicated, character case is used to distinguish characters at the third level of the French

Canadian sort, so the third level consists of the collating-symbols <LOWER>, <UPPER>, and <NOCASE> among others.

The collating symbols fall at the beginning of the LC_COLLATE section. Each one consists of a line with the keyword "collating-symbol" followed by the name of the symbol in angle brackets. These symbols can fall in any order.

While we don't use collating elements in our French Canadian sort, they are useful in others. A collating element is a combination of characters that sort as one. For instance, the letters *ch* in Spanish sort as a single character that falls after every *c* and before every *d*. This can be represented as follows:

```
collating-element <ch> from \
<LATIN_SMALL_LETTER_C><LATIN_SMALL_LETTER_H>
```

So *czech* should sort before *chinese* in a Spanish collation (although this isn't the intended usage), since <ch> would be defined greater than <c>.

Some collations also need to handle one-to-many characters such as the German sharp-s character. This is a single character, ß, which should sort as *ss*. In this case, we use two characters at each level of the collation. See the sharp-s entry in the French Canadian sort, which falls right after <LATIN_CAPITAL_LETTER_S>.

After the list of collating symbols is the ordered list of characters and symbols. This begins with the order_start line, which indicates that the collating information begins on the next line. The rest of the line contains one flag for each level of the sort indicating the directionality of the level. We'll take a look at these flags after we look at the collating information itself.

The order section begins with the list of collating-symbols in the order in which they should appear in the collation. As you can see, <LOWER> falls before <UPPER>, so lowercase characters will be sorted in front of the same uppercase letters. For example, *a* is less than *A*.

Next comes a complete list of characters and collating elements, one per line. Each line consists of the symbol of the character followed by collation information for each level of the sort. The levels are separated by semicolons. The collation information can be a character symbol, a collating symbol or a collating element, indi-

cating that at that level, the character should be sorted with every other of the same character, collating symbol, or collating element. Or the collating information can be the word *IGNORE,* indicating that the character should be ignored for that level of the sort. Let's look at the character *a:*

```
<LATIN_SMALL_LETTER_A> <LATIN_SMALL_LETTER_A>; <NO_DIACRITIC>;\
<LOWER>; IGNORE
```

At the first level, it should be sorted with every other character that is described as a <LATIN_SMALL_LETTER_A>. If you take a look at the locale definition, you will find that all these characters sort the same as *a* at the first level:

```
<LATIN_SMALL_LETTER_A>
<LATIN_CAPITAL_LETTER_A>
<FEMININE_ORDINAL_INDICATOR>
<LATIN_SMALL_LETTER_A_WITH_ACUTE>
<LATIN_CAPITAL_LETTER_A_WITH_ACUTE>
<LATIN_SMALL_LETTER_A_WITH_GRAVE>
<LATIN_CAPITAL_LETTER_A_WITH_GRAVE>
<LATIN_SMALL_LETTER_A_WITH_CIRCUMFLEX>
<LATIN_CAPITAL_LETTER_A_WITH_CIRCUMFLEX>
<LATIN_SMALL_LETTER_A_WITH_TILDE>
<LATIN_CAPITAL_LETTER_A_WITH_TILDE>
<LATIN_SMALL_LETTER_A_WITH_DIAERESIS>
<LATIN_CAPITAL_LETTER_A_WITH_DIAERESIS>
<LATIN_SMALL_LETTER_A_WITH_RING_ABOVE>
<LATIN_CAPITAL_LETTER_A_WITH_RING_ABOVE>
<LATIN_SMALL_LIGATURE_AE>
<LATIN_CAPITAL_LIGATURE_AE>
```

At the second level, *a* sorts as the collating symbol <NO_DIACRITIC>. In the above list, there are only two such characters:

```
<LATIN_SMALL_LETTER_A>
<LATIN_CAPITAL_LETTER_A>
```

At the third level, *a* sorts as the collating symbol <LOWER>. Of the two above characters, only *a* is <LOWER>.

The fourth level is <IGNORE>. This level will be significant only if the only difference between two strings is in control characters. We'll see how this works in a minute.

As with collating symbols, precedence is determined by the order in which characters appear in the list. The character

<LATIN_SMALL_LETTER_A> falls before <LATIN_SMALL_LETTER_B> in the list, and thus sorts in front of it.

Coming back to the order_start line, there is one flag for each level of the sort. These flags indicate the directionality of that level. In our example, there are four levels, and so there are four flags:

```
forward; backward; forward; forward, position
```

These are used as follows:

- **forward:** Indicates that the string should be examined from beginning to end, or that differences at the beginning of the string are more significant than differences later in the string.
- **backward:** Indicates that the string should be examined from end to beginning.
- **position:** Indicates that the string with the first non-ignored character comes first in the sort order. If the flag is **position** or **forward, position,** then we start from the beginning of the string; if the flag is **backward, position,** we start from the end of the string. If we find two non-ignored characters, precedence is based on the relative weight at that sorting level.

So what does this mean in terms of our French Canadian collation? The first weight level is for letters and it's forward. So the first nonequal letter in the string determines which string comes first in collation order.

The second weight level is for diacritic marks and it's backward. This means that if all the letters are the same, then the *last* accent difference determines precedence. In French, the reason that this is important is that accents that fall late in a word tend to indicate a grammatical concept (to create an adjective or a noun from a verb, for instance), whereas accents earlier in a word tend to be an indication of pronunciation. For collation purposes, grammatical differences are deemed more significant than pronunciation differences.

Let's look at the words *pêche* and *péché* (the only real-world example we could think of that would illustrate this collation difference). Note that the pronunciation of the first letter e of the first word differs from that of the second, but this difference is less interesting than the notion that *péché* is a noun created from the verb *pécher* based on the accent of the second *e*.

At the primary level these words are equivalent. (*PECHE* equals *PECHE*.) At the secondary level, we start at the end of the string and work backwards. Since <NO_DIACRITIC> (the last character of *pêche*) comes before <ACUTE> (the last character of *péché*), *pêche* sorts before *péché*. If we started from the beginning, the first letters *e* would take precedence and the sort order would be the opposite.

The third level tests case differences. It is forward and works similarly to the first level.

The fourth level tests control characters and is positional. Let's look at the strings "Bananes, Pommes" and "Bananes Pommes". Since <COMMA> and <SPACE> are ignored at the first three levels, these strings are equivalent until we get to the fourth level. At that point, we examine the strings from the beginning. The first seven letters in each string ("Bananes") are ignored at this level. Next, we compare <SPACE> and <COMMA> and discover that <SPACE> comes before <COMMA> and that's what determines the precedence—the second string comes first in the sort order.

If instead we had "Bananes, Pommes" and "Bananes, Pommes", we get to the fourth level as we did in the first example. The first nine characters appear in both strings ("Bananes, ") and are either ignored or are equal. Next, we compare <SPACE> in the first string to <IGNORE> (which is the *P* in Pommes) in the second string. Based on the positional rule, the first nonignored character takes precedence, so the first string sorts after the second.

You might wonder why describing collations in a locale definition is so complex. There are actually two problems. One is that sorting customs have been developed over a period of decades or centuries. For instance, you may want your phone book to group *MacDonald* with *McDonald*. This is a common practice, and one that's difficult to express without a flexible tool. The problem may be more acute in Japan, for instance, where the *Nobasu* character, which looks like a long hyphen, prolongs the sound of Katakana characters and sorts as the equivalent vowel. So <ka><nobasu> sorts in the same grouping as <ka><a>, and <ki><nobasu> sort in

the same grouping as <ki><i>. This is difficult to express because there are many Katakana characters and several Nobasu characters.

The second problem is that a lot of data already exists in orders that have been defined by other systems. If we want to access that data and not disturb the sort order, we need a very flexible tool to allow us to express the same order.

Multiple Categories

You might require two or more sort orders (or other category) in one locale. There is no problem with this; you simply name each category. For instance, you might have the following categories in a locale:

```
LC_COLLATE "dictionary" DEFAULT
LC_COLLATE "case-sensitive"
```

The first section would specify the collation for the dictionary sort order for this locale, and it will be the default sort order if the client application doesn't specify which sort order to use. The user may instead choose the second, case-sensitive sort. Of course, the client application will have to supply a mechanism for the user to choose the sort order.

Charmap Table Format

A charmap is the list of characters that appear in a code page and their corresponding code points. Please refer to the sample charmap in Appendix F to follow along with this discussion.

As with the locale, we use the "#" character in the first column to indicate a comment. We've included comments with the name of the file, information about the character set, and the date the file was created, but you may want to include other comments as well.

The <code_set_name> identifies the charmap to the locale compiler, and ultimately to the client application. Some client applications will display this information when requested by the user.

The <mb_cur_max> and <mb_cur_min> lines indicate the number of bytes that can make up each character (*mb* stands for multibyte). Because this is a single-byte character set, a character consists of exactly one byte. In the Japanese multibyte character set, called Shift-JIS, some characters are two bytes and some are one. In this case, the <mb_cur_max> value would be two and the <mb_cur_min> value would be one. For a double-byte character set such as Unicode, both values would be two.

A line that contains the word "CHARMAP" begins the list of characters and code points. This section is terminated with the "END CHARMAP" line.

Each of the lines in the charmap section consists of the symbolic name of the character followed by the code point value. The value can be expressed as a decimal value (such as "\d255") or as a hex value ("\xff").

Testing a Locale

There are several possible approaches to testing locale information. The trick is to have a reliable tool to access the contents of the locale in a straightforward manner. We could write routines in C to access the information, but this would require a fair amount of time and an engineer with good C programming skills to do the testing. Alternatively, we might have a stable database program that uses our locales. We could use this for our testing, with the caveat that when we find a bug, it's possible that the bug is in the database program or in the way that the program is using the locale as well as in the locale itself.

For our testing at Borland, we use a scripting language that allows us to create a list of functions related to locales, a list of inputs to each function, and a list of expected results for each input. So for our testing, we can use QA engineers who may not know C programming, and the script language is pretty bare-bones, so we're pretty sure that the bugs we find are in the locale and not in the calling program.

The scripting language allows us to open one or more locales, name a function, and then list a series of inputs with associated expected results. For instance, we might have something like the following:

```
TOUPPER @ 1
# The @ 1 refers to the locale that has been opened as "@ 1"
"A" = "a"
"B" = "b"
"A" = "A"
"B" = "B"
```

This means that if we call toupper("a") (where "a" is the character on the right), we expect the return value to be "A". There are similar formats for other functions.

Whether you use a scripting language or C code, there are a set of items that you will need to test in each locale. Let's take a look at some of these.

Character Classification and Transliteration

Testing character classification is simply a matter of listing all the characters and checking that the functions return the correct value for each one (either true or false for classification functions or the correct character for transliteration functions). Once you have determined that the results are correct, you will want to find a way to store the results as a baseline and compare them to subsequent test runs that you might do whenever the locale is rebuilt and before milestone releases.

Even for multibyte character sets, it's probably not necessary to partition your data and only test certain characters, since this testing is straightforward enough. If you decide to partition your data, you should include the first 255 characters, plus several from each grouping, including some Kana characters, some Kanji characters, some characters that contain upper- and lowercase letters as the second byte, and so on. (Please refer to Chapter 13 for more information.)

Formatting of Date and Time Values

For date values, it's important to include enough test cases. These should include 2/29 for several leap years, one date for each day of the week, one date in each month of the year, 12/31 and 1/1, and so forth. Include B.C. dates, and dates several centuries in the future. For Asian dates, it's important to include the day before and the day after each change in emperor eras plus several in between.

For each of these dates, you'll want to display each of the elements of the format individually and in all the expected combinations. Please refer to Chapter 6 for ideas on testing date formats and to Appendix B for formats to test.

In addition, you should test several invalid test cases. You might want to see how your function handles 2/29 in a non-leap-year, or 2/30 in a leap-year. Try 4/31; try 13/1, 0/1, 1/0, and so on. You should test dates in the far past and the far future.

Similarly, you need to test a variety of time values. Try 00:00, 23:59, 24:00, 11:59, 12:00, 24:01, 25:00, –01:00 plus several other times. Again, you should display each element of the time value separately and in a number of formatted strings. Please refer to Chapter 6 for ideas on testing time formats.

Formatting of Numeric and Monetary Values

Choose a wide variety of numbers as test cases. These should include 0, 1, –1, .1, .111, .999, .5, 10, 100, –10, –100, some very large positive and negative numbers, and some very small positive and negative numbers.

After you have these test cases, display them as numbers, as monetary values, and as international monetary values. For numbers, check that you get the correct decimal point and thousands separator characters, and that the grouping is correct. For monetary and international monetary values, check the same things, plus the monetary symbol used, the plus and minus sign used, the number of fractional digits, and the formatting of the currency symbol.

String Collation

Depending on the number of sorting levels, testing collation can be very complex. For a single-level sort in a single-byte character set, it's sufficient to sort the 256 code points and check that they come out in the right order. To do a complete test of a two-level sort, it's not too difficult to create a list of all combinations of two characters and check that these 65,536 values come out in the correct order.

As you can see, though, testing a five-level Japanese dictionary sort that includes some 12,000 Shift-JIS characters and collating elements is not straightforward.

For any sort, we have to know what our baseline is. We have several options:

- ✦ If we're trying to match existing data, then we will probably have a program with which we can compare sort results. This is the most straightforward way to test collation.
- ✦ Some countries publish national standards that contain collation information. Canada has an excellent set of standards for French Canadian sort orders.
- ✦ To some extent, we may be able to use a dictionary, a phone book, or other reference work as a baseline.
- ✦ We may be able to find a native of the target country with knowledge of sorting to tell us if the results are reasonable. Unfortunately, it's very difficult to find people who are sufficiently familiar with their sorting customs. In many cases the sort order will be clear enough, but there are many subtleties that even linguists won't be familiar with.

In any of these cases, we need to isolate a number of examples that demonstrate subtle differences in collation. For French Canadian, the examples would probably include some strings that differ only in accents, some that differ only in case, and strings that differ only in control characters. The examples provided in the description of the locale are good ones in that they demonstrate a particular characteristic of the sort, and the results would be different if the directionality of a level were wrong.

How many of these examples are required? Our approach has been to test collations by level. We test the primary level first by sorting all single characters (256 for single-byte code pages, 12,000 or more for multibyte code pages). We don't really expect to find problems with this test, since it's trivial to make the sort work to this level. But if we do find problems, it doesn't make sense to

move forward with any other testing. (Note that for a single-level sort such as a code-point sort, this level of testing is sufficient.)

Once the first level works properly we combine the characters into groups of two. For single-byte code pages, we use all combinations; otherwise, we start with a subset of single characters and combine those. The subset we use includes the first 256 characters, all the Kana and Nobasu characters (for Japanese), plus a sampling of Kanji and other characters. This testing can find many problems, including those below the second weight level.

At the third level, it starts to become prohibitive to test every combination. We have a tool that will combine character combinations from a database in multiple ways. By choosing our characters carefully, being more selective this time and choosing subsets of character types, and combining up to three characters, we can generate on the order of 100,000 test cases and find bugs that the two-character combinations don't find.

At the same time, we need to be creative and choose test cases based on our knowledge of the collation definition. There are thousands of possibilities. We look at the collating symbols, collating elements, and 1-to-2 characters and choose test cases that involve each of these in many combinations.

CHAPTER 8

Localization Decisions

Several fundamental questions need to be answered as part of the process of deciding to localize.

- Should we localize or not?
- If so, should we localize everything, or just some parts?
- Should we localize in-house, or through a translation agency? at our distributor's office, or at an agency? a combination? If we use an agency, should it be one here in the United States, or in the target country?
- Should we try to localize the product so that it is ready at the same time as the U.S. product? What extra work is involved in this type of localization?

This chapter discusses these questions in detail.

Making the Decision to Localize

The primary decision, of course, is whether to localize at all. The decision can be simple, but more often is it a complex one, based on many factors, including the following:

- *Incremental revenue:* You need to get a firm estimate of the expected incremental revenue from the localized product, and compare this to the expected revenue in that country if the U.S. product were the only one available to sell. This figure is in itself made up of many factors and is generally best derived by your marketing specialists in the target country.

- *Costs of localization:* This figure must take into account the cost of the translation of the documentation, help, UI, sample files, the cost of R&D, QA and management resources involved in the project, the cost of the hardware and software required to perform the localization, and any other costs associated with the localization process. (It shouldn't take into account the costs of enabling the product, since this is an important process whether or not the product is localized; such enabling, or internationalization, costs should properly be charged as part of the core development process.)

Most of the localization costs are highly variable depending on the decisions you make about how to localize your product. These decisions include:

- *Full versus partial localization:* This is the extent of the localization. In some cases, full localization of the product is a requirement, but in others, it may be reasonable to localize only certain aspects of the product.
- *In-house versus external localization:* The differences in cost between these two methods are not always obvious, but instead are a tradeoff of schedule and localization quality as well.
- *Translations: Agency or Subsidiary:* Each has advantages at different times in your company's growth.
- *Simultaneous shipment versus post-U.S. model:* If we ship the localized version on the same day, or even within a month of the U.S. ship date, the cost of localization goes up significantly; yet the potential increased revenue of a simultaneous shipment may far outweigh the additional costs.
- *Extent of localization enabling in the product:* Localizing a well-enabled product won't cost much more than the

cost of translation. Localizing a poorly enabled product will incur high costs in R&D and QA.

The last item is detailed in Chapters 9 and 10. The rest of this chapter describes in detail the other issues summarized above.

Full versus Partial Localization

Full Localization

Full localization is generally preferred over partial. With a full localization, your customers in the target country will have access to your product in the fullest and most specific way possible—with the exact same level of quality as your U.S. customers have. Of course, full localization is more expensive than partial, and you'll have to carefully evaluate the cost differences depending on the features you require to have localized.

As a full localization,

- Your product will address a broader audience.
- Your product will be more accessible to your customers, so it will be easier to use, better accepted, easier to support, and will sell more copies.
- You can generally charge more for a full localization.
- Government agencies in some countries (such as Spain) will only purchase fully localized products.

A full localization includes at least all of the following:

- The entire user-interface (UI) of the software, including but not limited to menus, dialogs, title bars, status messages, error messages, any other strings that the user will see, icons, and bitmaps
- On-line help
- CBT materials
- Documentation

- ✦ Sample programs or files
- ✦ Macro language

Partial Localization

In many cases, it may not make sense to translate every aspect of the product. Even many "full" localizations are actually partials, as when the entire UI, on-line help, and documentation set are translated, but sample code and macro languages are not. Depending on your product, such localizations may very well satisfy your target market's perceived need for a fully localized product. It's critically important that you determine in advance exactly what your target market expects—and what it does not expect—when your market research tells you that a full localization is required. In fact, often such markets are satisfied with UI, documentation, and on-line help, which can save you substantial translation effort and money by not having to translate the other parts of the product.

Decisions about partial localization are usually based on several factors:

- ✦ *Type of product:* Generally, it is more critical to fully localize end-user-oriented software, since these products address a wide audience, many of whom do not speak English. On the other hand, many software developers in various countries speak English, often out of necessity. For example, while there are vast quantities of technical materials available in English on C++ programming, there are very few available in Spanish.
- ✦ *Market demands:* This decision also depends on the target market. In certain countries, many people speak English and are tolerant of English software. Sweden is one of these; the Swedes will generally prefer the localized product if available, but many purchase English software otherwise, especially if your competition is also not localized. In other countries, very few customers will purchase nonlocalized versions. For instance, in Japan, many people speak English, but very

little English-language software is suitable for Japanese requirements. French customers, including French governmental agencies, also tend to have a strong preference for localized products.

- *Market size:* If the target market is small but growing, it may not make sense to invest in a full translation, but partial translation might create a niche for your product and establish it as a standard.
- *Extent of localization enabling:* Certain modules of your program may be very expensive to localize. It might make good business sense for you to leave those modules in English, assuming that this won't be confusing to your customers or appear inconsistent. An example might be a program that is accessed only by the network system administrator who is likely to speak English.
- *The investment your company is willing to make in localization:* No matter what the potential return on investment is, your company may not be in a position to invest in a full localization. In some of these cases, it might still be worthwhile to do a partial localization. If your company is not willing to hire R&D and QA engineers to work on the UI, you could still have an outside agency translate the documentation.
- *Product areas:* There may be areas of the product where localization is undesirable. For example, depending on your application, it may or may not make sense to translate the commands of your macro language. While users may prefer to use a command such as "@ouvrir()" in a French spreadsheet, translating such commands could limit the portability of the code across localized versions of your product. (While it may be possible to store commands such as these as tokens to avoid the portability problem, this approach is not suitable to all applications.)
- *Preference for English:* In the Middle East, users generally prefer English product but require special support for bidirectional input.

In-house versus External Localization

Localization and the associated translation work can be performed in-house, by permanent or contract employees, or externally, by professional translation agencies. The costs and quality associated with each differ.

Costs

In general, in-house localization, much like in-house programming or technical writing, is cheaper on a per-project basis than working with agencies. Highly trained employees, permanent or contract, are much more knowledgeable about both the individual company's policies and the product than an agency ever can be. In-house localization employees can work on several projects over the course of a year, effectively filling in the slack time between releases of any single product. The other significant advantage of an in-house staff is that their training can be leveraged over many projects, and the growing experience of your employees gets applied to all your future localizations. With an external agency, you effectively have to pay to train the agency's employees each time, unless you are lucky enough to maintain a solid relationship with an agency that will assign the same personnel to all of your projects.

However, working with external agencies can be cost effective as well, depending on the project. The major advantage of working with an agency is that you don't have the overhead costs of in-house employees—especially important during a quarter when there is less or even no revenue from a localized product. With agencies, the costs associated with localizing a product are spent in the fiscal quarters immediately preceding the product's release, and there is no in-house overhead during subsequent quarters when there is no revenue for that localized product.

From a cost-only standpoint, there is no correct answer. If you are doing only a few localizations, or if the localizations will be done with major gaps between them, then an external agency is the best bet. But if you are doing many localizations, especially of a

single product, or if you are localizing products continually or every quarter, an in-house staff will be cheaper both in the long and short runs.

Other Translation Issues

Cost is one of the most important issues in determining whether to use an external agency or in-house employees to perform your localization. But cost is by no means the only issue.

Quality is another major factor. While most agencies have a very high standard of quality, only by employing your own staff on site will you have direct control over the quality of your localization work.

A third important factor is scheduling. If your project is on a tight schedule, or if the product changes often during development, then you will need to be very flexible with employee assignments, last-minute changes in what is being localized and what is not, and with moving critical milestones. In almost every case, such flexibility demands in-house work. The best agencies can work around your changes, but they will make you pay for it.

Additional discussion of the differences between agencies and in-house personnel is presented in Chapter 5. That discussion focuses specifically on the translation component of the localization project.

Translations: Agency or Subsidiary?

Another factor in considering the performance of the localization is whether your translation should be done by personnel in your company's subsidiary in the target country, or by an agency. Of course, this applies only if you have a subsidiary; but this is an important issue for any company that may grow to have a subsidiary. Historically, almost all companies start small, and that means starting with an agency, moving to several agencies in several countries, and perhaps eventually opening a subsidiary in one of the more important countries (usually Germany), followed by additional subsidiaries in other countries.

At some point after creating the first subsidiary, the question arises: Should I have my employees at the subsidiary do the localization work; or should I continue to use the agency?

The advantages and tradeoffs of external translation agencies versus in-house employees is discussed above and in other chapters. The issue to consider here is the same as considering whether to do your localizations in-house or with an agency. The difference is that your in-house proposal will usually be far away from you, at the subsidiary, and more difficult to manage effectively. Other issues to investigate are:

- Is management at the subsidiary able to manage localization?
- What are the costs of hiring individuals at the subsidiary? Are they substantially greater or lesser than at home?
- What methods of communication do we have in place to support localization at the subsidiary? Is e-mail enough? What about file transfer: modem to modem, or do we have a leased-line network? Is a daily or weekly conference call enough? Should we be considering video conferencing?

Simultaneous Shipment versus Post-U.S. Model

We use two models for localization projects: the simultaneous shipment model and the post-U.S. shipment model. The goal of the simultaneous model is to ship the localized product at the same time as the U.S. product. The post-U.S. model is used for all other projects.

The model used depends on the needs and potential revenues of the localized product for that target country. In most segments of the software industry, for example, Germany is the most important revenue-generating country after the United States. Closely following in European revenue importance are usually France and Spain, or Italy. Therefore, software localization projects often target simultaneous shipment for Germany, and if possible, France, with subse-

quent localizations following periodically using the post-U.S. shipment model.

Why Is Simultaneous Shipment Important?

One reason for the importance of simultaneous shipment is obvious: The sooner the localized versions are available, the sooner they can be sold and generate revenue. But there are more important considerations as well. Two linked facts illustrate these considerations: (1) Localized products are usually sold at a much higher price than the U.S. product, and (2) if the localized product is not available very soon after the U.S. product is shipped, then customers in the target country will purchase the English-language (U.S.) product. The latter is particularly true in Germany, where many computer users are both proficient in English and technically focused and motivated to use the latest available version.

Customers who then buy the U.S. product—often on the gray market—usually don't spend additional money later to buy the localized product when it does finally become available. Therefore, the company gains the sale of a U.S. product, but loses the additional revenue they would have charged for the localized product. This revenue is then lost forever—so simultaneous shipment is not a method to pull in "deferred" revenue—it is a method to bring in substantial additional revenue. Multiply this by the large numbers of customers that often buy newly released or upgraded products, and this additional revenue becomes so substantial that the extra problems and costs associated with simultaneous shipment are easily justified.

Also, it is the higher price of the localized product that pays for the localization itself. If customers buy the U.S. product at the lower price because the localized product is not yet available, the cost of localization per localized unit goes up, further reducing the effectiveness of the investment in the localization versus the total revenue for that country.

There are additional motivations for simultaneous shipment. If the localized product is not available soon after the U.S. product, then there is a substantial risk that the customers in that country will not purchase the U.S. version of your product; but they may well purchase a competitive product, which may already be localized.

Problems Involved in Simultaneous Shipment

If simultaneous shipment is so important, why don't we do it for all localizations? The two answers are cost and time.

Simultaneous shipment provides a lot of financial benefit, but not without substantial costs. Most of these costs are related to the problems inherent in the development process, and the costs involved in working around these problems.

First, let's describe the very straightforward post-U.S. model, and contrast it with the involved simultaneous model.

The Post-U.S. Model

In the post-U.S. model, translation efforts don't have to start until the U.S. product is complete. When the books go to the printer in the United States, the book sources can start being translated. When the user interface and the help are complete and the U.S. product goes to Release to Manufacturing, then the UI strings and the help sources can start being translated. With diligent effort on the part of the translators, the project manager, and the localization team, a localized product can be completed and ready for testing within a few weeks.

The Simultaneous Model

In the simultaneous model, the luxury of waiting for the UI, help, and books to be done is not available. The volume of translation is large, so that the translation must start before the U.S. products are completed. Furthermore, the translated UI must undergo beta cycles and the documents must undergo review cycles of their own if the product is to have an acceptable quality level. In the simultaneous model, these cycles need to start early enough in the development process so that they can be completed in time to ship concurrently with the U.S. product.

For the UI, the translation starts when the localization team delivers a translation kit based on one of the U.S. beta versions. For

the book and help sources, the translation starts at a point when the technical writers and the localization project manager agree that the material is stable enough for translation to begin.

After translation has begun, problems occur when the inevitable changes occur. The user-interface always undergoes changes and additions after the beta cycle when translation has already started. Development managers usually try to plan so that these changes are minimal, but competitive pressures and unforeseen technical issues often make substantial change necessary late in the cycle.

Whenever the user-interface is changed, the documentation—both books and help—must be updated to reflect these changes. Often the cycle of UI-change-causing-documentation-change is repeated several times after translation has started.

For the UI translation, updated translation kit software is provided at subsequent beta and gamma milestones, and within hours of each United States Release to Manufacturing candidate build, so that in-house translators can make the final changes as soon as possible. This fast update of the kit software is important during the first phases of product development when new builds are often done every few hours. Good localization kit software can identify changed and added strings and make the updating as easy as possible, so that updated builds can be created within days and even hours of new U.S. builds.

For the documentation and help translations, the updating is not nearly so easy. To manage the changes, an agreement is made between the localization project manager and the technical writers at the time of the translation-start milestone for each chapter or help source file. When the writers hand off a chapter or file for translation start, they agree to track the technical changes that will follow. Usually changes are made late in the cycle for technical reasons, and for proofreading and editorial corrections as well. The translators, having already started translating the material, care only about the technical changes or additions that have been made since they started translation. Therefore, the writers agree to track the technical changes between the translation-start handoffs and the final handoffs, and the translators incorporate the technical changes to their already translated book and help files to create the final localized versions ready for delivery to RTM or to the printer.

All this updating means increased costs for the translation, as the translators must in many cases retranslate material that has already been made obsolete by the later technical changes. This usually leads directly to increased vendor bills. Other additional cost is due to the extra work that must be done by the localization manager, the technical writers, and the localization teams both in the United States and at the translation agency and subsidiary.

Chapter 9

Localization Enabling

As discussed earlier, all software is localizable. What varies is the length of time required to complete the job and the costs involved. In some cases you might very well need to rewrite the entire product.

When designing a product, it is very important that people are aware that a properly enabled product can be localized quickly with minimum cost. A poorly designed product will require almost as much work as writing a new one, with the associated higher expenditures.

Localization Models

To date, most efforts at localization have been largely limited to ensuring that a particular program is enabled for a particular country. For example, Paradox DOS for Germany is specifically localized for the German market, and the same binary is not targeted for any other country—the program is recompiled for each country's localization. This is a *static* approach and is only a partial solution, as it addresses only one market.

Ideally, the application should *dynamically* adapt to the user's native language and cultural conventions. For example, dBASE for Windows can dynamically switch its user-interface to different languages. This is done by using resource files, called dynamically loaded libraries (DLLs), containing all user-interface text, which are completely separate from the executable file. At runtime, it's possible for dBASE for Windows to load different resource files at the user's request.

While Borland ships only a single resource file with each localized version, using the same executable for all localized versions—including the U.S. version—saves substantial development, testing, and translation time.

Regardless of whether you choose the dynamic or the static model, a great deal of preparation is required to have an effective and successful translation cycle. Just as in building a house, if the foundation is not done properly, there is little chance that a good house can be built on top of it.

In this section, we will discuss the levels of localization enabling into which your software may fall. These levels are based on the status of the UI and *cultural conventions* contained in your product. These may be:

- ✦ Hard-coded throughout the source (difficult translation, full recompilation)
- ✦ Hard-coded, but contained in header files (easier translation, full recompilation)
- ✦ Hard-coded, but limited to a few source files (recompile only the source files and relink with the other object files)
- ✦ Resourced, but statically linked (no recompilation)
- ✦ Resourced and loaded dynamically at runtime (no recompilation, no relink)

✦ Hard-coded throughout the source (difficult translation, full recompilation)

Programs that are not well-enabled for localization fall into this category. Often, they consist of code written and modified on the fly, where messages, strings, prompts, and dialog boxes are embedded throughout the code. This adds a tremendous amount of complexity to the translation process in that the strings must be extracted from the sources before they can be translated, then merged back into the baseline code. This becomes especially tricky if the baseline changes after the strings have been extracted because there is no reliable way to upgrade and maintain the links to the source. Simultaneous release is not reasonable, revisions of the product require full retranslation, and it is very difficult to main-

Type	Location of translatable strings	Compilation	Linking (object files or resources)	Amount of source code required to build translated product
Hard-coded throughout the source	All sources	Full	Full	All
Hard-coded, but contained in header files	Header files only	Full	Full	All
Hard-coded, but limited to a few source files	Few modules	Partial	Full	Some
Resourced, but statically linked	Resources only	None	Partial	None
Resourced and loaded dynamically at runtime	Resources only	None	None	None

tain consistency with previous versions. Tools for parsing and merging will be described later in this chapter.

In products like these, you might find problems such as the following:

- Strings that belong to the user-interface (UI) are spread throughout the program and intermixed with code.
- In some cases, translations in different areas of the program must match in order for the program to function properly. An example is a program that uses strings as tokens where the parser requires a string that matches its corresponding function call.

- Memory allocated for strings is hard-coded. If the developer has defined a buffer to contain a string and the size of the buffer is the number of chars that the string in native language contains, the program will crash if translation contains more characters than the original program.
- Yes/no questions are spread throughout the code, and each time, the result is compared with "Y" or "N". Even worse are programs that use the equivalent characters expressed in decimal, HEX, or OCTAL ASCII. In both these cases, the strings to translate will be difficult to find and the translator will have to translate the same strings many times.
- Dialog boxes contain components that use hard-coded coordinates. This requires the translated version to have each one of its coordinates reengineered.
- Strings are constructed from multiple concatenated strings. In other languages, the strings won't fall in the same order, so the translated version will require a change to the source code or the translation won't be correct. For example, the string "File %s is not found in directory %s" might translate to the equivalent of "Directory %s does not contain file %s" in some languages. This might appear to the user as "Directory AUTOEXEC.BAT does not contain file C:\".

  While there are solutions to this problem (see below), another problem is that when a string is built out of multiple concatenated strings there may be no way a translator can know which string represents which parameter. The above example might be easy enough to translate, but many times, strings don't contain as much context. It might be difficult for a translator to deduce that "%s of %s, Record %d of %d" should result in the string "Standard form of table CUSTOMER.DB, Record 1 of 250".
- Similarly, some programmers assume that plurals are formed by adding an *s* to the end of a word, but this isn't the case in most languages.
- Error messages come from standard runtime libraries. It is important to resource all messages that the user might see

```
int yesno(pmsg,defresp)
char *pmsg;
int  defresp;
{
     int row,col;        /* Position of user response */
     char *presp,*calloc(),*cgets(),*ifixit();
     int resp,done;
     presp = calloc(BUFSIZE + 2,1);
     cputs(pmsg);        /* Output the prompt */
     cputs("?");
     sccurpos(10,25);    /* Hardcoded location, if prompt gets */
     do                  /* longer code change will be needed */
     {
      done = TRUE;
      *presp = BUFSIZE; /* Max BUFSIZE characters accepted */
      presp = cgets(presp);
      if((*presp == 0) && ((defresp == 0) || (defresp == 1)))
               resp = defresp; /* Null response is OK */
      else
      {
               presp = ifixit(presp); /* Remove blanks and shift up */
               sccurset(10,25);
               scwrite(BLANK,80 - 25); /* Clear the old response, and */
               cputs(presp);    /* write the converted one. */
               if(*presp == 'Y')
                  resp = YES;
               else if(*presp == 'N')
                  resp = NO;
               else
               {
                done = FALSE;
       }
      }
     }
     cputs("\x0d\x0a"); /* Carriage return/line feed */
     free(presp);
     return(resp);
}
```

Figure 9.1 Example of code that is poorly enabled.

so that they can be translated. Some programs use error messages from the C runtime libraries (such as "File not found," "Abort, Retry, Ignore"). These strings are not readily accessible to the translators and can't be resourced.

There are a number of steps that you can take to resolve such problems. Even if you aren't able to resolve all the problems in the next revision of your product, each of these steps will facilitate your translation process and help you deliver cleaner localized versions more quickly.

- *Move strings to a header file:* By moving all strings that the user might see to header files in which each string is a macro, you simplify the parsing and merging process (Figure 9.2).

  This can be modified as shown in Figure 9.3.

  Note that the model in Figure 9.4 solves some of the problems in that it moves translatable items out of the source code, but it still requires full recompilation of the product.
- *Allocate extra memory for expansion and extra space on the screen:* Usually, a string will require more space when translated from English. If you dynamically allocate string buffers, and if you design your user interface with sufficient space from the beginning, you will save a large amount of redesign when it comes time to translate the product. The shorter the U.S. strings, the more extra room you should allow. The table in Figure 9.5 shows typical expansion that is expected on translated strings.

```
* HELLO.C--Hello, world */
#include <stdio.h>
int main()
{
   printf("Hello, world\n");
   return 0;
}
```

Figure 9.2 HELLO.C with unresourced strings.

```
/* HELLO.C - Resourced Hello, world */
#include <stdio.h>
#include "Hello.h"
int main()
{
   printf(Hello_string);
   return 0;
}
```

Figure 9.3 HELLO.C with resourced strings.

```
/* HELLO.H - Hello world header */
#define Hello_string "Hello, world\n"
```

Figure 9.4 HELLO.H containing string in macros.

- *Define standard procedures for common tasks:* Instead of comparing yes/no responses to "Y" and "N" throughout your code, you can call a single function that displays a prompt, accepts a response, and returns the answer as a flag. In this way, the translation need be done only once.
- *Use dynamic dialog boxes:* When reasonably possible, create dialog boxes that resize according to their contents. Alternatively, create dialog boxes using a visual editor that your translators can also use.

English length	Additional growth
1–4 chars	100%
5–10 chars	80%
11–20 chars	60%
21–30 chars	40%
31–50 chars	20%
over 50 chars	10%

Figure 9.5 Expected expansion of strings when translated from English.

- *Avoid strings that are built out of multiple strings:* In many cases, you have to dynamically compose a string from two separate strings, but you shouldn't have more than two. In our International API, we have a version of the sprintf() function that parameterizes the substitution strings. In the previous example, "File %s is not found in directory %s", we would instead have, "File %s1 is not found in directory %s2", which means that the %s1 is replaced by the first parameter and the %s2 is replaced by the second parameter. This can be translated to "Directory %s2 does not contain file %s1" and will still work correctly. The user will see "Directory C:\ does not contain file AUTOEXEC.BAT".
- *Never make plurals by adding* s *to the end of words:* Instead, use separate strings.
- *Make sure that all messages are controlled by your application:* Rather than calling RTL or other standard library routines that might display a message, use your own routines that display a message that you control.

✦ Hard-coded, but contained in header files (easier translation, full recompilation)

Once we've cleaned up the problems discussed above, we will end up with a product that contains all the strings in header files. This is a milestone stage in that all strings to be translated appear in a common format and in only a few files. This allows us to:

- Extract the strings to a common format.
- Create a safe environment for the translators to work in, isolated from code. This might be in the form of a database with one field for the English strings and one for the translated strings.
- Make use of tools to check spelling and translation consistency among other things.
- Reincorporate the translated strings into our executable and build a translated version of the product.

The suite of tools that addresses these tasks is called the Software Translation Kit and is described later in this chapter.

At this stage, we have a much safer process for translating the strings in the product, and we no longer require that the translators be programmers. The code itself will be very close to the core version, so the early localized builds are likely to be much more stable than in the previous model, and will require less QA work.

To reach the next level, you will need to move all strings to separate source modules. In this way, all the modules that do not contain strings can be delivered as a library and linked to the translated modules.

✦ **Hard-coded, but limited to a few source files (recompile only the source files and relink with the other object files)**

If we remove the strings from header files and restrict them to a handful of C source modules, we've reached another milestone. We still have the advantages of the previous model, but we no longer require access to the complete set of source code to build a localized version. At this point, it is possible to send the Software Translation Kit and a set of object files to an external translator without having to send complete source code. The translator can build a localized version to test it, but doesn't have access to sensitive information and therefore has less opportunity to introduce bugs. The initial localized builds are likely to be more stable than in the previous model, because they will be closer to the core version.

To reach the next level, we can resource our strings separately from source code (Figures 9.8, 9.9, and 9.10).

```
/* HELLO.C - Resourced Hello, world */
#include <stdio.h>
int main()
{
   printf(getString(Hello_string));
   return 0;
}
```

Figure 9.6 HELLO.C with resourced strings.

```
/* HELLORes.C - Hello world strings */
char* getString(int token)
{
   switch (token)
   {
         Hello_string: return("Hello, world\n");
         Other_string: return("Other string\n");
   }
}
```

Figure 9.7 HELLO.H containing string in macros.

While this is a Windows-specific example, similar concepts can be used on other platforms.

✦ **Resourced, but statically linked (no recompilation)**

This next stage is similar to the previous one, but no recompilation is required. Messages are contained in resource files that are linked to the executable. Since no source code is changed, there are fewer opportunities to introduce bugs.

The whole process of translation may now be handled by the distributor and translator, who can create and test localized versions. While we still require testing by our international QA engineers, we tend to find a relatively small number of bugs.

To improve these products, we can:

- ✦ Make better resource editors.
- ✦ Create menu builders and software interface emulators.
- ✦ Improve consistency checking in resource editors.

```
/* HELLO.C - Resourced Hello, world */
#include <stdio.h>
int main()
{
   printf(Hello_string);
   return 0;
}
```

Figure 9.8 Resourced HELLO.C

```
/* HELLO.H - Hello world header */
#define Hello_string LoadString(1)
```

Figure 9.9 Alternative HELLO.H, used with the resourced HELLO.C (Fig. 9.8), but retrieves resources from a resource file.

- ✦ Make improved resource file compilers, and improve size of final object and accessing speed.

In addition, we can move to the next level by binding the RC file to a separate dynamically loaded library.

✦ Resourced and loaded dynamically at runtime (no recompilation, no relink)

This final stage is what we consider to be a product that is fully enabled for localization. We have a single executable file that ships worldwide. This executable can choose which resource file to load based on user-selection or based on a flag in a configuration file. While it is still possible to introduce bugs during the translation process, these bugs are likely to be less serious than in other models, and we have a much higher confidence level in the quality of the product.

Localization: By Design or Retrofit?

Localization by Design

Software can be designed with localization requirements in mind. Typically when a new product is being developed, this represents very little additional effort and provides high gain. In fact, it pro-

```
/* HELLO.RC - Hello world header */
STRINGTABLE
{
1, "Hello, world"
}
```

Figure 9.10 HELLO.RC with the resources for HELLO.H.

vides benefits to the maintainability of the core product as well.

Good coding standards are encouraged by localization enabling, including having strings separated from main code, having clear boundaries between modules (which will later facilitate internationalization, for example, if support for additional peripherals is required), and creating modular code. Note that similar work is needed to write portable code if one plans to move code from one platform to others.

UI design, when done with international needs in mind, ensures that little or no work has to be done to fit longer strings and bitmaps to all cultural needs.

Samples that are sensitive to international needs are also important. One example of what not to do is to use labels with U.S.-formatted addresses (which include ZIP code).

Localization as a Retrofit

This represents the category of software that has been designed with little or no attention given to the needs of localization. Expect to do major work to prepare the product for localization, starting from basic enabling, such as:

- Adding support to date, number, printer, currency
- Adding support to different code sets (437, 850, 862, ANSI)
- Creating resource strings (separate the executable sources out of the code)
- Creating rewrite samples

For more details, please refer to Chapters 8 and 11.

CHAPTER 10

Managing Localization

This chapter discusses how to manage the localization process. Proper management of the localization process is critical to the success of any localization project. More than any other single factor, management can make or break the project.

Often, with the pressures of time, revenues, and staffing resources, careful management can end up taking a back seat to these seemingly more immediate concerns. This is a critical mistake. Enough time must be set aside early in the project to plan, supervise, and implement during the entire project. This time must be protected and guarded, so that the person taking the role of project manager does not get moved onto other, seemingly more pressing tasks.

Role of the Localization Project Manager

Critical to the success of the localization project is a single person assigned as the project manager. Ideally, this person should have no other responsibility but localization project management and related duties, but often this role must be taken on by a software development project manager or one of the programmers on the project.

Management of the documentation issues is a major responsibility of the localization project manager. Usually, dedicated resources have been allocated for programming and testing the localization of the software, but documentation is often left to the project manager. For this reason, the project manager needs to be fully aware of the documentation issues for localization as detailed in Chapter 4.

Responsibilities of the localization project manager include the following, in chronological order:

- Provide input on, review, and evaluate the various plans created by other group managers: the product plan or specification, the QA plan, the documentation plan, the marketing plan, and the distribution plan.
- Work with the international marketing teams to determine the number and order of localizations to be done for the product.
- Talk with other group managers, developers, technical writers, testers, internationalization and localization teams, translators, representatives for the target countries, and upper management to determine the needs of the localization project.
- Create the localization project plan, get it reviewed by appropriate team members, and incorporate review comments to produce a final plan.
- Create a localization schedule based on the product schedule, and make sure it includes specific dates for translation kit handoff dates, documentation source handoff dates, and milestone dates—beta, gamma, release to manufacturing (RTM)—for each country in the localization plan.
- During the design stages of the development cycle, work with the developers and the documentation teams to avoid implementations that will cause localization problems or added expenses.
- During the delivery stages of the product, work with the international team members to ensure delivery of the translation kits and other source files as planned.
- Also during the delivery stages, work with the documentation teams to deliver the translation start (80%) and final documentation sources (for books, help, and readme files) for translation.

- ✦ Work with the translators and the international team members to ensure delivery of the translated product as scheduled at all appropriate milestones: beta, gamma, and final RTM.

Managing Translators

The task of translation itself is almost always given to a particular translation agency. It is strongly recommended that a single agency, with substantial professional translation experience, be contracted to translate all three major parts of the product:

- ✦ The user-interface, using the software translation kit
- ✦ The help, translating directly from the help source files
- ✦ The books, translating directly from the documentation source files

It's often tempting to save costs by having one person or group translate the software and others translate the documentation, but this is often a mistake. For example, sometimes an in-house engineer may be a native speaker of the target language, and so it may seem smart to have him or her translate the software, and then send the documentation out to a vendor. Sometimes, companies try to save even more money by sending the documentation to university students for translation. These examples illustrate two different kinds of mistakes: (a) using multiple parties for the translation, and (b) using inexperienced translators.

Using the same agency for the entire translation will help avoid problems with terminology and glossary issues between each part of the translation. With more than one translation site, you have additional work to do coordinating the results of each site, and if you are not fluent in the target languages, doing this properly is impossible. Further, it is much easier to manage a single agency during the translation effort. Negotiating the contract, determining the total costs, and keeping costs down are all much easier when working with a single agency. When schedules change and motiva-

tion—positive or negative—must be strong to ensure meeting the new dates, it's far easier to implement with a single translation agency.

Using inexperienced translators is very tempting due to the potential cost savings, but it is very risky. Conventional localization wisdom dictates that translations must be physically done in the target country by native speakers who use the language daily. Native translators on assignment here in the United States have admitted to losing some of their speed after only four or five months here. This is due, of course, to the lack of everyday use, in both conversation and print, of the native languages. This is particularly true of technical terms, which often have translations that are not obvious or have no cognates to the English. When the translator isn't able to read the technical periodicals of the target language, or to converse with other native speakers about technical subjects, the translator's efficiency is reduced.

Most of us readily accept the argument for native speakers, but the temptations of lower-cost translations can push us to try using inexperienced translators for some small segment of the project. Even if the inexperienced translators are themselves native speakers, if they have lived away from their home country for a long time, they can be significantly affected by the loss of efficiencies as just described. Additionally, their lack of experience in translation will be a heavy burden. Professional translators have learned a variety of methods of performing translations quickly, using various glossaries and other techniques to ensure quality and consistency while getting the job done on schedule. Inexperienced translators don't bring this level of expertise and problem-solving. What this means is that your whole project can be sidelined by fix-it work required for problems that a professional translator would have identified and prevented. Multiply this by a few more problems, and the potential savings of the cheaper translation are soon eaten up by the fix-it hours.

It is best to use professional translation agencies on your first few localization projects. After you've worked with translators for a while, you can use your experience to decide whether to take the risks of cheaper translation.

Information Flow and Communications

The most important job performed by the localization project manager is *coordinating the information.* It is his or her responsibility to ensure that all members of the team have the information they need to get their jobs done on schedule and at the expected level of quality. He or she must make sure that the team members have access to the tools and the people they need to do their jobs properly. Ultimately, the localization project manager has one job from which all other responsibilities derive: *to deliver the localized product on time and within budget.*

Managing the flow of information across the team is the critical component to this task. As the localization project manager usually does not have direct authority over the various people involved with the project, he or she has to *manage by influence.* The localization project manager not only must keep all team members aware of the tasks to be done, but also must continually remind people of the importance of the localization project. This is especially important in regard to people whose cooperation is critical, but whose level of understanding of internationalization is not a priority: development managers, programmers, documentation managers, and technical writers.

As a practical matter, the localization project manager needs to attend all project meetings. There are several important reasons: to spare the localization team members from wasting their time on meetings where their presence is not required, to defend the interests of the localization project and the international group, to represent the localization team as a knowledgeable and able asset to the entire company, to assess the impact of changes to the product or the project schedule, and to provide immediate estimates of impacts to the localization project.

Of particular concern are schedule changes. Changes to the core project's schedule have an immediate and critical impact on the schedules for the localization project. The localization project needs to be rescheduled immediately, and to do so the localization project manager needs to meet with all team members to accurately evaluate the impacts of the core schedule change. No one must be forgotten in this information flow, or the project can be plunged into critical danger. For example, a simple change to the U.S. feature complete date will usually cause changes to all the documentation dates, which will subsequently cause changes to the translation dates, the localized to-print dates, and the final delivery dates for the localized product—even if the *only* U.S. date changed is the one feature complete date. Therefore, the localization project manager must be sure to discuss the impacts with the technical writers and publications managers, the documentation translators, the software translators and R&D engineers, the QA engineers and management, the internationalization department management, the management of the subsidiary or distributor in the country, the marketing team for the localized product, and upper management. If any of these extended team members don't know about the new feature complete date, their assumptions about the schedule and delivery will be obsolete, causing more problems later in the project.

The localization project manager should maintain an updated mental checklist at all times:

- Is the localization project schedule updated? Does everyone have a copy of it?
- Does everyone on the localization team understand the currently defined contents of the core product?
- Does everyone on the team understand what components of the product are being localized, and what components are not?
- How confident are the localization team members of their delivery dates?
- How much padding currently still exists in the schedule? How many more changes can we take without the dates slipping again?
- Do the core R&D and publications managers remember that I have to be involved in any discussions that could result in content or schedule change?
- Do the translators know and "own" their current delivery dates? Are they telling me everything I need to know to predict problems that may occur?

Good management is the single most important component of the localization project. With good management, all problems can be handled effectively. Without good management, the project will be unfocused, overly expensive, and almost certainly behind schedule—regardless of how good the rest of the localization team or the core team are. Make sure that you put your best people and your best efforts behind your localization project management.

Translation Preparation

Proper preparation before the start of translation is the key to a successful project.

Identification of General Requirements

As in any well-managed project, the first phase is the definition of the scope of work. Many of the questions have already been addressed in previous chapters: Localize in-house, with an agency, or a combination? Use the simultaneous or post-U.S. localization model? Where will the work be done? What are the modules that will be localized? How many languages will the product be translated? What are the localization processes we will be using? Have we checked for legal concerns (such as encryption algorithms)? Are there additional features needed for specific markets (such as specific graph types, spell-checking engines)? Should we delete some features that might not be appropriate for the target market? Have we identified all of the third party's software and any specific issues relating to it (access to source code, proper internationalization support, rights to sell it in foreign countries)? What is the applicability of samples and collateral material?

Having these questions answered in advance will greatly facilitate the work to come, and will allow management to do the proper preparation up front on the marketing plans and revenue forecast, and realistic goal setting for release.

Localization Planning

After the general requirements have been identified, you are ready to do your first draft of your localization plan. This is usually comprised of the test plans, documentation localization plan and software localization plan. Contents of the localization plan should include, but not be limited to, the following:

- Lists of contacts and responsibilities
- Lists of resources (people and capital equipment)
- Schedule with key milestones
- List of modules to be translated
- High-level word count
- Description of all work expected to be done

Glossary Development

This is one of the most important phases of any localization project. In all software localization, many parts of the user-interface are referred to by terms that are used correspondingly in the documentation and on-line help. Since these different parts of the project are translated by different people, a glossary must be developed early in the localization project. The glossary contains all the phrases that are used in more than one place in the product. This should be the first text translated, and the translation should be placed in the glossary so that the English and translated terms are together. This way, the various translators all work from this central glossary to ensure consistent translation of all terms across all parts of the product: UI, documentation, and help. The glossary will also save time later by reducing time needed to test the product as well as avoiding the need to fix linguistic bugs when testing cycles start.

Tools Definition and Development

Most new releases will need new tools to be developed, either to address a new type of module, or to improve the process used in

the past. If your company has multiple products, it is a good idea to develop or acquire a set of tools to be used for all your software translation kits. This is especially helpful if your linguistic translation work force will be doing multiple projects and the required training on new tools is costly and time consuming.

Integration/Build Process

If you plan to release multiple localized versions, which is true for most of the cases, having a well-defined integration/build process will be of extreme importance. It is important to have a proper "version control" system in place (as you would when you are developing the core product), as well as clear boundaries and procedures that describe exactly how the Software Translation Kit (SWTK) will be sent to translation site, received back, integrated into the product, and delivered to QA—all the steps until the product is ready to be released to the market.

This is even more critical if you are trying to achieve simultaneous shipment, as the core source base can be changing constantly until very late in the core development project. It is highly recommended that the domestic integration process be integrated into the localization integration process.

Software Screen Translation

The next step, in parallel with documentation translation, is to work toward a stable user-interface that can be used to produce screen shots as well as validate the glossary. During this phase, changes will be done to the "localizeable" items: menus, dialog boxes, messages, icons, bitmaps text, status bar, functions/macros, and more.

As the UI becomes more stable, translation of the sample applications or code should begin, with the goal to have all software translations completed when the product is delivered to the last outside cycle (gamma).

Help Translation

Help is a major component of any localization work due to the increasing volume of on-line help systems. Most companies are putting more information into on-line forms in order to provide better on-line support to the user, as well as to reduce cost of goods (COGs). Translation of this help proceeds in parallel with the software translation.

Stabilization of the help depends heavily on how soon the main development effort freezes: The product has to be done before it can be fully documented. Because of this lateness of help, when using the simultaneous localization model, the help is likely to be on the critical path and as such it must be managed very carefully.

This is becoming even more true as modern release cycles of PC-based software are being scheduled much quicker than before—between 9 and 18 months—forcing very tight schedules with consequential late freezes on the feature set.

Document Translation

Documentation translation is also performed in parallel with the software translation. As the software goes through the testing phases and product stabilization, the core documentation is stabilized and sent to printer. See Chapter 5 for a detailed discussion of documentation translation issues.

Resources for Localization

Localization projects require close cooperation from all team members. The following paragraphs describe the role of each team member. Keep in mind that for small localization projects, one person may act in several, or even all, of these roles simultaneously. If possible, however, at least one person should be assigned to each of these roles.

- *R&D engineers.* These are the software engineers who are responsible for developing the tools to enable the prod-

uct, for adding necessary international support (such as resource strings, separating localizeable strings out of the executable), and developing the SWTKs so translation can be done with minimum impact to the functionality of the product. They are also responsible for fixing the bugs created in the localization process.

- *Integration engineers.* These are software engineers who are responsible for making the formal builds that are delivered to Quality Assurance. In some cases, these engineers are also responsible for making the easier bug fixes (with support from the translator: incorporate spelling fixes, dialog box resizing, and resolution of pickletter conflicts). In other cases, the integration engineers are also responsible for creating the build environment, and ensuring that builds delivered are fully reproducible and properly backed up.
- *QA engineers.* These engineers are the champions of quality, and indeed are responsible for the quality of the localized product. In some cases, they also take on integration responsibilities and are responsible for ensuring that the code base of the localized product can be reproduced.
- *Translators.* The translators are responsible for the linguistic translation of the product, the creation and maintenance of the glossary, linguistic consistency, and in some cases, testing of the product for linguistic translation quality. Their work can be focused on one of the following areas:
    - *Software.* For this task it is important that the people assigned are not only linguistically capable, but also have good grasp of technology, as they will be using an SWTK as well as doing some minor debugging work. Because translation of samples is usually included, knowledge of the specific product being translated is highly desirable.
    - *On-line files, such as help and on-line documentation.* For help files, if the system to be translated is

an MS-WINDOWS application, the translator should be experienced in building and maintaining Windows help systems.

- *Manuals.* Usually, this is the bulk of the translation work and as such becomes the critical path item. Proper management of this work is critical for a timely and successful localization project.

✦ *Project managers.* See the detailed discussion earlier in this chapter for specifics of the project manager's responsibilities.

CHAPTER 11

Performing Localization

As noted in previous chapters, careful planning and solid management are the foundations for a successful and cost-effective localization project. The actual work of the project—the localization—must also be performed as carefully as possible. This chapter describes the issues and tools associated with actually performing the localization.

Localization Tools

Localization enabling work can be greatly facilitated when the proper tools are used. Some of the basic tools include ready-made utilities and widely available tools, including the following:

- *A good programmer's editor:* If your editor contains good macro support (such as Borland's Brief), you can write macros that can help you search for specific problem areas and perform merges and updates.

  Examples include searching for single-quoted strings ('Y') and runtime library functions instead of locale-sensitive functions when dealing with strings (strcmp, isalpha,).
- *Grep:* This is a simple but effective tool that can be used to locate hard-coded strings in source code and in function calls that will cause problems for localization.
- *AWK and SED:* These are a class of tools that can be used for global replacement of code, which is often necessary for localization.

- *Resource Workshop:* If the application is a Windows application, use of a resource tool such as Borland's Resource Workshop will help you to walk through all the UI components of the product so you can ensure that bitmaps are international in nature, and that menus and dialogs have proper layout to allow expansion and translation.
- *Resource linkers:* Tools such as Borland's BRCC allow you to extract the resource information out of both executable and library files. These resources can later be parsed for hard-coded strings.
- *Spreadsheets and databases:* These can be used as a data repository, where translatable items can be stored and manipulated. Given that most of the high-end databases provide powerful macro language support, you can build most of the translation environment using them and also check and manipulate all the data to be translated.
- *Document comparison tools* (e.g., Docucomp, by Advance Software, Inc.): These tools can help identify changes from version to version. This type of tool can also be useful during the localization work for tracking help and documentation changes, and can also be used on source code files.

There are also some tools developed specifically to help fix sources that were not built with localization in mind. Some of them provide parsers that go through the source and replace the translatable items with macros. These macros point to strings that are then moved into resource files.

Translation Tools

Most important is a standard set of tools, defined by and used for the translation process. Such standard tools provide the translators a common user-interface and translation platform, so there is no need to keep learning new tools every time a new product needs to be translated.

Ideally (as discussed in detail in previous chapters) all products should have resource file sources that are in a standard format, and all products should have external resource files, so the translation work does not interfere with the executable binary. Unfortunately, this is not always the case despite the best intentions. Various parts of the product can be developed by internal resources; but they can also be acquired or written by third parties, or a particular piece might not fit in the localization template that has been set. Examples of this include:

- Application macro languages
- Binary objects created by the application
- Sample applications or code, where proper resourcing might make the sample too complex and defeat its purpose

Translation work is often done by a wide array of people with a variety of technical skills. Therefore, translation tools need to be characterized by the following qualities:

- *Easy to use:* They should address translators who might not understand the compilation and linking process, or how to load a debugger to trace through C or C++ sources.
- *Standard:* Training should be minimized so the same translators can be applied to different projects with minimum retraining and downtime.
- *Powerful:* They should give the translator the ability to manipulate translation data, provide contextual information, provide ability to see the translated product (this can be an emulation or an actual build of the product), and ideally, check if the final product is functional.
- *Flexible:* They will probably need to address several different types of resource files.

In order to achieve all of these things at the same time, translation tools should be designed very carefully, so they can be shareable across different application resource needs.

Translation is *datacentric.* In other words, during the translation process, the main object being worked on is data that will need to be extracted from resource files, translated to the local language, manipulated, reinserted to sources, and used to build the final localized product. The following requirements should be kept in mind:

- *Standard format:* You should define standard formats to which translation *data* should be extracted, the data *structure* in which the data should be stored, and *editors* that will provide to the translator the interface on which he or she will work.
- *Upgradability:* As translation work is expensive and consistency across upgraded versions is a must, it is critical to ensure that translation work done for one version of the product can automatically be carried forward to future versions. Therefore, it is key that every translatable item be uniquely identifiable, and that this ID remain static through the life of the product so that every item extracted to the data structure can also be uniquely identified.
- *Extraction (Parsing) tools:* These should be as generic as possible, so that when a new object is encountered the extraction tool can handle it. If new tools are needed, they should follow similar architecture, so they can be easily maintained and generate standard data.
- *Editors:* These should also be generic, so they can be used across platforms and modules. For example, a menu or dialog box editor written for Windows should also be able to deal with OS/2-style menus or dialog boxes.
- *Flexibility:* As tools are developed, translatable items are always being enhanced—due to improvement, need to deliver a better product, or the fact that code is written by different programmers. Therefore, the tools should be as generic and flexible as possible so they can support different styles or easily be adapted as the need arises.
- *Consistency:* The translation of UI elements will certainly have to be consistently rendered in other parts of the prod-

uct, such as help and documentation. For example, if the "Search" menu item is changed to "Find" in the UI, then the corresponding documentation and help will need to be changed to reflect this. Therefore, a glossary tool is highly desirable, if not a must. Such a tool must be available during the translation process for each one of the elements.

Focusing on a Windows Translation Project

MS-Windows applications follow Microsoft resourcing standards. As Windows applications are the fastest-growing group of products being localized, in this section we present some translation specifics for Windows applications.

The basic user-interface components of an MS-Windows application are menus, dialogs, strings, icons, and bitmaps. These are compiled with a resource compiler. The resource editor creates a .RES file that can then be bound to the executable or (preferably for localization purposes) to a resource DLL, where all localizable items reside.

The major translatable items for a Windows product are as follows:

- *Menus:* Ideally, translation of menus should be done in-context. In other words, provide a way to show the translator exactly how the menu item appears in the final product—while the translation is being done.

  The major problems encountered in menu translation are the need to ensure that for a given menu level all pick-letters are unique, and provision for the translator to change shortcut selections. Therefore, an ideal tool should emulate the menu, as well as provide warnings where there are pickletter conflicts.
- *Dialogs:* In dialog boxes, strings are not the only objects that might need to be translated. As strings get translated, areas in the dialog boxes might not be large enough to fit the longer translated strings. This creates a need for those dimensions to be modified. In these cases, we have two objects that need translation:

  - *Strings:* Most of the same considerations for menus apply here again in terms of pickletters, and in "tab" order as each one of the selections can be reached using the tab key.
  - *Dimensions:* These should be treated the same way as translatable items, with the main difference that what is actually being translated are not strings, but *dimensions* and *location,* which are usually represented by four numbers (x and y coordinates and height and length). These numbers need to be carried forward the same as is done for strings.

Therefore, this creates a need for dialog box editors, or an equivalent mechanism, in which the resizing happens automatically or can be done by the translator. Automatic resizing does not always produce the best results.

- *Messages:* These are all the strings that represent error messages, annotation lines (hint lines), and reserved names. It's best to provide the translator as much information about obscure strings as possible.

  Maximum string length, context information, and any other hint that would help the translator is highly desirable. As sources are continually upgraded, it is important that the proper information is written and maintained by the original developer who knows the code and the context, and who can ensure that the strings in the source code do not get lost, and provide the extraction tools to extract the strings into the translation tables.
- *Bitmaps and Icons:* Any bitmap that appears in the product should be internationally acceptable: No country-specific icons or bitmaps should be used to represent generic items, such as using an American flag to represent a country field. Even when bitmaps are properly internationalized, bitmap editing tools, such as Borland's Resource Workshop, should be provided in case it becomes necessary to modify them.

CHAPTER 12

European Localization QA

There are two fundamental areas of quality in our localized software that interest us: We want to ensure that the software works properly, and that the messages are translated accurately and consistently. As an engineering organization, our focus is primarily on the functionality of the software; we provide the translators tools to help them with their work, but we rely on them to a large extent to proofread their own work. In other words, we separate the primarily engineering task of functionality testing from the primarily documentation task of reviewing the translation. These are very different tasks and require very different skills and aptitudes. We will discuss the proofreading tasks to some extent at the end of this chapter.

Note that this chapter focuses primarily on European localization. In most areas, you can consider localization for the Asian market to be a superset of this. Please refer to Chapter 14 for more information.

How Localization QA Differs from Core QA

There are several items that we must focus on during localization QA:

- That core functionality is maintained
- That strings in the UI are displayed appropriately and dialog boxes are properly sized
- That the localized product runs properly under local environments

- That the help screens have been translated appropriately and that the correct help screen comes up throughout the program
- That sample programs are translated cleanly and are fully functional
- That the installation program is localized properly and installs all the files to the correct directory

The scope of testing a localized version is the same as for the core version—we have to test every aspect of the product to be sure that it functions correctly. However, we need to test more or less deeply depending on how deep the changes are for localization. Testing a Western-European localization of a product that is well enabled and properly resourced can be fairly straightforward. While we need to cover the whole product, we don't expect that many bugs will have been introduced in the localization process. This means that we don't test as many boundary cases, and we don't do as much stress testing, and the testing we do requires less time because there are fewer bugs to isolate and report.

On the other hand, testing a localized product that is not well enabled can be much more involved. If the source code needs to be modified for the localized versions, the chance to introduce bugs goes up tremendously and testing will have to be deeper. Similarly, a multibyte product will require extensive testing. (Please refer to Chapter 14 for more information.)

Planning Localization QA

As with other QA tasks, it's important to plan out the process ahead of time. This is usually done by figuring out the work that will be required, then describing an overview of the task in a *test plan*. Writing the test plan should help you define the process involved in testing a localization. You should be able to use the same test plan for QAing each similar language. For instance, we might write a test plan for Western Europe that we can apply to each of the ten or so countries for which we may localize our product.

The test plan should contain a list of all tasks required for the localization effort on a per-language basis. These include:

- A list of engineers required for the task, and a list of hardware and software resources required.
- A list of what your group is responsible for and a list of what you plan on excluding from your area of responsibility plus a list of all groups related in any way to the localization effort, and what their responsibilities entail. An important aspect of this is a description of how much testing you expect your translators to do and what tools you can provide to help them with their testing. (See the section on the test kit, below.)
- A list of all product areas and how you plan to test each one.
- An overview of the test automation that you are planning on using and the source of your test suites (whether you plan to write new ones or port existing ones).
- A definition of other tools and systems you will need, such as a bug-reporting program.
- Information on the level of testing you expect to do and the basis for your decision. For instance, we can justify fairly shallow testing for a resource-only European localization effort.
- A description of beta tests and bug hunts you are planning and how they will be administered.
- A statement of the quality level you expect to achieve at each milestone release, including the final one.

The Test Kit

The test kit consists of standalone tools that can be run easily by nontechnical translators. It is sent to the translators along with the translation kit to be used to test the basic functionality of the translated UI and allow the translator to view the translated strings in context. There are several requirements for the test kit:

- The translators must be able to build a translated version of the product. In the case of a cleanly resourced Windows program, they can simply link the resources to the executable. However, in products that are not well-enabled, a test kit may not be a realistic goal since the translators will require full access to the sources.
- The translators must schedule time to run the test kit and review the results. While this may seem obvious, it is easy to overlook in scheduling a tight simultaneous release.

So what is included in the test kit?

- There is a set of instructions for installing the kit, making it run on translated versions of the software, and analyzing the results.
- Typically, a set of test suites is selected from those used for localization testing and packaged in a form that can be run easily by a nontechnical translator.
- The suites must be resourced so that they can effectively test localized versions. For instance, rather than hardcoding pickletters in the tests, the pickletters should be in a separate test script. The process for making these tests run on localized software must be well documented.

  It's quite possible to build testing tools based around the Software Translation Kit such that test suites access translated resources automatically, although we've yet to do so.

  If it's not reasonable to include a set of test suites, it may be sufficient to include a written set of test outlines for the translators to work through.
- If possible, a context checker should be included in the test kit. This is a tool that will run the executable and surface all the messages automatically. A tool such as this can be used to check that messages are correct in the context of the product, that the menu is correct on the screen, that prompts and status bars fit in the space allocated, that dialog boxes are sized properly and dialog items are aligned,

that text mixed with graphics fits properly, that translated function or macro names work properly, and so forth.

For instance, the tool would display all the menus systematically and pause for each menu item so that the translator can review its status line in context. In addition, the context checker would bring up all the dialogs and cycle through all the controls on the dialog to verify their status lines and also check the layout of the dialog, the length of the strings in the dialog, and that the tab order is correct. Finally, the context checker should surface as many error messages as is reasonable to allow the translators to check them in context. Often, the core team will have a similar tool to check their error messages that can be adapted for this purpose.

- There may be other tools that are useful to include in the test kit. One is a pickletter checker that automatically goes through each menu and dialog and verifies that no pickletter conflicts with another. This can be done in numerous ways; Windows tools can operate directly on the resource file or a test tool can be used in the context of the executable.
- The test kit must include the means for the translator to set up a standardized environment. This might include standard configuration files so that the system will produce consistent results no matter how the computer has been set up in the past.
- The test kit must contain a full set of instructions describing how to set up the computer, how to install and run the test suites, how to make them work for translated versions of the product, and how to analyze the results.

Types of Bugs

There are basically three types of bugs that we find during localization testing:

- *Core bugs* are basic functionality bugs that exist in the core product. We often find core bugs in the localized version. It's important to have a core version of the product readily available while doing localization QA so that we can test bugs in both versions and report core bugs appropriately. Otherwise, we waste the time of the localization engineers when they try to fix bugs that don't belong to them.
- *International enabling bugs* are core bugs that primarily affect countries other than the country of origin. Our goal is generally to have a fully internationalized product. In other words, a European should have full access to accented characters in the U.S. version and in all other versions of the product. If an accented character isn't displayed or sorted appropriately, we call it an *enabling bug.* We distinguish enabling bugs from core bugs because they will sometimes look like localization bugs and, depending on the structure of the QA group, are usually found by a different set of engineers than other core bugs. Like other core bugs, these should be tested in the core version of the product and reported appropriately.
- *Localization bugs* are bugs introduced by the translation process. If a bug doesn't occur in the core version, it is probably a localization bug. Types of localization bugs include functionality that gets broken by the localization process and dialog sizing problems where the strings don't appear appropriately.

  It's possible to have a core bug that only shows up in the localized version. An example might be a crash that occurs when we put a string that's too long into a fixed-length buffer. It's especially important to report these types of bugs early so that they can be fixed before the core version is released.

It's important that QA engineers recognize each type of bug and report each one appropriately in order to keep the bug reporting process pure. These bugs are usually reported to a different R&D

engineer or a different group of R&D engineers. Also, localization bugs are generally not counted in the bug metrics for the core product.

Elements of Localization QA

Core Functionality of the Product

The most important aspect of localization QA is to verify that core functionality does not break as a result of the localization process. This will require the most work on your part. It consists of testing the complete product systematically over each build of the product. There are a number of strategies that can be followed, ranging from fully automated testing to ad-hoc testing. Please refer to the next section on test suite Automation.

Clean Translation

As discussed earlier, we rely on our translators to proofread their work and we provide them with tools to verify their translations in context. However, we test the UI to be sure that the strings can be displayed properly in all applicable video modes. We generally do this by hand, using the context checker that we supply in the test kit.

Compatibility Testing

Clearly, we need to be sure that the product runs properly on localized versions of the operating system and can use products that are common to the target region, such as printers and network cards. While European-specific compatibility bugs may not be common, they do exist. And this type of testing is especially important for Asian markets.

A minimum requirement should be a complete round of testing using localized versions of the operating systems set to local conventions. It would be a good idea to have people in your group testing under a variety of video modes and using a variety of settings. For more extensive compatibility testing, please refer to Chapter 14.

Testing Help

While we rely on the translators to translate the contents of the help file correctly and to proofread their own work, we as QA engineers need to at least check that the connections between the program and the help file have not been broken. There are several ways to automate this process, but it is often quicker to do the work by hand. This is simply a matter of bringing up the help screen for every menu item and dialog item and verifying that the title of the help screen roughly corresponds to the item.

If your product involves a programming language, you will also need to test the context jumps from the language elements.

Testing Samples/Tutorials

Again, we rely on the translators to translate any sample programs or sample files included with the product. But sometimes the translators are careless, and sometimes (during a simultaneous ship project) changes to the UI cause the samples to break. It's important to check the samples to ensure that they work as expected.

We generally accomplish this by stepping through all the samples after they've been delivered from the translators and at several other points during the development cycle, particularly before releases (leaving time to fix any problems that come up). We focus on functionality problems in the samples, but also pay attention to the format of addresses of phone numbers to ensure that they're appropriate for the target country.

When we find bugs in the samples, it's tempting for us as QA engineers to fix the bugs ourselves and submit our fixes. However, it's important to have a single person who owns each sample and is responsible for any bug fixes. When QA engineers find bugs, they should submit a bug report just as for program bugs.

✦ If we switch between test mode and fix mode, we tend to lose focus on our testing and we often don't get full coverage.

- If we fix the problems ourselves, we run into versioning problems; the next time the translator fixes a problem, his fix will overwrite our fix.
- Fixing bugs locally can cause contention between the QA engineer and the person who originally translated the sample.

Rather, we should report the bugs to our bug database and the translator should make fixes based on these reports.

Installation Program

Testing the installation program consists of stepping through the UI systematically to be sure that each dialog is functional, that the UI works properly, and that the translation is clean, and also verifying that the installation works for all options selected and under a variety of environments.

It's often useful to do a complete install and a minimal install (assuming your product has these options) and to compare the results to similar core installations to be sure that the same files are installed.

In addition, you should do some testing under the localized version of the operating system using local conventions, and you should do some testing in a variety of video modes.

On-line Files

As part of the final installation testing for a release, it's important to check all on-line files that are installed. While the responsibility of the contents of these files lies with the translators and you may not have the expertise to read the file or check the wording, you can at least check to be sure that the contents of the file compare roughly to those in the same file in the core version and that the file is complete.

Test Suite Automation

The most important aspect of localization QA is to verify that the core functionality has not been broken in the localized product. Often, the most efficient way of accomplishing this is to automate as much of the testing as possible. There are several automation strategies to choose from for testing your localized versions, presented here in order of preference:

- Decide early in the development of the core product to use test suites to automate localization testing and enable the core test suites accordingly.
- Port core test suites that have already been written.
- Write new test suites.
- Leverage test outlines from the core team.
- Forgo automated test suites and rely on ad-hoc testing.

Let's take an in-depth look at each of these.

Enabling Test Suites

It makes sense that if we're planning to invest in the development of automated test suites for the core version of the product, we would want to be able to use those same tests across all of the localized versions of our products. Achieving this goal, however, requires careful planning, coordination, and training. We need to set the goal early in the development of the product and devise a strategy for implementing it, we need to make sure that all the QA engineers who will be developing test suites are signed up to follow the strategy, and then we need to train them in the implementation.

While we've used a couple of different strategies for enabling our test suites, we've found that the best strategy is to proceduralize all the menus and dialogs. All the UI procedures reside in a single script file that we call the resource script. Rather than using keystroke commands to access menu and dialog items, test scripts make calls to the UI test script.

This has two primary advantages. Unrelated to localization QA, as the design of the product changes during the early development stages of the product, it is relatively easy to modify test suites to accommodate the modifications. More importantly (as far as localization QA is concerned), when it comes time to test a different language, we need only make changes to one file and our test suites will continue to run.

The goal is that the test scripts do not need to be modified to test localized versions. The process for localizing the test scripts is to modify in the resource script all the keyboard commands that open and select menu and dialog items. While we haven't taken it to this extent, it would even be possible to use a resource extraction tool (discussed in Chapter 11) to generate a table that the resource script could use so that localization of the test scripts does not need to be done by hand.

There are alternatives to using pickletters. One (for Windows programs) is to use the F10 key to activate the menu, then arrow keys and ENTER to select the menu item. In dialogs, tab keys and arrow keys can be used to select the dialog item. The advantage of this approach is that the same UI script can often be used for localized versions without alteration. The disadvantages are that it sometimes needs to be modified for localized versions anyway (if menu items or dialog items are modified dynamically), it doesn't work as reliably, and it can be difficult to track down problems when they occur.

There are object-oriented test environments that may provide more robust tools for UI testing, but they are beyond the scope of this book.

Once you've localized the UI script, you will need to run the full set of test scripts to create a new baseline and verify that the new baseline is correct. You will need to follow the same process for doing this as for the core product.

Porting Core Test Suites

If you aren't able to enlist the cooperation of the core QA engineers, or if you've decided to use test automation on localized versions after the core test suites have already been written, it may still be possible to port those test suites, although it may be time-consuming depending on the design of the test suites. Also, you will get a snapshot of the test suites and will have to reimplement any updates yourself. This may be too expensive for a resource-only localization; because you will probably have to make only a few test passes through the product, it's probably more efficient to do the testing on an ad-hoc basis. But if your localization project requires modifications to the core code base (as with most Asian localization projects, or if the product isn't properly resourced), it may be necessary to port the core test suites in order to achieve a reasonable degree of confidence in the product.

The process of porting the test suites will probably involve running each one by hand on your localized version and making changes to the parameters of keystroke commands as required. Probably the best way to do this is to have the script in a text editor on one system and the localized product running on another system. The QA engineer walks through each step of the script on the localized version by typing the commands in the script and making changes in the editor. Once this is done, you will need to run the full set of test suites to verify that they work properly and to create a new baseline, then verify the new baseline.

Writing New Test Suites

While development cycles are shorter for localized versions than they are for the core version, we normally localize a product into a number of different languages. In this case, you probably don't want to do the same testing over and over again and it might be worthwhile to develop new test suites for some areas even if the core QA engineers decided not to automate those areas.

Let's face it—the costs of test automation can be high. Here's what will be involved:

- ✦ We need to train our engineers in the scripting language.
- ✦ We need to develop a consistent test environment in which to run the test suites.

- ✦ We need to write the test suites.
- ✦ On each build of the product, we need to run the test suites, analyze the failures, fix any test suites that are broken, and report any bugs we find.
- ✦ We need to maintain the test suites as the product changes.

So how do we decide when it makes sense to automate? If we look at the automation process, we might get some ideas. When an engineer is assigned an area of the product to cover, she or he might do the following:

When Testing Using Automated Test Suites	When Ad-hoc Testing
1. Read through the specs for the area.	Same
2. Play around with the program to see what it does and how it works and to find any surface bugs that exist.	Same
3. Discuss the area with the appropriate R&D engineers to discover problem areas.	Same
4. Write a quick outline of the expected coverage.	Same
5. Generate a set of test cases with associated test data.	Same
6. Write test scripts to automate the test cases on one computer while running through the same steps on a second computer.	Methodically step through each of the test cases in the area.
7. Run the test script to make sure it works properly.	
8. Verify that the correct results are produced.	
9. On each build, run the tests, analyze the failures, report bugs, fix test suites.	On each build, methodically step through each of the test cases in the area (although we tend to fudge here and not do full coverage on each build).

So where is the cost of automation? If I assign an engineer to cover an area, I would expect him or her to do steps 1 through 5 regardless of the decision to automate. Step 6 overlaps for both methods, although writing the test script takes significantly more time. Steps 7 and 8 are unique to automation.

In step 9, automation starts to pay off. When we automate, we get full coverage on each build, and the cost is relatively low compared to achieving the same coverage by hand. Because we get consistent coverage, we can often pinpoint regressions as soon as they are introduced.

The actual decision to automate depends on many factors including:

- The type of localization project it is: A well-resourced Windows application will require few iterations for European localizations, so only a few test passes should be required to deliver a product. A product that requires extensive modifications to the core source code may require many test passes, so automation is more likely to pay off.
- The number of localizations you will be doing: It might be difficult to justify the cost of automation for up to three resource-only localizations unless it would be difficult to achieve sufficient coverage by other means.
- Lead time: If you need to deliver a product in a very short amount of time, it may be impossible to develop a bed of test suites.
- The skill level and aptitude of your QA engineers: If your QA engineers aren't experienced programmers or if they haven't written test suites before, the learning curve may be steep. As in programming, the difference in productivity between a very good engineer and a mediocre engineer can be large.
- Whether your engineers are already trained in the scripting language, and whether a test environment exists for maintaining, running, and analyzing the results of test scripts.

It's important to remember that this doesn't have to be a black-and-white issue. In many cases, it might make sense to automate only the most automatable or the riskiest areas, or to automate most of the product but not certain areas.

Test Outlines

If you decide that it's not practical to automate your testing, probably the next best thing is to use detailed test outlines developed by the core QA engineers, or if necessary, to write new ones for the localization testing.

A test outline should cover an autonomous area that is owned by a single engineer. Depending on the size of the area and the scope of the coverage required, an engineer may own one area or several areas or many areas. The outline must be comprehensive and provide at least several test cases for each aspect of the area. It should be as detailed as possible without being unwieldy. As a new QA engineer, I carefully wrote out the specific keystrokes required to test my area. This quickly became very tedious to write and even more tedious to test. In addition, as the design of the product changed, I found that I didn't have time to maintain my test outline and still achieve the coverage I needed, so my outlines became hopelessly out of date.

Each engineer should use his or her own judgment and his or her own style, but the best strategy seems to be to list every aspect of the test area, then list a set of test cases for each aspect.

Ad-hoc Testing

Finally, if all else fails, we rely on ad-hoc testing. While I feel that ad-hoc testing has a place on every project as a supplement to automated test suites, it is difficult to consistently get complete coverage with ad-hoc testing alone. It's a little like driving down a winding mountain highway late at night when we're very sleepy. There are many hazards that come up along the way, but we'll generally be awake enough to see these and swerve to avoid them. But sooner or later, we'll doze off and we won't see one that should be

obvious to us. This could lead to a slightly embarrassing fender-bender, or it could lead to more serious problems. While we need to stay awake even if we have good test automation, it can point out the most obvious of these hazards.

Milestone Releases

Depending on the scope of your localization project, it is probably a good idea to include one or more milestone releases into your schedule. While these are often tied to external testing efforts (see next section), they're really as much for making sure that the project is staying on track. Also they offer an opportunity to test the process of building a full version of the product, cutting to diskettes, and verifying and releasing the diskettes. And they provide a stable baseline for your translators to work from.

It's up to the QA manager or the QA department to define the quality expectations for these milestone releases. While there are a number of metrics that can be used to determine readiness, there is also an imprecise element of whether the product "feels" ready. Here are some examples of metrics you might use:

- ✦ *Percentage of the UI that has been translated:* Particularly in the simultaneous-ship model, it's often useful to send out a version that's mostly translated. Generally, the core pieces of the product will be fully translated, but some modules may not yet be stable, so we ship them in English.
- ✦ *Correctness of the help file:* Because it is often on the critical path of a localization project, it's important to translate as much of the help as possible as early as possible. While you may or may not want to tie this to your milestone releases, it's important to gauge progress on translation. You could define levels of correctness of the help file as (1) that all the help topics are reachable through some means and (2) that all the context-sensitive help jumps are functional.

- *State of translated samples:* It's desirable to translate the samples as early as possible in the development cycle. This is sometimes difficult if the core versions don't stabilize early. Depending on your expectations, you may be able to use the percentage of samples that have been translated as a criteria for milestone releases.

- *State of international enabling:* If there are still many hard-coded strings in the product, and if the product doesn't properly handle accented characters in many places, beta testers in other countries will have a difficult time testing and assessing your localized beta version. You should aim to have your product reasonably well enabled before releasing betas.

- *Level of usability:* We don't expect our beta test releases to be 100 percent usable; there are bound to be crash bugs, nonfunctional areas, and many other problems that the user will encounter. As we test our software, we have a sense of what the user will be able to accomplish with it. Will the user usually be able to accomplish a set of day-to-day chores without too much frustration? Will the software function as long as the user doesn't do anything unexpected? Will the user be able to use the software on a daily basis and only rarely encounter an anomaly? We often rely on touchy-feely "metrics" such as these to determine whether our software is ready for a milestone release.

- *QA metrics:* There are many numbers that you can derive from a database of bug reports that may be helpful for determining readiness to release. These include number of bugs found, bug find rate, number of bugs fixed, bugs found versus bugs fixed rate, and so on. Frankly, we've found that there are many factors involved in the development of a software; while we continue to generate statistics such as these for reference, we haven't found them to be a reliable indicator of readiness to ship.

External Test Cycles

Beta Tests

Please refer to Chapter 6 for more information on beta tests.

Depending on a number of factors, a beta test for a localized product may not be as beneficial as that for the core version of the product, and the costs may be higher, but in certain cases it's still a good idea to do a beta test:

- ✦ If there are functional changes to the product (as is often the case when localizing for Asian countries), beta testers can help identify design problems and bugs.
- ✦ If coverage is light on the localized version, it may be useful to have beta testers look at the product to give you a sense of how close it is to being ready to ship.

Once the beta test sites have been selected, milestone builds should be selected to send out externally. Beta test releases should be tested thoroughly and deemed appropriately stable for the level of that release. Beta testers should be made aware of the level of the product and what they should be expected to do and not do given the state of the product.

During the beta test cycle, the beta testers should be contacted on a regular basis. They should have a local contact they can call to ask questions to come up to speed. Feedback should be requested regularly. Often, we provide a questionnaire along with the beta version that the beta tester must fill out in order to participate in future beta tests. This questionnaire might ask about specific features of the product, what changes the customer liked most or liked least, and so forth.

Bug Hunts

Bug hunts can be used to test localized versions of your software as well as the core version. In this case, the rules should state clearly that you will pay only for localization bugs, although core bugs should be reported as well.

Localization bug hunts work effectively with one of two groups: core engineers who know the product but not the language, or engineers in the target country who may not know the product but who can speak the language. Tech-support engineers make excellent candidates in the United States and in subsidiaries—they know the product well and they are eager to see its next revision.

Please refer to Chapter 6 for more information on bug hunts.

Beta Tests versus Bug Hunts

Should you use beta testers? Should you hold a bug hunt? There are certain costs and certain benefits associated with each, and you will need to decide if they make sense for your project.

Basically, a beta test will provide you with information about how actual customers will use your product on a daily basis. A bug hunt will quickly provide you with a large number of bug reports.

For our European localization projects, we generally have one or two beta cycles plus a gamma cycle. In the larger countries, these will involve up to 20 customer sites.

We generally only use bug hunts for the core versions of our products or for the larger or more involved localization projects. If we hold a bug hunt for a European version, we don't hold one in other European countries, based on the assumption that most of the bugs we'll be looking for can be found in any version.

Skill Set of Localization QA Engineers

Given this discussion of what localization QA entails, what should we look for when we hire a localization QA engineer?

- ✦ A programming background, which helps in developing test suites and in understanding the process of developing software.
- ✦ Knowledge of test automation tools.
- ✦ Analytical skills for isolating bugs and reporting them accurately.

- Diplomatic and communication skills for negotiating bug fixes with R&D engineers and for defining test areas with core QA engineers and international QA engineers.
- Engineering skills, not linguistic skills. Because we work extensively with the product, we learn it well enough so that we can do functional testing even if we don't speak the language in which the product is written.
- Experience with localization QA is desirable, but difficult to find.
- Sensitivity to and interest in international issues.
- A willingness to do similar work over many localized versions of the same product.

As with international QA engineers, these skills correspond pretty closely to what we look for in a good UI QA engineer.

Proofreading the Localized Product

The task of verifying the text is an important one, but it is a different kind of task from the QA engineering work that we've described in this chapter. For this reason, we require that it be done by the linguistic experts, usually the translators themselves or our representatives in the subsidiaries.

The QA team might be able to provide tools for covering the UI systematically. The proofreader must check all the menu items, dialogs, status lines, error messages, and any other strings that the user might encounter. The translations must be checked for accuracy and the must be compared against the glossary for consistency across the UI, help, and documentation.

Chapter 13

Asian Localization

Technical Complexity

For the most part, all the localization issues involved with European localization of a software product are included in the issues involved with Asian localization, although there are a few differences. For example, Japanese date formats include emperor era where the years are counted from the start of each emperor's reign. So, 1995 is year 7 of the Heisei era.

Emperor	Time Period
Heisei	January 8, 1989–
Showa	December 25, 1926–January 7, 1989
Taisho	July 30, 1912–December 24, 1926
Meiji	January 1, 1873–July 29, 1912

Additionally, Asian localization includes the following major technical complexities that are not associated with European localization:

- Large multibyte character set
- Character versus byte
- Nonalphabetic collation
- Input method editors
- Hardware issues

Asian languages, such as Thai, that use a single-byte character set have their own peculiarities. However, most of the complex localization issues are associated with far-eastern languages like Japanese, Korean, and Chinese, which use multibyte character sets. We will use Kanji (written script for Japan) as an example in this chapter since many of the issues are common to Hangeul (written script for Korea) and traditional (Taiwan) and simplify (China) Chinese.

Multibyte Character Sets

Unlike European languages, Kanji uses thousands of characters in the written script, which raises problems in many areas including encoding scheme, keyboard input, editing text, and word wrapping.

A single byte is capable of representing only 256 distinct characters. A single byte is not sufficient to represent the thousands of the characters required by Kanji. There are three primary multibyte code sets used in Japan:

- JIS (Japanese Industry Standard)
- Shift-JIS
- EUC (Extended UNIX Codeset)

All three code sets represent Kanji characters from the JIS-X208 and JIS-X201 standards. EUC is used primarily on UNIX systems. JIS is currently used primarily for printers. Shift-JIS is the most important code set for Japanese PCs. Most applications will deal with the conversion between these three code sets in one way or another. Regardless of the internal code set used by an application, it may have to perform one or more of these six possible conversions:

From/To	SJIS	EUC	JIS
SJIS		SJIS to EUC	SJIS to JIS
EUC	EUC to SJIS		EUC to JIS
JIS	JIS to SJIS	JIS to EUC	

All the conversions in this table can be done through functions rather than lookup tables. In fact, these conversion functions are

quite simple and are readily available for download on many public sites. Many of the Kanji support issues are similar regardless of the code sets your application has to use. This chapter will use Shift-JIS in the discussion.

Generally, Shift-JIS represent Kanji characters with two bytes and ASCII characters with one byte. The table below shows a detailed breakdown:

Single Byte	Double Byte
alphanumeric	alphanumeric
Katakana	Kana (Katakana & Hiragana)
	Kanji

Shift-JIS Byte(s)	Code Points
Leading (first)	0 × 80 – 0 × 9f and 0 × e0 – 0 × fc
Trailing (second)	0 × 40 – 0 × fc

The important thing to remember in dealing with multibyte character sets is that the software must treat a character of text as a whole and not necessarily as a byte.

For example, when the cursor is under a double-byte character, and the user wants to delete that character, two bytes (a single character) should be deleted from the internal buffer, and the cursor shape should change accordingly depending on whether the previous character is single or double-byte. If the internal structure, like a string buffer structure, was not designed to handle a multibyte character set, the changes required could be extensive (especially in replacing a double-byte character with a single-byte character in overwrite mode or vice versa).

Additionally, since the trailing byte of a Shift-JIS double-byte character can overlap with ASCII, further complication can occur in manipulating Shift-JIS strings. For example, ASCII represents the backslash character "\" as 0 × 5c. However, there are a few Shift-JIS double-byte characters that have 0 × 5c as the trailing second byte. If an application is parsing a pathname for a filename, the application should not interpret the trailing byte of a double-byte character as a backslash. This can be done by checking the type of the preceding byte.

```
/*
 * returns:
 *              0xc1 11000001 ANK
 *              0x52 01010010 KANJI 1st
 *              0xa2 10100010 KANJI 2nd
 *              0x54 01010100 HALFDBL 1st
 *              0xa4 10100100 HALFDBL 2nd
 *
 *              :1               0
 *        ---------------------------------------
 *        bit 0 :ANK        not ANK (ANK or HALFDBL)
 *        bit 1 :KANJI      not KANJI (ANK or HALFDBL)
 *        bit 2 :HALFDBL    not HALFDBL (KANJI or ANK)
 *        bit 3 :(reserved)
 *        bit 4 :dblbyte 1st        dblbyte 2nd or ANK
 *        bit 5 :dblbyte 2nd        dblbyte 1st or ANK
 *        bit 6 :dblbyte 1st or ANK dblbyte 2nd
 *        bit 7 :dblbyte 2nd or ANK dblbyte 1s
 *        ---------------------------------------------------------
 *
 */
int fstrctype(const char far *s, unsigned width)
{
   int type = 0xc1; //set to ANK initially
   unsigned n = width;
   const unsigned char far *p = (const unsigned char far *)s;
   for (; n >= 0 && *p; p++, n--)
      {
      if (*p >= 0x80 && (*p < 0xa0 || *p >= 0xe0 && *p < 0xfd) )
         {
         if (n < 2)
            {
            type = 0x52; //Kanji 1st Byte
            if (*p == 0x80 || *p == 0x85 || (*p == 0x86 & p[1]<0xa0))
               type = 0x54; //HALFDBL 1st
            if (n != 0)
               type += 0x50; //Kanji or HALFDBL 2nd Byte
            break;
            }
            n--;
         p++;
         }
      }
         return type;
}
```

The function fstrctype() returns the type of character located at s + width. The term *ANK* (alphanumeric Kana) in fstrctype() is

commonly used to denote single-byte character (ASCII and Kana). The term *HALFDBL* means double-byte characters with a display width of 1. These characters are called half-size Kanas and are often used for aesthetic reasons.

There are many areas that require changes in the code to process Shift-JIS, including editing, displaying, line wrapping, searching, and windows overlapping. Some applications may require more changes than others depending on the features involved. However, the key point to remember is to process a character as a whole entity and not as a byte. This is simple in theory but difficult in practice. It requires a mental shift for many western programmers.

Wide Characters and Unicode

As you can see from the previous section, processing multibyte character sets requires changing the application logic in dealing with text data. Wouldn't it be ideal to process Kanji characters the way an application currently processes ASCII characters? This is possible with Unicode. Unicode, as mentioned previously, is a 16-bit encoding scheme where every character is represented by a fixed-length double-byte. An application can process the Unicode Kanji and English characters in the same way that it currently processes ASCII characters. Moving a character forward and backward within a string can be done easily, as with ASCII processing. Editing and other types of string manipulations can be done just as easily. The only difference is that the data type is now two bytes in length each, instead of one byte, as in ASCII. Using Unicode as a processing code requires code conversions between Unicode and other code sets upon entering and leaving the application boundaries (please see Figure 4.2 in Chapter 4).

Borland chose to have the Asian version of dBASE for Windows process generic (not Unicode) wide characters internally, where the bit pattern of the wide-character representation was not fixed. The only guarantee is that a wide character is 16 bits in size. Why wasn't Unicode chosen? Originally, Borland had planned for dBASE for Windows to process everything internally as 16-bit wide characters and our wide-character representation was going to be Unicode. However, we discovered a round-trip conversion problem.

One of the important criteria for dBASE for Windows is to transparently access dBASE for DOS data. The dBASE table (.dbf) is stored in DOS. There are two important DOS systems in Japan: MS-DOS/V (the *V* stands for VGA; it has software fonts instead of in ROM) and NEC-DOS. NEC-DOS runs on NEC PC hardware, which commands about 50 percent of the PC market in Japan. Both DOS systems have code points for extended Kanji characters that are outside of the JIS-X208 standard. Unfortunately, both systems have different code points for the same extended Kanji characters. For example, the "Ming" Kanji character is represented by 0 × fb61 on MS-DOS/V and by 0 × ee45 on NEC-DOS. MS Windows 3.1J represents the same Ming Kanji character by both 0 × fb61 and 0 × ee45 since the MS Windows 3.1 J Kanji font can have the two glyphs be identical for display. The Ming Kanji character is represented by 0 × 73c9 in Unicode.

The problem is that dBASE for Windows sits on top of MS Windows 3.1J. There is no way for dBASE for Windows to know if the dBASE table (.dbf) came from an MS-DOS/V or a NEC-DOS system. Regardless of the system that dBASE for Windows is running on, the dBASE DOS table could have come from the other DOS system or the dBASE DOS table could be sitting on a network server. If dBASE for Windows uses Unicode internally, it must convert the Ming Kanji character into Unicode from the file system, process it, and convert the same Ming Kanji character from Unicode out to the file system. This is not possible without knowing the original DOS system that the dBASE table (.dbf) came from.

You can guarantee round-trip conversion of dBASE for Windows maps the extended Kanji characters to different code points in the user-defined area of Unicode. In other words, map 0 × fb61 to 0 × yyyy of the user-defined area of Unicode and 0 × ee45 to O × zzzz of the user-defined area of Unicode. The problem is that there are many extended Kanji characters outside of the JIS-X208 standard. Additionally, it seems to defeat the purpose of Unicode's being the universal code set.

Borland chose to use generic wide characters internally. Instead of doing code conversion to some specific code set internally (e.g., Unicode), we would zero-pad the single-byte characters coming into dBASE for Windows and pass through untouched the double-

byte characters. This would maintain the importance of having the internal processing code be a fixed length of two bytes for each character (for string manipulations). We would be able to guarantee the round trip between MS-DOS/V and NEC-DOS to and from Unicode. We would zero-pad the characters coming into dBASE for Windows based on the locale being used and the character mapping associated with the locale (e.g., Shift-JIS, KS5601). An added benefit is that the transformation to and from wide characters is faster than the table lookup conversion to and from Unicode.

Nonalphabetic Collation

Far-Eastern languages like Kanji have ideographic characters. Ideographic characters represent concepts. As mentioned in Chapter 2, the western alphabetic notion of collation does not apply for languages like Kanji. There are three different ways of sorting Kanji characters: by radicals, by strokes, and by phonetic order. Often, a combination of the sort orders is used: by strokes within radicals, or by radicals within strokes. You can also sort Kanji characters strictly by code points, as with ASCII sort. This may be sufficient for many applications since the Shift-JIS code points are reasonably sorted already: JIS level 1 is sorted phonetically and JIS level 2 and 3 are sorted by strokes within radicals.

Input Method Editor

The Shift-JIS character set contains thousands of characters. There is no keyboard with keys representing all the possible Kanji characters in Shift-JIS. To input all the possible Kanji characters, an IME is desirable. An IME is a software Front End Processor (FEB) that intercepts the keyboard inputs, performs some intermediate processing, and outputs to an application. Specifically, an IME:

- Parses keyboard input
- Converts to Kanas if keyboard input is Romaji

- ✦ Performs Kana-Kanji conversion (KKC)
- ✦ Displays possible Kanji homophones for user selection
- ✦ Sends Kanji selection to application

There are three main levels of integration between an application and the input method editor (IME).

1. A user can input Kanji characters into an application even if the IME is not integrated with the application. The IME simply works as a front-end processor that captures all keyboard inputs, performs the necessary conversion and user selection, and gives in to the application. The IME will usually show up at the bottom of the screen in a separate window from the application.
2. You can integrate the IME with an application such that when the user turns the IME on, the input and editing is done on-site where the cursor is positioned (Figure 2.4 in Chapter 2) instead of in a separate window at the bottom of the screen.
3. The application and IME can also be integrated such that the application controls the turning on and off of the IME. For example, in a database application where you specify a particular column to contain Kanji strings, the application can automatically turn on the IME when the cursor enters the column edit field.

Hardware and Other Issues

The hardware base is not always compatible outside the United States. For hardware like Sun and HP, there are no compatibility problems outside of the United States. However, in the Intel PC arena, hardware can be totally incompatible with that of the United States, like the NEC 9801 PC computers in Japan. The only layer in which PC-9801 is identical with IBM-PC in functionality is the MS-DOS system call layer. At the BIOS level, the NEC 9801 and IBM PC are incompatible. Any DOS program that bypasses the DOS system

call to make IBM BIOS calls needs to change in order to run on the NEC-9801. Note that the number of BIOS calls on the PC-9801 is smaller than that of the IBM-PC. Additional differences are in video resolution, memory map, and keyboard.

There are other complexities in dealing with Asian localization; we have listed the major issues in this chapter.

CHAPTER 14

Asian QA

In many ways, testing of Asian software is a superset of European localization QA. While it is necessary to do the basic level of QA outlined in Chapter 12, there are a number of additional issues to be aware of:

- Core source code is usually modified at a deep level, so we must test at a deep level.
- We must test handling of multibyte characters throughout the product.
- Our product must know how to handle non-Western date formats.
- Usually, new functionality is added to the product to support IMEs, Asian word-wrapping rules, vertical writing, auto-furigana, and possibly other Asian-specific features.
- Hardware and software compatibility testing are more critical and more involved in Asia due to more diversity in platforms and standards.
- For cultural and historical reasons, the Japanese market is particularly sensitive to quality. The tolerance for bugs is lower than in many other countries, including the United States, and ease of use is particularly important.
- It's necessary to have some engineers on the team with some level of language expertise.

In some ways, testing an Asian product is broader in scope and magnitude than testing a core product. There is new functionality

in the Asian version that doesn't exist in the core version, and the multibyte testing requires deep testing throughout the product. For this reason, it is particularly important to leverage as much of the work of the core team as possible.

Testing Full Functionality

If the product is not double-byte enabled initially, it must be modified extensively to handle Asian characters. At the same time we're testing the enabling functionality we need to test the core functionality to find bugs that have been introduced during the enabling process. Because a lot of code is modified, it's not unusual to have many new bugs introduced.

As discussed in Chapter 13, there are advantages to making your product multibyte, and there are advantages to making it widechar. From a QA perspective, enabling a single-byte product for multibyte should be significantly quicker and easier than enabling it for widechar (although there are other tradeoffs as discussed in Chapter 13). In other words, a lot more bugs will be introduced by converting a product to widechar than to multibyte because the modifications required are deeper and more extensive. Ultimately, however, this doesn't change the QA process. You will need to do the same amount of testing for each, although you should allocate more time for the widechar conversion because more builds will be required and it takes a lot of time to isolate and report all those bugs.

Here are some ideas for testing the core functionality:

- ✦ Create an Asian-enabled English version of the product that contains no new functionality, only the ability to properly handle double-byte characters. Once this version starts to stabilize, have the core QA team do several full functionality test passes on it, including running a complete battery of test suites. While complete functionality testing will still need to be done on later localized versions (which probably contain new functionality

also), this process will certainly shake out a large number of bugs.

- With Asian software, test automation can be particularly helpful because of the large number of builds required and because so many hard-to-find bugs can be introduced. See the section on test automation in Chapter 12 for strategies to share or port test suites from the core team, or to create new test suites.
- In areas where automation is not available, there may be test outlines developed by the core QA engineers that will be helpful for testing the localized version.
- In areas where automation is not an option and outlines are not available, engineers will need to outline the full functionality of the product in order to get complete coverage.

Testing Keyboard Handling of Double-Byte Characters

Every field in the product where a string can be entered must be tested to verify that double-byte characters are properly handled. Handling double-byte characters means that these characters must never be split. You can see some of the problems by running a non-double-byte-enabled U.S. Windows product under Japanese Windows and entering Kanji characters. Depending on the how the product was designed, the characters may display properly but there will be other problems. All of these must be tested in every field of your double-byte product:

- Place the caret at the beginning of a string containing a mixture of double-byte and single-byte characters and move it a little to the right, then to the left. You should move a full character at a time. In a nonenabled product, the caret will land in the middle of a Kanji character.
- If you click with the mouse in the middle of a Kanji character, the caret should be placed either in front of or after the character, but never in the middle.

- Similarly, when marking a section of text with the mouse or with the keyboard, you should be allowed to mark only whole characters, never half characters.
- If you place the caret in front of a Kanji character and press DELETE, the whole character should be erased. In a nonenabled product, the first half of the character will be erased and the second byte will display as a single-byte code point.
- Similarly, if you backspace over a Kanji character, U.S. software will allow you to erase the second byte of the character. Japanese software shouldn't allow this.
- In a fixed-length field enter Kanji characters to fill up the field. If the field length is 10 bytes, for example, you should be allowed to type no more than 5 Kanji characters.
- In the same fixed-length field, type a single-byte character (assuming the width of the field is an even number), then enter some Kanji characters to fill up the field. If the field length is 10 bytes, you should be allowed to type only 4 Kanji characters after the single-byte character, with room left for a single-byte character at the end of the string.
- With a Kanji character in the last position in the field, press the HOME key, then the END key, and verify that you moved past the last character. Try this with an even number as well as with an odd number of bytes in the field.
- In an edit control, type some Kanji characters and then press the HOME key. Type some single-byte characters to move the Kanji characters out of the display window and check that each one moves out of the display as a whole character. In nonenabled software, the character moving out of the window will display as a block character or a garbage character.
- If your operating system uses an underline cursor (as does PC-DOS), the cursor should appear as double-width

when it is placed on a double-byte character and single-width when it is placed on a single-byte character.

Testing Other Double-Byte Issues

There are other classes of double-byte enabling bugs:

- When the software handles a string as bytes rather than as characters, several problems will occur. Strings won't be uppercased (or lowercased) properly, since the function won't know if the byte value of 0x61 is the letter *a* or the second half of a Kanji character. So the character at SJIS code point 0x8E61 (see the table in Figure 14.1 for pronunciation and the character) will be uppercased to code-point 0x8E41, whereas it should be left as is. You should test all transliterated strings with these two characters. (Note the similarity between this testing and the transliteration testing in Chapter 6. There may be some tools created by the internationalization QA engineers that you can share.)
- Also when your software handles a string as bytes, some characters in filenames will produce incorrect results. If you save to a filename that contains code point 0x955C in a DOS or Windows program, for instance, your program will see the 0x5C and interpret it as a backslash. This could simply cause the save to fail with an error message, or it could create a directory with an invalid code point that can't be deleted from your system. In every place that

Codepoint	Pronunciation	Character
0x8E41	satuei	撮影
0x8E61	zantei	暫定
0x955C	hyou	表

Figure 14.1 DBCS test characters.

your product uses a filename, you should test it with this character plus the two characters mentioned in the last paragraph.

- ✦ If your product allows the use of wildcards in searches, you must test how they handle double-byte characters. If the question mark character "?" matches a single character, you must check that the pattern "A?B" finds the string "A<hiragana-A>B". Also, the pattern "*\" should match the full string "<hyou>\", not just the Kanji character "<hyou>" (whose second byte is the backslash character).
- ✦ In every place that a font is selected (by the program), the program must use a font capable of displaying double-byte characters. The table in Figure 14.2 lists two such fonts. It's not uncommon to have fonts hard-coded in the source code. In this case, Kanji characters will show up as garbage characters. To find these problems, you will need to enter double-byte characters everywhere you can and check that every control that can display a string will display double-byte characters properly.
- ✦ If your program uses a macro language or a programming language, the language will need to handle double-byte data, and you will probably want to have the language-support double-byte characters for variables and function names also. Select a good set of characters (including those in Figure 14.1), and use each one to test each item your parser might misinterpret.
- ✦ Many programs need to pass data to and from other programs through data file input and output, DDE, OLE, and other means. The double-byte handling at each of these points needs to be tested thoroughly by passing data to

Font name (Roman letters)	Font name (Japanese)
Minchou	明朝
Gothic	ゴシック

Figure 14.2 Japanese font names.

another program, checking that the correct information shows up, then passing the information back and checking it again. Note that it isn't sufficient to pass the data out and back and only check the final results. You could end up with the right values even though the other program received garbage.

Emperor Eras

In Japan and China, dates are expressed in emperor eras rather than in years. Just as we checked a variety of date formats in internationalization QA, you will need to check the Japanese formats in the table in Figure 14.3.

In addition, you will need to verify that your program is using emperor eras appropriately. Use the table of eras in Chapter 13 and test all the border dates between each era, plus dates before the first era and long past the current era to verify that they display correctly in your program.

Asian Functionality

IME

IME testing depends on the level of implementation that your program is using. Our goal is to determine that the IME handling has been implemented properly and consistently throughout the program. If your program supports Level 2 IME handling, it should do so throughout.

Japanese Date Formats
1995年 2月 9日
7年 2月 9日
平成07年 2月 9日

Figure 14.3 Japanese date formats.

Level 1: Allow the operating system to handle the IME. In this case, double-byte characters will be input in a buffer that displays at the bottom-left-hand corner of the screen.

Level 2: Double-byte characters are entered at the same place as the edit control. Checking the functionality for each edit control is generally straightforward:

- ✦ Check whether the IME is in-line, that is, whether the IME is at the cursor point or in the bottom-left-hand corner of the screen.
- ✦ Check what happens when we move the window while entering double-byte characters. Ideally, the double-byte buffer should move along with the window. Alternatively, the double-byte buffer can be placed at the cursor after the window has been dropped.
- ✦ Check what happens when we click on another edit field as we type double-byte characters. Either the characters should be dropped, or the double-byte buffer should be moved to the new edit field intact. The behavior needs to be defined in the spec, but we need to check that the behavior is correct and consistent throughout the product.
- ✦ Check that the font and color of the double-byte edit window is the same as for the original window.
- ✦ Check that the edit window grows appropriately for the number of characters entered. Oftentimes, if a window is intended to grow, it does not work properly with double-byte characters.

Level 3: The UI turns on the IME when the cursor moves into certain fields.

- ✦ Check all level 2 functionality.
- ✦ Check all fields in the product by turning off the IME, then moving directly to the field. If the field is a string field, the IME should be turned on (at least for most string fields); otherwise, the IME should not turn on.

Word Wrapping

As we know from the previous chapter, word-wrapping Japanese text is fundamentally different from word-wrapping English text. Rather than word-wrapping on word boundaries looking for spaces, we can wrap any character. The only restriction is that certain characters (such as open quotes) cannot appear at the end of the line and other characters (such as close quotes and small Kana characters) cannot appear at the beginning of the line (see Figure 14.4 for a list of Japanese open and close characters).

As the user types, the editor must never wrap a line right after the "open characters" in the first column of the table. These characters must wrap with the following character. If the wrap should occur at one of the close characters, we must wrap both the close character and the previous character.

Open Characters	Close Characters
[	)
｢	]
“	}
〔	｣
｛	｡
《	､
『	ｧ
{	ｨ
‘	ｩ
（	ｪ
［	ｫ
〈	ｬ
「	ｭ
【	ｮ
	ｯ
	ｰ
	ﾞ
	ﾟ

Figure 14.4 Japanese word-wrap characters.

Probably the easiest way to test this is to have a test file that contains all of these characters alternated with other characters. For the other characters, you should choose a variety of single- and double-byte characters, spaces, and tabs. Start typing in front of the characters to push each one off the line. Verify that the open or close character jumps to the next line at the appropriate time and that the character after the open character or the character before the close character jumps to the next line at the same time.

Vertical Writing

In order to accommodate computers, many Japanese and Chinese users have become accustomed to writing horizontally. But in some applications such as word-processing, vertical writing is important.

When we type vertically, we start in the top-right corner and type down. When we press the ENTER key or when the line wraps, the cursor should move to the top of the column to the left of the first column. All of our movement keys must change to take this into account. Here are some things to look for:

- We need to verify that we start at the upper-right-hand corner and wrap to the top of the next column to the left when we press the ENTER key or when we reach the bottom of the window.
- We need to verify the behavior when we hit the end of the left-hand column. The columns should appropriately scroll to the right.
- We need to check the cursor movement keys. PageUp and PageDown should move horizontally rather than vertically (but the Up and Down arrow keys should still move up and down). The behavior of Home and End and Control-Home and Control-End keys needs to be modified to accommodate the orientation.
- If word-wrapping depends on the size of the window, we should rewrap whenever the top or bottom of the window are sized, but not necessarily when the sides are sized.

- Marking text should be done by columns rather than lines.
- If we enter data into a vertical field, we need to test that the field properly expands and that it can handle our text.

Vertical Printing

When printing vertically, we need to verify that we use a vertical font so that the characters print right-side up, that alignment of text is correct, that text is wrapped appropriately, that pages break at the correct place, and so on.

We should have vertical printing covered by our body of printer tests. Please see the section on printer tests for more information.

Auto-Furigana

To type Kanji characters, users type syllables and convert them to Kanji. For certain applications, it is useful to capture the syllables that the user types in the form of Katakana characters. This is called *furigana*. If the program automates the process, we call it auto-furigana. For instance, if we have a database of names, we might want to store both the Kanji characters in one field and the furigana in another so that we can sort the records by pronunciation and provide multiple means of finding records.

To test this functionality, we must verify that we can attach the auto-furigana field to the source field, that we capture the Kana characters at the appropriate time (usually when we leave the field), and that the correct characters are captured.

Compatibility Testing

For the Japanese market, the biggest issue with compatibility testing is the different platforms, at least as far as DOS and Windows are concerned. Currently, NEC holds 50 percent or more of the PC market share. As discussed in Chapter 13, this machine is different at the BIOS level compared to the IBM PC. While there are particular differences that we must test for, it's critical to do full functionality testing on both the NEC and the DOS/V machines. In

addition, if you wish to sell to Epson and Fujitsu FMR users, you will need to test on these machines as well, since these also have differences.

Let's examine the differences that we specifically need to test for.

Drive Letter

The first hard disk is drive A: and not drive C:, and, in fact, some of the older NEC machines have only a drive A:, which is a hard disk, and a drive B:, which is a floppy drive. This can be a problem throughout the product and it's important to test on a machine that does not have a drive C:, starting with an install to drive A: and running through full functionality testing.

Video Modes

In DOS, the standard video mode for DOS/V and NEC is 24×80 characters rather than 25×80 to allow one line at the bottom of the screen for the front-end processor. You need to check that your program doesn't inappropriately scroll off the screen and that it doesn't compete with the FEP for the twenty-fifth line.

In Windows, the only video mode on the older NEC machines is 640×400 (instead of 640×480, which is the lowest resolution available on DOS/V machines). While more and more computer users are switching to a higher-resolution video mode, others still have only this mode available. You should consider 640×400 as the baseline for your Japanese product. You should check that all your dialogs fit in this mode. This can be a problem particularly with computer-based training, which requires a lot of screen real estate.

There are other video modes:

640 × 400

640 × 480

800 × 600

1024 × 768

1280 × 1024

While you should do some cosmetic checking on each of the video modes, the ones on which you should spend most of your time are 640 × 400 24 point and 1024 × 768 24 point. The reason is that in these modes, the least amount of text fits on the screen, and so it's in these modes that text is most likely to be chopped off in dialogs and status lines.

You do need to check all of your dialogs in these modes and you need to check all the status lines for all menu and dialog items. See Chapter 12 for more information.

Printers

For most products, it makes sense to create a body of printer tests that test all aspects of your program's output. These tests should be automated so that they can be run easily against a large number of printers. These tests should print single pages and multiple pages, graphics, tables, in several different fonts and in a variety of sizes, in landscape mode and portrait mode, using different paper sizes and with a variety of margin settings. If your program allows printer codes to be entered manually, this should be covered. Every place in your program that allows printing should be covered.

There are a wide variety of printers in Japan and you will need to support a certain set of them. Any of these printers can display distinct problems. You can treat these problems as printer driver bugs or you may choose to fix them in your product.

This printer test suite should be run on as many printers as possible. You may be able to have your beta testers or your distributor in Japan run this for you on equipment that they have available. It may also be possible to arrange to borrow a printer from the manufacturer if they are motivated to have your product support their printer.

The most common page size in Japan is A4, which is close in size to 8.5″ by 11″ in the United States. (See Appendix A for dimensions.) Also common are B4 and C4. In addition to these regular page sizes, it is common practice in Japan to print to preformatted forms and Japanese label sizes. Most database and word processing

products can handle these. If your program needs to address this, you will have to print extensively to these forms.

Quality Level in Japan

The Japanese market has evolved in a very service-oriented way with many small developers writing custom software. As a result, the Japanese tend to have high expectations for the software they use and they have a lower tolerance for bugs than do other cultures. In addition, the market is consumer-oriented, and ease of use is particularly important.

It is important to take this into account when you are deciding whether or not to defer a Japanization bug, and it's also important to consider when deciding whether you should fix some core bugs in your Japanese version. While it's difficult to lay out definite guidelines, a borderline bug that has been deferred in the core product should probably be fixed for the Japanese product.

One thing to keep in mind is that the Japanese market is less price sensitive than other markets. One option may be to spend more to clean up your product, then charge more for it.

Language Skills of the Engineers

When it comes to Asian software, it isn't enough to know the operating system and the product. Installing software and interpreting error messages can be very difficult or impossible without knowledge of the language.

We've found that if about half the engineers on the QA team have the ability to read and write Japanese, we should be able to have a fully productive team. The goal is to have enough Japanese speakers available so that the non-Japanese speakers always have someone available to answer questions. One of the Japanese engineers can be an entry-level engineer who helps install software, answers language questions, does cosmetic testing, and so on. In addition, it's important to have an engineer with experience testing double-

byte software. It's also useful to have an engineer with knowledge of your product category in the Japanese marketplace.

Double-Byte QA Documentation

Because of the extent of the testing, and because of the coordination efforts required, documentation of the QA process is very important. Please refer to Chapters 6 and 12 for information on writing a test plan and a set of test outlines.

Test Automation

As in European localization QA, the ideal situation is to be able to use the core test suites directly to test the localized version, but the other automation options may apply as well. Because many builds of the product will be required before it stabilizes, test automation is particularly important for Asian QA.

APPENDIX A

International Tables

Paper Sizes

Name	Width (mm)	Length
Legal	215.9	355.6
Letter	215.9	279.4
A0	841	1189
A1	594	841
A2	420	594
A3	297	420
A4	210	297
A5	148	210
A6	105	148
A7	74	105
A8	52	74
B0	1030	1456
B1	728	1030
B2	515	728
B3	364	515
B4	257	364
B5	182	257
B6	128	182
B7	91	128
B8	64	91

Envelope Sizes

Name	Dimensions
	120 × 180
	138 × 230
	160 × 230
	230 × 341
	260 × 360
B4	250 × 353
B5	250 × 176
B6	125 × 176
C3	458 × 324
C4	229 × 324
C5	162 × 229
C6	114 × 162
C65	114 × 229
DL	110 × 220
E4	310 × 220
E5	220 × 115
E65	110 × 220
Italian	110 × 230
M5	155 × 220
M6	110 × 155
M65	110 × 220
Monarch	$3\frac{7}{8}$ in × $7\frac{1}{2}$ in
Size 10	$4\frac{1}{8}$ in × $9\frac{1}{2}$ in
Size 11	$4\frac{1}{2}$ in × $10\frac{3}{8}$ in
Size 12	$4\frac{3}{4}$ in × 11 in
Size $6\frac{3}{4}$	$3\frac{5}{8}$ in × $6\frac{1}{2}$ in
Size 9	$3\frac{7}{8}$ in × $8\frac{7}{8}$ in

Values in mm unless otherwise stated.

Code Pages

CODE POINT	CODE PAGE 437	850	852	857	860	861	863	965	866	ANSI
128	Ç	Ç	Ç	Ç	Ç	Ç	Ç	Ç	Ђ	■
129	ü	ü	ü	ü	ü	ü	ü	ü	Ѓ	■
130	é	é	é	é	é	é	é	é	‚	■
131	â	â	â	â	â	â	â	â	ѓ	■
132	ä	ä	ä	ä	ã	ä	Â	ä	„	■
133	à	à	ů	à	à	à	à	à	…	■
134	å	å	ć	å	Á	å	¶	å	†	■
135	ç	ç	ç	ç	ç	ç	ç	ç	‡	■
136	ê	ê	ł	ê	ê	ê	ê	ê		■
137	ë	ë	ë	ë	Ê	ë	ë	ë	‰	■
138	è	è	Ő	è	è	è	è	è	Љ	■
139	ï	ï	ő	ï	Í	Ð	ï	ï	‹	■
140	î	î	î	î	Ô	ð	î	î	Њ	■
141	ì	ì	Ź	ı	ì	þ	‗	ì	Ќ	■
142	Ä	Ä	Ä	Ä	Ã	Ä	À	Ä	Ћ	■
143	Å	Å	Ć	Å	Â	Å	§	Å	Џ	■
144	É	É	É	É	É	É	É	É	ђ	■
145	æ	æ	Ĺ	æ	À	æ	È	æ	‘	‘
146	Æ	Æ	ĺ	Æ	È	Æ	Ê	Æ	’	’
147	ô	ô	ô	ô	ô	ô	ô	ô	“	■
148	ö	ö	ö	ö	õ	ö	Ë	ö	”	■
149	ò	ò	Ľ	ò	ò	þ	Ï	ò	•	■
150	û	û	ľ	û	Ú	û	û	û	–	■
151	ù	ù	Ś	ù	ù	Ý	ù	ù	—	■
152	ÿ	ÿ	ś	İ	Ì	ý	¤	ÿ		■
153	Ö	Ö	Ö	Ö	Õ	Ö	Ô	Ö	™	■
154	Ü	Ü	Ü	Ü	Ü	Ü	Ü	Ü	љ	■
155	¢	ø	Ť	ø	¢	ø	¢	ø	›	■
156	£	£	ť	£	£	£	£	£	њ	■
157	¥	Ø	Ł	Ø	Ù	Ø	Ù	Ø	ќ	■
158	Pts	×	×	Ş	Pts	Pts	Û	Pts	ћ	■
159	ƒ	ƒ	č	ş	Ó	ƒ	ƒ	ƒ	џ	■

Figure A.1 Code_PG1.pcx.

CODE POINT	437	850	852	857	860	861	863	965	866	ANSI
					CODE PAGE					
160	á	á	á	á	á	á	¦	á		
161	í	í	í	í	í	í	´	í	ў	i
162	ó	ó	ó	ó	ó	ó	ó	ó	ў	¢
163	ú	ú	ú	ú	ú	ú	ú	ú	J	£
164	ñ	ñ	Ą	ñ	ñ	Á	¨	ñ	¤	¤
165	Ñ	Ñ	ą	Ñ	Ñ	Í		Ñ	Ґ	¥
166	ª	ª	Ž	Ğ	ª	Ó	³	ª	¦	¦
167	°	°	ž	ğ	°	Ú	¯	°	§	§
168	¿	¿	Ę	¿	¿	¿	Î	¿	Ë	¨
169	□	®	ę	®	Ò	□	□	□	©	©
170	¬	¬	¬	¬	¬	¬	¬	¬	Є	ª
171	½	½	ź	½	½	½	½	½	«	«
172	¼	¼	Č	¼	¼	¼	¼	¼	¬	¬
173	i	i	ş	i	i	i	¾	i	-	-
174	«	«	«	«	«	«	«	«	®	®
175	»	»	»	»	»	»	»	¤	Ï	¯
176	░	░	░	░	░	░	░	░	°	°
177	▒	▒	▒	▒	▒	▒	▒	▒	±	±
178	▓	▓	▓	▓	▓	▓	▓	▓	I	²
179	│	│	│	│	│	│	│	│	i	³
180	┤	┤	┤	┤	┤	┤	┤	┤	ґ	´
181	╡	Á	Á	Á	╡	╡	╡	╡	µ	µ
182	╢	Â	Â	Â	╢	╢	╢	╢	¶	¶
183	╖	À	Ě	À	╖	╖	╖	╖	•	•
184	╕	©	Ş	©	╕	╕	╕	╕	ë	¸
185	╣	╣	╣	╣	╣	╣	╣	╣	№	¹
186	║	║	║	║	║	║	║	║	є	º
187	╗	╗	╗	╗	╗	╗	╗	╗	»	»
188	╝	╝	╝	╝	╝	╝	╝	╝	j	¼
189	╜	¢	Ż	¢	╜	╜	╜	╜	S	½
190	╛	¥	ż	¥	╛	╛	╛	╛	s	¾
191	┐	┐	┐	┐	┐	┐	┐	┐	ï	¿

Figure A.2 Code_PG2.pcx.

CODE	CODE PAGE									
POINT	437	850	852	857	860	861	863	965	866	ANSI
192	└	└	└	└	└	└	└	└	А	À
193	┴	┴	┴	┴	┴	┴	┴	┴	Б	Á
194	┬	┬	┬	┬	┬	┬	┬	┬	В	Â
195	├	├	├	├	├	├	├	├	Г	Ã
196	─	─	─	─	─	─	─	─	Д	Ä
197	┼	┼	┼	┼	┼	┼	┼	┼	Е	Å
198	╞	ã	Ă	ã	╞	╞	╞	╞	Ж	Æ
199	╟	Ã	ă	Ã	╟	╟	╟	╟	З	Ç
200	╚	╚	╚	╚	╚	╚	╚	╚	И	È
201	╔	╔	╔	╔	╔	╔	╔	╔	Й	É
202	╩	╩	╩	╩	╩	╩	╩	╩	К	Ê
203	╦	╦	╦	╦	╦	╦	╦	╦	Л	Ë
204	╠	╠	╠	╠	╠	╠	╠	╠	М	Ì
205	═	═	═	═	═	═	═	═	Н	Í
206	╬	╬	╬	╬	╬	╬	╬	╬	О	Î
207	╧	¤	¤	¤	╧	╧	╧	╧	П	Ï
208	╨	ð	đ	º	╨	╨	╨	╨	Р	Ð
209	╤	Ð	Đ	ª	╤	╤	╤	╤	С	Ñ
210	╥	Ê	Ď	Ê	╥	╥	╥	╥	Т	Ò
211	╙	Ë	Ë	Ë	╙	╙	╙	╙	У	Ó
212	╘	È	ď	È	╘	╘	╘	╘	Ф	Ô
213	╒	ı	Ň		╒	╒	╒	╒	Х	Õ
214	╓	Í	Í	Í	╓	╓	╓	╓	Ц	Ö
215	╫	Î	Î	Î	╫	╫	╫	╫	Ч	×
216	╪	Ï	ě	Ï	╪	╪	╪	╪	Ш	Ø
217	┘	┘	┘	┘	┘	┘	┘	┘	Щ	Ù
218	┌	┌	┌	┌	┌	┌	┌	┌	Ъ	Ú
219	█	█	█	█	█	█	█	█	Ы	Û
220	▄	▄	▄	▄	▄	▄	▄	▄	Ь	Ü
221	▌	¦	Ţ	¦	▌	▌	▌	▌	Э	Ý
222	▐	Ì	Ů	Ì	▐	▐	▐	▐	Ю	Þ
223	▀	▀	▀	▀	▀	▀	▀	▀	Я	ß

Figure A.3 Code_PG3.pcx.

CODE POINT	437	850	852	857	860	861	863	965	866	ANSI
224	α	Ó	Ó	Ó	α	α	α	α	а	à
225	ß	ß	ß	ß	ß	ß	ß	ß	б	á
226	Γ	Ô	Ô	Ô	Γ	Γ	Γ	Γ	в	â
227	π	Ò	Ń	Ò	π	π	π	π	г	ã
228	Σ	õ	ń	õ	Σ	Σ	Σ	Σ	д	ä
229	σ	Õ	ň	Õ	σ	σ	σ	σ	е	å
230	µ	µ	Š	µ	µ	µ	µ	µ	ж	æ
231	τ	þ	š		τ	τ	τ	τ	з	ç
232	Φ	Þ	Ŕ	×	Φ	Φ	Φ	Φ	и	è
233	Θ	Ú	Ú	Ú	Θ	Θ	Θ	Θ	й	é
234	Ω	Û	ŕ	Û	Ω	Ω	Ω	Ω	к	ê
235	δ	Ù	Ű	Ù	δ	δ	δ	δ	л	ë
236	∞	ý	ý	ì	∞	∞	∞	∞	м	ì
237	φ	Ý	Ý	ÿ	φ	φ	φ	φ	н	í
238	∈	¯	ţ	¯	∈	∈	∈	∈	о	î
239	∩	´	´	´	∩	∩	∩	∩	п	ï
240	≡	-	-	-	≡	≡	≡	≡	р	ð
241	±	±	˝	±	±	±	±	±	с	ñ
242	≥	‗	˛		≥	≥	≥	≥	т	ò
243	≤	¾	ˇ	¾	≤	≤	≤	≤	у	ó
244	⌠	¶	˘	¶	⌠	⌠	⌠	⌠	ф	ô
245	⌡	§	§	§	⌡	⌡	⌡	⌡	х	õ
246	÷	÷	÷	÷	÷	÷	÷	÷	ц	ö
247	≈	¸	¸	¸	≈	≈	≈	≈	ч	÷
248	°	°	°	°	°	°	°	°	ш	ø
249	•	¨	¨	¨	•	•	•	•	щ	ù
250	•	•	˙	•	•	•	•	•	ъ	ú
251	√	^{1}	ű	^{1}	√	√	√	√	ы	û
252	^{n}	^{3}	Ř	^{3}	^{n}	^{n}	^{n}	^{n}	ь	ü
253	^{2}	^{2}	ř	^{2}	^{2}	^{2}	^{2}	^{2}	э	ý
254	■	■	■	■	■	■	■	■	ю	þ
255									я	ÿ

Figure A.4 Code_PG4.pcx.

Country Information in MS-DOS 6.0

Preparing Config.sys and Autoexec.bat for NLS Support

Config.sys

Country: Syntax: *country = ccc[,[ppp][,drive:][path\filename]]*

where:

ccc—is the 3-digit country code for the telephone system.

ppp—is the codepage for the country.

filename—specifies country-specific information file, usually COUNTRY.SYS.

For example:

```
COUNTRY = 033,,c: \dos\country.sys
```

Display: Syntax: device – [drive:][path]DISPLAY.SYS CON[:]= type[,hwcp][,n,m])

where:

type—specifies display adapter type (MONO, CGA, EGA and LCD).

hwcp—specifies code page supported by hardware.

n—specifies number of additional code pages that can be supported (between 0 and 12).

m—specifies the number of subfonts supported for each page.

For example:

```
Device=c: \dos\display.sys con:=(ega,850,2)
```

Autoexec.bat

Nlsfunc: Syntax: nlsfunc [[drive:][path]filename]

where:

filename—specifies country specific information file (COUNTRY.SYS).

For example:

```
nslfunc c: \dos\country.sys
```

Mode: Syntax: mode device codepage prepare = ((cp) [drive:][path\filename)

where:

device—specifiles CON, PRN, LPT#.

cp—specifies codepage number, or list of codepages.

filename—identifies name of codepage information file (CPI).

For example:

```
mode con codepage prepare = (850,c: \dos\ega.cpi)
```

To activate or select a codepage, use **mode select** command.

Mode select: Syntax: mode device codepage select = cp

where:

device—specifies CON or LPT#

cp—identifies code page to be activated.

For example:

```
mode CON select=850
```

To select codepage that DOS will use you can use **chcp.**

CHCP Syntax: chcp [ppp]

where:

ppp—specifies desired codepage.

For example:

```
chcp 850
```

If you want to enable a different keyboard driver, you should use the **keyb** command.

keyb Syntax: keyb [xx[,yyy],[[drive:][path\filename]]]
where:

xx—specifies a two-letter country code.

yyy—specifies numeric definition of character set.

filename—identifies keyboard definition file KEYBOARD. SYS.

For example:

```
keyb sv,,c: \dos\keyboard.sys
```

Locales Information

Currency
Dates
Numbers
Time tables (listed under Dates.doc).

APPENDIX B

International Date Formats

Defaults per Country

	Dates	Most Used	Currency	Most Used	Currency Fraction
Austria	2.Januar 1990		ATS		groschen × 100 (g)
	2.1.90		A$		
	900102		AS		
	2.Jan.1990		öS		
	2 Jan 1990		Sch		
			ÖS		
			S		
Belgium (Flanders)	31-12-90	X	BEF	X	centime × 100
	31-jan-90		BF	X	
	31/12/90	X	BEF		
	31 januari 1990	X	F		
	31.12.90	X	fr.		
	31 jan 90				
Belgium (French)	31-12-90	X	BEF	X	centime × 100
	31-jan-90		FB	X	
	31/12/90	X	BEF		
	2 janvier 1990	X	F		
	2 jan 90				
Canada (English)	January 2 1994		CAD		cent × 100
	2-jan-94		$	X	
	1/02/90 (mm/dd/yy)		$		
Canada (French)	2 janvier 1994		$		
	90-01-02 (yy-mm-dd)				
	90 01 02 (yy mm dd)				
	2 janv. 1990				

	Dates	Most Used	Currency	Most Used	Currency Fraction
Denmark	31.januar 1990	X	DKK		øre × 100
	1990-1-31		Dkr		
	1990 01 31		Kr.		
	31/1-90		kr.	X	
	90-12-31 (Standard EEC Date Format)		Dkr		
	31-1-90	X	k	X	
Finland	2.1.1990	X	FIM		penni × 100 (Pia)
	2.1.90	X	FMK		
	1990-01-02		FMK		
	2. tammikuuta 1990		FIM		
	EEC Date Format		mk		
			Fmk		
France	2 janvier 1990	X	FRF		centime × 100
	2 jan 90		FFR		c
	02.01.90		FFR		ct
	02/01/90	X	F	X	cs
	02-01-90		FF		
Germany	2. Januar 1990	X	DEM		pfennig (Pf) × 100
	2. Jan. 1990	X	DM	X	
	2.1.90	X	DM		
	02.01.90				
	2.1.1990				
Iceland	2.januar 1990	X	ISK		eyrir × 100 (plural: aurar)
	2. 1. 1990		ICK		
	2. 1. '90	X	ISK		
	020190		Kr.	X	
	900102 (ISO 2014)		kr.		
	90 01 02 (ISO 2014)				

Ireland	2-January-1990		IEP		penny × 100
	2.1.90		IR£		p
	020190		IR£		
			£		
Italy	2-GEN-90		ITL		centesimo (ctmo)
	2/1/90		LIT		
	2 Gennaio 1990		LIT		
	29.1.90		L.	X	
			Lit		
Netherlands	31-12-90	X	NLG		cent × 100
	31-jan-90		Dfl.		
	31/12/90	X	NLG		
	31 januari 1990	X	FL		
	31.12.90	X	fl	X	
	31 jan 90		F		
	31.12.1990		f	X	
			Hfl	X	
			gld	X	
			DFL		
Norway	2.januar 1990	X	NOK		øre × 100
	2.1.90	X	NKR		
	20190		NKr.	X	
	02.01.90		Kr.	X	
Portugal	90.01.02		kr.		
	2.1.90		PTE		centavo × 100
	02.01.90		ESC		
	2.JAN.90	X	ESC		
	2/1/90	X	Esc.	X	
	02/01/90		-$- Eg. 1$50		
	2/JAN/90				
	2/1/1990				

	Dates	Most Used	Currency	Most Used	Currency Fraction
Spain	02-01-90 (civil)	X	ESP		céntimos (cts)
	02.01.90 (military)		PTA		
	02/01/90		Pts.	X	
	2 de Enero de 1990	X	Pta, plural Pts		
	2 Ene 90				
Sweden	2 januari 1990 (long Swedish standard)	X	SEK	X	öre × 100
	1990-01-02 (Swedish standard)	X	SEK		kronor
	90-01-02 (often used short form)	X	Kr	X	
			kr	X	
UK	2nd January 1990	X	GBP		new penny × 100 (p) (plural: pence)
	2-January-1990	X	GB£		
	2/1/90	X	GB£		
	2.1.90		£	X	
	020190				
	2 Jan 90				
USA	02-Jan-90	X	USD		cent × 100
	January 2, 1990	X	US$		¢
	2/20/90	X	USA		
	second of January '90		$	X	
	31-Month-1990 (military)				
	90/12/31 (military)				

Legend

For Currency the first three represents:

a) ISO 4217 Symbol

b) International Symbol

c) EEC symbol

Delimiters: Note that thousand separator as well as decimal separator varies from country to country.

APPENDIX C

Internationalizing Microsoft Windows 3.X Applications

Overview

When writing a Microsoft Windows 3.X application, the developer must take into consideration several key issues to ensure that the program can be translated into different languages:

- Use country-specific numbers, list, date, time, and currency formats. Locate text strings separately from source code to facilitate the translation work as well as to minimize risks of introducing bugs when the product gets translated.
- Design code that is data independent so that it executes correctly in any language. Place items on the display and printed page in accordance with the size of the items. Make sure that applications run properly with any language keyboard.

There is also a need to physically separate the files that will have to be modified during translation.

Country Information

Country information includes the country, language, character set, and the language-dependent layout of the keyboard.

The language and keyboard layout are initially specified in the Windows Setup program and the character set is usually static for Windows programs. However, all selections may change and should be considered when writing an application. Some are statically linked to the version of Windows you are using, and some can be changed by the user at any time by choosing the International icon from the Control Panel application.

These selections instruct the Windows system as to which keyboard and language drivers to use by copying the appropriate kbdXXX.dll and langXXX.dll files to the windows\system subdirectory. These filenames are recorded in the system.ini file and are read at system initialization time. The following code illustrates how an application can retrieve this information:

```
char szFile[156], szKeyboardDLL[13], szLanguageDLL[13];
GetWindowsDirectory (szFile, 145);
if (szFile[lstrlen(szFile)-1] == '\\') lstrcat (szFile, "system.ini");
else                                   lstrcat (szFile, "\\system.ini");
GetPrivateProfileString ("keyboard", "keyboard.dll", "", szKeyboardDLL,
  13, szFile);
GetPrivateProfileString ("boot", "language.dll", "", szLanguageDLL, 13,
  szFile);
```

The country can also be set in the international windows. This selection is stored as a string in the win.ini and also as an integer based on international-phone calling codes and can be queried by interested applications.

The following table provides list of values for country names (sCountry) and country codes (iCountry):

iCountry	sCountry
Australia	61
Austria	43
Belgium (Dutch)	32
Belgium (French)	32
Brazil	55
Canada (English)	2
Canada (French)	2
Denmark	45
Finland	358
France	33
Germany	49

Iceland	354
Italy	39
Mexico	52
Netherlands	31
New Zealand	64
Norway	47
Portugal	351
South Korea	82
Spain	34
Sweden	46
Switzerland (French)	41
Switzerland (German)	41
Switzerland (Italian)	41
Taiwan	886
United Kingdom	44
United States	1
Other Country	1

The following code illustrates how an application can retrieve this information:

```
char szCountry[25];
int CountryCode;
GetProfileString ("intl", "sCountry", "United States", szCountry, 25);
CountryCode = GetProfileInt ("intl", "iCountry", 1);
```

Note that when any one of these settings changes, the Control Panel writes the new information to the win.ini and sends the WM_WININICHANGE message to notify all top-level windows. An application may elect to read this information only at startup and respond to this message.

Country-Specific Formats

These allow the user to specify to Windows applications which separator character should be used for lists, and to specify desired formats for time, date, currency, and numbers. This is done by selecting the International icon from the Control Panel to enter the information. As changes occur, the Control Panel stores the new settings in the win.ini file and sends WM_WININICHANGE messages to notify all top-level windows.

The following section contains descriptions of each of the international settings that are stored on win.ini file. Note that if the settings are U.S. defaults, the Control Panel may not store them in the win.ini file beyond the sCountry field, so when the desired field is not found, applications should use the U.S. defaults.

Rather than rereading it every time it is needed, applications may read this information on initialization and in response to WM_WININICHANGE messages and so be assured of having up-to-date values.

The **list separator** character partitions items in a list, such as a series of numbers. This character will be used only when creating a list or a series within the application. Note that static text, which may contain lists, will be translated by the translator. Users enter the desired character in the List Separator edit box. The Control Panel application limits this field to one character. The selection is recorded in the win.ini file as sList.

```
char szListSep[2], chListSep;
GetProfileString ("intl", "sList", ",", szListSep, 2);
chListSep = s zListSep[0];
```

When creating a list, insert the chListSep character between the items.

The Metric/English measurement flag specifies to applications whether the user is working with metric or English measurement values. Most applications can support both, and this flag is used to define the default mode. The user sets this by selecting either Metric or English from the Control Panel's Measurements box. This selection is recorded in win.ini as iMeasure. The value is:

- 0 if the user selects Metric
- 1 if the user chooses English

```
BOOL bMetric;
bMetric = !(GetProfileInt ("intl", "Measure", 1));
```

The **time** format defines how the user wants to display the time of the day, including 12- or 24-hour format; whether or not the hour

should include a leading zero; which character to use for separating hours and minutes; and the trailing string, such as AM, PM, or PST. This information is entered in the International-Time Format dialog box. These selections are recorded in win.ini as iTime, iTLzero, sTime, s1159, and s2359.

iTime results from the "12 hour" and "24 hour" radio buttons. The values are 0 and 1 for the 12- and 24-hour formats respectively.

iTLzero results from the "Leading Zero" radio buttons. iTLzero is 0 if the user chooses the 9:15 format—meaning, do not display a leading zero when the hour is less than 10; iTLzero is 1 if the user chooses the 09:15 format—meaning attach a leading zero when the hour is less than 10. Minutes and seconds less than 10 always contain a leading 0.

sTime is the separator placed between the hours, minutes, and seconds of the time. This string is usually just one character; however, the Control Panel application allows a string that may include spaces to be entered. The width of the edit box limits the number of characters that can be entered.

s1159 is the string that follows times between 12:00 A.M.—midnight—and 11:59 A.M. This string is specified in the "00:00–11:59" edit box if the user selected 12 hour, or is copied from s2359 if the user selected 24 hour. This string may contain spaces and is limited by the Control Panel application to 8 characters.

s2359 is the string that follows times between 12:00 P.M.—noon—and 11:59 P.M. This string results from the "12:00–23:59" edit box (note that this is the "00:00–23:59" edit box if the user selected 24 hour). This string may contain spaces and is limited to 8 characters. The iTime field defines whether to display these times as 12:00–23:59 or 12:00–11:59. If iTime is 1, time is presented in 24-hour format. The previously mentioned times would be displayed as 12:00–23:59 (with the s2359 string trailing). If iTime is 0, time will be displayed in 12-hour format. Consequently, this time range would be displayed as 12:00–11:59 (with the s2359 string trailing). The following code retrieves the time format information from the win.ini file:

```
BOOL b24Hour;               // TRUE if time is to be written in 24 hour
   // format, FALSE if 12 hour format (times after   // noon are to be
written as 12:00-11:59)
```

```
BOOL bLeadZeroHour; // TRUE if the hour is to contain a leading 0
   // when < 10
char szTimeSep[5]; // The string to use to separate the hours,
   // minutes and seconds of the time, such as a    // ":" in English
(this string will most often                       // be just one character)
char szAM[9];                 // the trailing string for times between
   // midnight and just before noon (00:00-11:59 on  // the 24 hour clock)
char szPM[9];                 // the trailing string for times between noon
   // and just before midnight (12:00-23:59 on the       // 24 hour clock)
b24Hour = GetProfileInt ("intl", "iTime", 0);
bLeadZeroHour = GetProfileInt ("intl", "iTLzero", 0);
GetProfileString ("intl", "sTime", ":", szTimeSep, 5);
GetProfileString ("intl", "s1159", "AM", szAM, 9);
GetProfileString ("intl", "s2359", "PM", szPM, 9);
```

There are two date formats: short—a numeric-only form of the date; and long—a format that may include the day of the week and the month name.

The **short date** format specifies the order in which to present the month, the day, and the year as well as the separator to place between them. The user enters this information in the "Short Date Format" group box in the International-Date Format dialog box. Selections are recorded in win.ini as sDate, iDate, and sShortDate.

sDate results from the "Separator" edit box. This separator is placed between the month, the day, and the year of the date. It is limited to one character.

iDate specifies the presentation ordering of the month, the day, and the year of the date. This results from the set of "Order" radio buttons. iDate is:

- ✦ 0 if the user chooses MDY
- ✦ 1 for DMY
- ✦ 2 for the YMD button

sShortDate describes how the short-date will be displayed. All information for displaying the numeric date is available in this string and it is unnecessary to check sDate and iDate. This string also incorporates information from the "Day Leading Zero," "Month Leading Zero," and "Century" check boxes. sShortDate will contain fields for the day, month, and year as described below. The sDate separator is placed between each field.

The day field is one of the following:

- ✦ dd—Display the day of the month with a leading zero if <10.
- ✦ d—Display the day of the month with no leading zero.

The month field is one of the following:

- ✦ MM—Display the number of the month, with a leading zero if <10.
- ✦ M—Display the number of the month with no leading zero.

The year field is one of the following:

- ✦ yyyy—Display the year including the century, such as 1990.
- ✦ yy—Display the year without the century, such as 90.

For example, January 3, 1969:

sShortDate	Displayed Date
M/D/yy	1/3/69
yy-MM-dd	69-01-03
d.MM.yyyy	3.01.1969

To read the short date information from the win.ini file:

```
char szDateSep[2], chDateSep;
int DateFormat;                    // 0 for MDY, 1 for DMY, 2 for YMD
char szShortDate[11];
GetProfileString ("intl", "sDate", "/", szDateSep, 2);
chDateSep = szDateSep[0];
DateFormat = GetProfileInt ("intl", "iDate", 0);
GetProfileString ("intl", "sShortDate", "M/d/yy", szShortDate, 11);
```

The **long date** format specifies the order in which to display the month, the day, and the year; the format of the month, the day, and the year; and the separators to be placed between the fields. This format also allows an optional day of the week. Users enter this information in the "Long Date Format" group box in the International-Date Format dialog box. Selections are recorded in win.ini as sLongDate.

sLongDate is a format string that describes how to display the date. This string includes an optional first field for the day of the week; fields for the month (M's), the day (d's), and the year (Y's); and the separator strings placed between each field. The month, day, and year fields may be in any order.

The following code reads the long date format from the win.ini file:

```
char szLongDate[40];
GetProfileString ("intl", "sLongDate", "dddd, MMMM dd, yyyy", szLongDate, 40);
```

The **day-of-week field** is optional. When present, it is the first field in the format string. Do not display the day of the week when this field is not at the beginning of the format string. Count the number of d's in the field to identify the difference between the day-of-week optional first field and the day as the first field.

The day-of-week field is one of the following:

- ✦ dddd—Display the day of the week, such as Sunday or Wednesday.
- ✦ ddd—Display the abbreviated day of the week, for example Sun or Wed.

The day field is one of the following:

- ✦ dd—Display the day of the month with a leading zero if <10.
- ✦ d—Display the day of the month without a leading zero.

The month field is one of the following:

- ✦ MMMM—Display the name of the month, such as March or December.
- ✦ MMM—Display the abbreviated name of the month, such as Mar or Dec.

- ✦ MM—Display the number of the month, with a leading zero if <10.
- ✦ M—Display the number of the month with no leading zero.

The year field is one of the following:

- ✦ yyyy—Display the year including the century, for example, 1990.
- ✦ yy—Display the year without the century, such as 90.

There is a separator between each field (day of the week, day, month, year). The separator can be of any length, may contain spaces, and may be enclosed in single quotes.

For example:

sLongDate	Date to Display	Comments
dddd, d. MMMM yyyy	Saturday, 6. October 1990	(German default)
dddd, MMMM dd, yyyy	Saturday, October 06, 1990	(U.S. default)
dd' of 'MMMM, yyyy	06 of October, 1990	(Taiwan default)

Number format allows the user to specify the format for the presentation of numbers. This includes the separator character placed between the thousands and the hundreds place (a comma is used in the United States); the separator character placed between the whole and fractional parts of a number (a period known as a decimal point in the United States); the number of digits to display in the fractional part; and information on whether to display a 0 for the whole part when the number is less than 1. The user enters these settings in the International-Number Format dialog box. Selections are recorded in win.ini as sThousand, sDecimal, iDigits, and iLzero.

sThousand results from the "1000 Separator" edit box and is limited to one character. This is the separator character to place between the thousands and the hundreds place in the presentation of a number.

sDecimal results from the "Decimal Separator" edit box and is limited to one character. This is the separator character that is displayed between the whole and the fractional parts of a number.

iDigits results from the "Decimal Digits" edit box. This value ranges from 0 to 9, as enforced by the Control Panel application. iDigits specifies the number of digits to display in the fractional part of the number—that is, the number of digits to the right of the sDecimal character.

iLzero results from the "Leading Zero" radio button. This setting dictates how to display the whole part of values less than 1. If the user selects the "0.7" button, applications should display a leading 0 as the whole part, and iLzero will be set to 1. If the user selects the ".7" radio button, nothing should be displayed left of the sDecimal character and iLzero will be set to 0.

The number format is read from the win.ini file:

```
char sz1000Sep[2], ch1000Sep;
char szDecimal[2], chDecimal; // decimal point character
int Digits;     ·   // number of digits to display in the fractional part
BOOL bLeadZero;   // TRUE if numbers less than 1 are to be displayed
  with a whole part of 0, such as 0.5
GetProfileString ("intl", "sThousand", ",", sz1000Sep, 2);
ch1000Sep = sz1000Sep[0];
GetProfileString ("intl", "sDecimal", ".", szDecimal, 2);
chDecimal = szDecimal[0];
Digits = GetProfileInt ("intl", "iDigits", 2);
bLeadZero = GetProfileInt ("intl", "iLzero", 1);
```

Currency format is a user direction for displaying monetary values. This includes the symbol for currency; the placement of the currency symbol (left or right of the value); the number of digits to be displayed in the fractional part of the number (for the United States, 2 is used for displaying cents); and the format for presenting negative currency values. This is done in the International-Currency Format dialog box. This gets recorded in the win.ini file as sCurrency, iCurrency, iCurrDigits, and iNegCurr. When displaying currency values, characters separating the thousands and hundreds place and the whole and fractional parts of the value should be used.

sCurrency results from the "Symbol" edit box. This is the currency symbol. The string may contain spaces and is limited in length by the size of the edit box.

iCurrency results from the "Symbol Placement" combo box. It specifies where to display the currency symbol. The list box selections and the corresponding values for iCurrency are shown here:

Symbol Placement	iCurrency	Comments
$10	0	DM10 is the German default
10$	1	
$ 10	2	B-Z 10 is the Brazilian default
10 $	3	10 kr is the Swedish default

iCurrDigits results from the "Decimal Digits" edit box. It is the number of digits to display in the fractional part, limits of the range value is between 0 and 9.

iNegCurr results from the "Negative" combo box. It specifies the format of currency values less than 0. The possible choices (from the list box) and the corresponding values for iNegCurr are as follows:

Negative	iNegCurr	Comments
($10.50)	0	($10.50) is the United States default
–$10.50	1	–DM1,22 is the German default
$–10.50	2	f – 1,22 is the Netherlands default
$10.50–	3	
(10.50$)	4	
–10.50$	5	–1,22kr is the Swedish default
10.50–$	6	
10.50$–	7	

The following code illustrates how to read the currency information from the win.ini file—including the thousands separator and the decimal separator characters from the number format section:

```
char sz1000Sep[2], ch1000Sep;
char szDecimal[2], chDecimal; // decimal point character
char szCurrency[5];  // the currency symbol (e.g. $ in United States)
int CurrencyFormat;  // 0-3, see format table above
int CurrencyDigits;  // number of digits to display right of the    //
sDecimal character
int NegCurrencyFormat;       // 0-7, see format table above

GetProfileString ("intl", "sThousand", ",", sz1000Sep, 2);
ch1000Sep = sz1000Sep[0];
GetProfileString ("intl", "sDecimal", ".", szDecimal, 2);
chDecimal = szDecimal[0];

GetProfileString ("intl", sCurrency", "$", szCurrency5);
CurrencyFormat = GetProfileInt ("intl", "ICurrency", 0);
CurrencyDigits -= GetProfileInt ("intl", "ICurrDigits", 2);
NegCurrencyFormat = GetProfileInt ("intl", "NegCurr", 0);
```

Language Independence

All displayable text strings will be localized by the translator. The key objective is to store strings in a location away from the source code, which allows the translator to quickly identify data that must be localized, and avoids unnecessary code modification.

It is important to store strings in a fashion that maximizes the memory resource for all applications without sacrificing execution speed. For these reasons, it is important to store static strings that are known at development time in resources. Keep sentences together in the resources rather than loading individual words and building sentences within the application. Because the word ordering changes from language to language, the translator should be working with complete sentences.

MS-Windows provides a predefined resource, STRINGTABLE, which allows an application to use integers for storing and accessing strings in small, discardable segments.

Call the LoadString routine to instruct the resource manager to fill an application-supplied buffer with the specified string. The resource manager loads the section of the string table containing the requested string if the segment is not already in memory. Note that strings are brought in 16 at a time, based on their integer values. For example, strings with values 0–15, 16–31, 32–47 are loaded together. Strings that are used together at execution time should be numbered within the same group of 16 so that only one portion of the string table will be loaded while executing that section of code.

Examples where this is applicable include labels displayed on a particular window or titles of windows created simultaneously. By default, the STRINGTABLE is a discardable resource.

Each string in the string table is limited to 255 characters. If longer strings are needed, create application-defined resources.

The resource may specify load and memory options. The available load options include PRELOAD and LOADONCALL, which determine when the resource will be initially loaded into memory.

- PRELOAD implies that the resource will be brought into memory when the application is loaded.

- LOADONCALL dictates that the resource will not be brought into memory until the first access occurs.

The available memory options include FIXED, MOVEABLE, and DISCARDABLE, which instruct the memory manager how to treat the segment containing the resource.

- FIXED means that the segment will not be moved in memory.
- MOVEABLE implies that the segment can be moved while unlocked and always remains in memory.
- DISCARDABLE prescribes that the segment may be discarded while unlocked.

The segment will be automatically reloaded the next time it is accessed. In most instances, a resource is LOADONCALL DISCARDABLE.

The application must be able to detect the end of the resource data. The routine GlobalSize returns the size of the segment containing the data. However, due to the granularity of the segment sizes imposed by the memory manager, the reported size may be greater than the actual amount of resource data contained in the segment.

The following routines are used to access application-defined resources:

```
HANDLE hResInfo;        // set by FindResource, used only by LoadResource
HANDLE hResource;       // global handle for segment containing the resource data
LPSTR   lpResource;     // long pointer to the resource data

hResInfo = FindResource (hinst, szResourceName, szResourceType);
hResource = LoadResource (hinst, hresInfo);
lpResource = LockResource (hResource);
_ (use the resource data)
UnlockResource (hResource);
FreeResource (hResource);
```

Character Support

Language-specific character values are beyond the normal alphabetic ranges “a”..“z” and “A”..“Z”. The SDK routines take the current language into account and ensure that the application can properly determine and manipulate characters. These routines support alphabetic values, case conversion, and sorting. The language-specific characters may contain values greater than 7FH, so characters must be stored in an **unsigned type** (BYTE rather than CHAR). Rather than comparing alphabetic or alphanumeric values against a hard-coded range, use the **IsCharAlpha** and **IsCharAlphaNumeric** routines. Furthermore, use the **IsCharLower** and **IsCharUpper** routines to establish the case of a character. Use the **AnsiUpper, AnsiUpperBuff, AnsiLower,** and **AnsiLowerBuff** routines for case conversions. When sorting strings, use the **lstrcmp** and **lstrcmpi** routines. These routines understand how to sort the accented characters. This is significant; for example, Scandinavian countries sort accented characters to the end, while Germany sorts them equal to their nonaccented equivalents.

Some languages, such as Japanese, include more than 255 characters. These languages employ a double-byte character set (DBCS). In this system, some of the character values are designated as lead bytes while the following byte, or trail byte, defines the character. For example, in Kata-Kanji, lead bytes occupy the 81-9F and F0-FC ranges. DBCS strings contain a mixture of one- and two-byte-long characters. A key restriction is that the trail-byte value will never be 0. The standard string routines lstrcat and lstrcpy function as expected. The number of bytes returned by the lstrlen routine does not necessarily equal the sum of the characters. This caveat also holds true when calling GetWindowTextLength. DBCS strings are sorted first by the lead byte and then by trail byte. Both lstrcmp and lstrcmpi function correctly.

Use the **AnsiNext** and **AnsiPrev** routines to reposition the pointer through a string a full—possibly double-byte—character at a time rather than incrementing or decrementing the pointer.

When searching through a string for specific characters, such as the "/" in pathnames, check that the identified byte is not the trail byte of a double-byte character.

The Times Roman, Helvetica, and Courier fonts do not contain DBCS glyphs. When calling LoadFont or LoadFontIndirect, read the facename from a resource rather than hard-coding it in the application.

DOS uses the OEM character set. Windows uses the ANSI character set. Identical language-specific characters may employ different values in the two character sets. The filenames and the content of files created by DOS must be converted for proper display in Windows. Files created in Windows for use in DOS must also be converted. The **OEMToAnsi, OEMToAnsiBuff, AnsiToOEM, AnsiToOEMBuff** routines perform the conversion between the two character sets.

When displaying strings, use the **GetTextExtent** routine to establish the space required by the localized strings rather than hard-coding locations for each item on the display. Be wary of calculating the width of the string using **GetTextMetrics** and multiplying the average—or even maximum—character width by the length of the string. This approach is inexact for variable-pitch fonts. Even with fixed-pitch fonts, Istrlen for double-byte strings reports the number of bytes in the string. This value does not correspond to the number of characters to display.

When displaying a string that spans several lines, use **DrawText** to allow GDI to perform word wrapping, rather than hard-coding the line breaks using multiple **TextOut** calls. If an application performs its own word wrapping, isolate the code that handles this function. This is important because some languages define appropriate line breaks differently. For example, in Japanese, lines can break without waiting for a space.

Some languages read right-to-left and columnar such as Arabic and Chinese. Textual output placement for right-to-left support is simplified by using the text alignment field of the DC. Set this field by using the **SetTextAlign** routine. The text alignment value is comprised of three parts:

- Vertical placement (choose one: TA_TOP, TA_BASELINE, TA_BOTTOM)
- Horizontal placement (choose one: TA_LEFT, TA_CENTER, TA_RIGHT)
- Reference point (choose one: TA_NOUPDATECP, TA_UPDATECP)

Default text alignment is TA_TOP | TA_LEFT | TA_UPDATECP, whose values are all 0.

When painting a string using a routine such as **TextOut,** the string is placed so the reference point relative to the string is in the vertical and horizontal position as specified in the text alignment field of the DC. For example, if the text alignment is TA_CENTER | TA_TOP, the text string will be centered under the reference point. The reference point is the *x,y* position sent as parameters to TextOut if the text alignment contains TA_NOUPDATECP. The reference point is the current position if the text alignment contains TA_UPDATECP. The current position is set by calling MoveTo or LineTo. The current position also moves after the string is drawn when text alignment contains TA_UPDATECP. The new current position is to the right of the string if text alignment contains TA_LEFT, to the left of the string if text alignment contains TA_RIGHT, and remains unchanged if text alignment contains TA_CENTER.

There are no built-in routines for displaying columnar text. This type of textual display would be performed by displaying one character at a time and moving the reference point by the height of the character drawn. This can be accomplished by using the tmHeight field of the structure filled by GetTextMetrics.

To prepare for localizing of right-to-left and columnar languages, perform all textual output in a general-purpose routine. This routine should call TextOut, ExtTextOut, TabbedTextOut, or DrawText depending on the parameters. The code could be easily rewritten when localizing to right-to-left and columnar languages.

If the translator only translates strings in the dialog template—rather than also using the dialog editor to reposition the controls—the application should resize the dialog window, and size and place the controls appropriate to the localized strings. The WM_INITDIALOG message is delivered to the dialog box procedure after creating the dialog window and all controls, and prior to painting anything on the display. All the controls should be initialized, sized, and placed according to the strings that will be displayed.

For example, to determine the size of a localized control:

```
hdc = GetDC (hwnd);
hControl = GetDlgItem (hdlg, controlID);
hfont = SendMessage (hControl, WM_GETFONT, 0, 0L);
```

```
SelectObject (hdc, hfont);
GetWindowText (hControl, sz, maxchars);
lExtent = GetTextExtent (hdc, sz, lstrlen(sz);
ReleaseDC (hwnd, hdc);
cxControl = LOWORD(lExtent);      // width of the string (in pixels)
cyControl = HIWORD(lExtent);      // height of the string (in pixels)
```

After determining the required sizes of the controls, use MoveWindow to resize and place them in the dialog box.

A scrolling dialog is convenient for dialog boxes with controls that don't fit entirely within a single window. Placing a thickframe on the dialog is beneficial since the user may determine how much screen real estate to devote to the dialog—as one does with all the other windows on the display. Moreover, by scrolling, the user can maintain access to all the controls. Use ScrollWindow with IpRect set to NULL to scroll the dialog window so controls will be automatically scrolled. When the user sets focus to a control—by pressing Tab, Shift-Tab, or the ALT-letter mnemonic—scroll the dialog so the control with focus becomes visible. Finally, some controls, such as the OK and Cancel buttons, should always remain visible. To implement this, use the IpClipRect ScrollWindow parameter to define which pixels on the dialog box window should scroll. The IpClipRect rectangle excludes the OK and Cancel button areas of the dialog box. However, all controls are actually moved because IpRect is NULL. Use MoveWindow to return these controls back to their original position after calling ScrollWindow.

For example:

```
ScrollWindow (hdlg, xAmount, yAmount, NULL, &rcClip);
MoveWindow (GetDlgItem(hdlg,IDOK), xOk, yOk, cxOk, cyOk, FALSE);
MoveWindow (GetDlgItem(hdlg,IDCANCEL), xCancel, yCancel, cxCancel, cyCancel,
  FALSE);
```

When a user-sizeable dialog box is destroyed, the application should record the current size and placement of the dialog to reestablish the initial position and the size of the dialog the next time it is displayed.

```
case WM.COMAND:
-
case DOK:
-
GetWindowRect (hdlg, &rc);
```

```
x = rcleft;
y = rctop;
cx = rcright-rcleft;
cy = rc.bottom-rc.top;
...store the x,y,cx,cy for use next time the dialog is displayed...
...(in WM_INITDIALOG next time, call MoveWindow (hdlg, x,y, cx, cy, TRUE); ...
EndDialog (...);
return (TRUE);
```

Keyboard Independence

Scan codes are keyboard-dependent values that report which keys were pressed or released. Virtual key codes are the corresponding keyboard-independent values for the keys. Applications should use only the virtual key codes, thereby maintaining keyboard independence.

- Keyboard messages (WM_KEYDOWN, WM_KEYUP, WM_CHAR, WM_DEADCHAR, WM_SYSKEYDOWN, WM_SYSKEYUP, WM_SYSCHAR, and WM_SYSDEADCHAR) report both the scan and the virtual key codes.
- WM_MENUCHAR, WM_CHARTOITEM, and WM_VKEYTOITEM messages specify the key involved using the virtual key codes. Accelerators should always use virtual keys.

GetKeyboardType returns information about the currently attached keyboard, including the number of function keys. When the number of function keys available to the user is limited, the application may elect to provide accelerators or macros to recover the lost functionality.

The WM_DEADCHAR or WM_SYSDEADCHAR message is delivered when the user enters a diacritical mark followed by the character that should receive the mark. When the character key is pressed, a WM_CHAR or WM_SYSCHAR message containing the complete character is delivered. The application is not required to remember the deadchar messages. Some language keyboards have keys for the accented characters. The user presses only one key

rather than the accent key followed by the character key on these keyboards. In this case, a DEADCHAR message is not generated.

Printing

Paper sizes differ in various countries. Use the GETPHYSPAGE-SIZE Escape code to determine the physical size of the paper rather than hard-coding the page boundaries in the application.

The following code retrieves the physical paper size of the printer. The width and height are reported in physical units, just as GetClientRect reports the client area size in physical units.

```
HDC hdc ;           // DC for the printer
POINT ptPageSize;
int cxPage, cyPage; // width and height of the paper (in physical units)
Escape (hdc, GETPHYSPAGESIZE, NULL, NULL, &ptPageSize);
cxPage = ptPageSize.x;
cyPage = ptPageSize.y;
```

Help Files

The keywords, designated by K footnotes, along with titles, designated by $ footnotes in the help text files, will be localized as they are displayed to the user via WinHelp's Search mechanism. Applications invoking Winhelp using help keywords should store the keywords in resources as in the following source code example:

```
LoadString (hInst, ID_KEYWORD, szKeyword, maxchars);
WinHelp (hwnd, szHelpFile, HELP_KEY, szKeyword);
```

The translator will localize the resources to match the translation performed on the keywords in the help files.

.ini File

Applications store data used from one invocation to the next in either the win.ini file or a private .ini file using the WriteProfileString or WritePrivateProfileString routines. This data is read using the GetProfileString, GetPrivateProfileString, GetProfileInt and GetPrivateProfileInt routines. The .ini files are user editable, so the section and key names should be localized. Store these names in a resource like other static strings—either in the string table or an application-defined resource.

For example:

```
char szApp[10], szSizeKey[10];
char szSize[30];            // size = ... string from win.ini
LoadString (hInst, APPNAME, szApp, 10);
LoadString (hInst, SIZE, szSizeKey, 10);
GetProfileString (szApp, szSizeKey, szDefault, szSize, 30);
```

Application Filenames

All the application filenames, .exe, .hlp, .ini, and .dll, should carry the same names for the localized version of the application.

Changing the application name may affect the application name chosen for DDE communications and the application's section name in the win.ini file. If the .exe filename changes, the application must be relinked. The NAME in the .def file must be blank or match the new .exe filename exactly.

If the .hlp filename changes, the help filename should be stored in a resource that will be read when the application calls Winhelp.

If the .ini filename changes, the filename should be stored in a resource that will be read when the application calls WritePrivateProfileString, GetPrivateProfileString, or GetPrivateProfileInt.

If .dll filenames change, those libraries must be relinked. One must be certain that the LIBRARY name in the .def file is blank or matches the new .dll filename exactly. The .dll filenames should be stored in a resource to be read when the application calls LoadLibrary.

APPENDIX D

International Functional Requirements Document (IFRD)

Introduction

International sales account for more than half of Borland's revenue.

The International Functional Requirements Document (IFRD) is a series of checklists to help you verify that a given product meets the needs of users worldwide.

European Product Requirements

The IFRD focuses on European product requirements. Most checks can be made by running a product under the local language and country settings provided by the operating system. Other checks can be made by examining compiled files and external functionality, or examining the product's resource files with a resource editing tool.

The IFRD allows anyone involved in product development or acquisition to determine if a product is suitable for sale outside the US.

Products that fail IFRD tests will be problematic to sell in non-US markets and expensive for Borland to localize. If your product fails these checks, it should be redesigned as needed before Alpha, or before contract negotiations are complete on a license or acquisition.

Asian and Other Wide-Character Requirements

The IFRD does not cover Asian, Arabic, or other pictogram or cursive language requirements. These are not easily managed by the operating system alone, and require architectural review at the source file level, which is out of the scope of the IFRD.

These requirements will be defined in an upcoming *International Programming Reference,* a technical guide for implementing language- and country-independent software architecture. The reference will provide code examples of:

- "good" and "bad" programming styles for international
- retrofitting sources to support wide-character
- using the International API to design truly international software
- portability issues for NEC and alternate hardware

IFRD Checklists

The attached IFRD checklist is for Software, and covers:

- Resource Files
- Numeric and Monetary Formats
- Date, Time, & Calendar Formats
- Character sets
- Collation (Sorting)
- UI, Graphics & Bitmaps
- Integration & Configuration

Additional checklists will be created for:

- Help Systems
- CBT (Tutorials)
- Print Documentation
- Marcom/Inbox Materials

Resource Files

Definition

Resource files include the text and coordinate locations of *anything* that requires localization, such as menus items, status messages, error messages, dialog box components, speedbar panels, property settings, icons, and pickletters. Language and country settings must also be resourced, so it can be dynamically set and extendable.

Requirements

- ❑ **Resource File Format:** Resources should be in standard file formats so they can be edited with common tools available worldwide.
- ✦ **Windows resources** should be stored in a separate DLL and be able to be edited as text RC files.
- ✦ **DOS resources** should be linked to unique tokens and in a format that allows extraction to the translation shell for editing and revision management.
- ❑ **EXE-Independent and Dynamically Loaded:** Resource files should be loaded at runtime. The EXE should not depend on any particular resource file contents.
- ❑ **Unique String IDs:** All resource elements should have unique IDs that remain static for every version of the product. Adding a resource should never cause resequencing the resource file or changing the ID of another resource.
- ❑ **Pickletter Resourcing:** All pickletters must be resourced, and extended characters must be operable as pickletters.
- ❑ **No Hardcoded Strings:** In some cases, a product that the developer considers "resourced" still contains hardcoded strings. Yes/No, OK/Cancel, and other common confirm/abandon strings must not be hardcoded.
- ❑ **No Message Concatenation:** When a string is translated, the translation needs to follow the grammatical structure of the local language, which may have a different subject/object order than English.

Creating a string by adding two or more strings, or adding strings and variables, typically creates problems for translators. When you review the resource files, check for concatenated messages. The resources also must not depend on adding "s" to construct a plural, since not all languages add 's' for plurals.

- ❑ **Work with EXPIMP and TSHELL** (Windows products only):
- ✦ **EXPIMP,** Borland's resource extraction tool, moves resources from their native format to a database for editing and manipulation. Other parses can be developed following EXPIMP model where needed.
- ✦ **TSHELL,** the Borland translation tool front end, allows the correct editing tool to be associated with each type of resource. Editing tools must support extended characters, international sort orders, spelling checks, and so on.
- ❑ **Resource File Names:** All files that contain localizable resources should be named in accordance with the POSIX or WinNT standard, which assigns alphanumeric locale codes for language and country.

Numeric & Monetary Formats

Definition

Numeric formats differ from country to country. Many countries use a comma as the decimal separator and a period as the thousands separator—as in 1.234,56—exactly the opposite as in the US.

Monetary formats also differ, and may require more than one character for the currency symbol, or place the symbol after the numerals, as in 1.234,56 DM.

Concepts for numbers can differ too. For example, in the US, one billion equals 1,000 Million; in the UK, the word billion means 100,000 Million.

Requirements

- ❑ **Local Defaults:** The product should reflect the local numeric and currency settings at startup.
- ✦ **Windows format defaults** should be determined by the Control Panel settings, which are written to the WIN.INI file. All Windows applications should query WIN.INI for international settings at product launch. WIN.INI settings should be able to be overridden by a product-specific INI file.
- ✦ **DOS format defaults** are determined by the NLSfunc (National Language Support function) and CP (code page) settings. These should be able to be overridden by a product-specific configuration or setup file that is independent of the main EXE. (For more on loading NLS and changing code pages, refer to your DOS manual.)
- ❑ **Core EXE Supports All Formats:** Verify that all international formats can be set in the US product. Common examples include:

US/UK	1,234,456.89
German	1 234 567,89
Danish	1.234.567,89

- ❑ **Computations Are Format-Independent:** Make sure numeric parsing and calculations are correct, regardless of the display format.
- ✦ **Numeric Constants:** Products that include a programming language *must* use the original parameter delimiters, in most instances a comma, when evaluating numeric constants. If the parameter delimiter were configurable, function calls would not work the same in every country. Local numeric formats are *not* supported with numeric constants.
- ✦ **Numeric-String Constants:** These should take local formats into account. For example:

  string_to_float (“3.5”) = three and a half

string_to_float ("3,5") = three and a half

- ✦ **Variables:** These should be stored in the program's own internal bit pattern.

- ❑ **Format Properties:** The program can allow properties to be set at the application, file, page, field, cell, or other definable property level.

Numeric Format Elements

- ❑ **Thousands and Decimal Separator:** Each separator must be able to be defined as a space or any character.

  0 56

  0,56

- ❑ **Numeric vs List Delimiters:** Most products also support a list delimiter, for import/export, for example. Determine if there are interdependencies between thousands, decimal, and/or list delimiters; changing one may require changing the other. Verify all options, using a matrix like this:

Decimal	Thousands	List
,	.	.
,	.	,
,	.	;

  etc.

- ❑ **Number of Digits between Thousand Separators:** Some countries use different numbers of digits between separators.

1 23 45 67.89	(2 digits per place)
1.234,567	(3 decimal places)

- ❑ **Leading Zeros:** The number of zeros should be user-defined.

  0,56

  00,56

- **Percentage Symbol:** Symbol and placement should be user-defined and program independent. Common notations include:

    90%

    %90

    .90

- **Scientific Notation:** Some programs use the letter E to signify exponential notation. The letter or symbol chosen must be user-definable and program independent.
- **Fractions:** Common notations are fractional digits (as in ½), or decimal notation (as in .5).
- **Rounding and Math Functions:** Mathematical rules for rounding, amortization, and so on, may need to be changed to meet the needs of local users. The product should include a method for changing the algorithm or adding new functions without recompiling the EXE.

Currency Format Elements

- **Currency Symbol:** The currency symbol should be a user-defined string of one or more characters.

    £

    DM

    ¥

- **Symbol Before/After:** The currency symbol may appear before, after, or between digits (at the decimal or thousands place, for example).

    USD 1,234.56

    1.234,56 DM

    1F56

- **Spacing between Symbol and Digits:** Spaces can occur or be omitted between the currency symbol and digits.

    $ 1,234.56

    1.234,56DM

- **Accounting Format for Negation:** Negative numbers may be shown with a minus sign before or after, or in parentheses.

  -1.234,56

  1.234,56-

  (1.234,56)

- **Written Currency Units:** Many countries have more than one currency unit (for instance dollars and cents, pounds and pence, etc.) Software that includes written formats should support more than one written unit.
- **Multiple Currencies per File:** International corporations typically need to manage data in multiple currency formats at variable exchange rates. New products should be designed so the user can set the locale on the field, record, or cell level. The data should be able to be associated with a fixed or variable exchange rate.
- **Currency Display Space:** Some currency units are very small and require more space than English units to display. Software can support this by resourcing the default column size, or by allowing the default currency format to include scientific notation or the local currency abbreviation.

Date, Time, & Calendar Formats

Definition

In the U.S., the most common date format is month/day/year. International dates are often day-month-year, and separated by a dash (-) or a period, as in 25.12.95.

For written dates, as in check writing or calendars, the order of the MDY elements and acceptability of abbreviation and capitalization differs from country to country. In addition, some countries consider Sunday the start day of the week, others base the week on a Monday start date.

Time formats can be based on 12- or 24-hour time, and may require a text string to follow the digits, as in 18:00 Uhr.

Although most countries use the same calendar system as the U.S. for business applications, other calendar systems may need to be supported.

Requirements

- ❑ **Local Defaults:** The product should reflect the local date, time, and calendar settings at startup.
- ✦ **Windows format defaults** are determined by the Control Panel settings, as described above for Numeric formats.
- ✦ **DOS format defaults** are determined by the NLSfunc (National Language Support function) and CP (code page) settings, as described for Numeric formats.
- ❑ **Core EXE Supports All Formats:** Verify that all international formats can be set in the U.S. product. Here are a few examples:

US	MM/DD/YY
Sweden	DD.MM.YYYY
ANSI	YYYYMMDD

- ❑ **Computations Are Format-Independent:** Changing the date, time, or calendar format must not break date/time computations or functions. Verifying this typically requires *extensive and careful testing.*
- ❑ **Format Properties:** Date, time, and calendar formats should be able to be set at the application, file, page, field, cell, or other definable property level.

Dates

- ❑ **Internal Date Storage:** Dates should be stored internally as YYYMMDD based on the Julian calendar. (See "Calendars" below.)
- ❑ **Month-Day-Year Order:** Date elements should be able to be displayed and printed in all available orders. Here are a few examples:

DMY 13 mai, 1995
MDY August 12, 1994
YMD 1993.03.03
YMD 91.XII.31

- ❑ **ISO Format:** Include a configurable option for the International Standards Organization (ISO) format.
- ❑ **Date Separator:** The digits should be able to be separated by a space, punctuation, or any printable character.

  2/3/93
  12-03-93

- ❑ **Leading Zeroes on Day and Month:** Provide options to display or omit the leading zero on day or month numbers less than 10.

  02.12.93
  Sunday, 02 September 93

- ❑ **Century Digits:** Display or omit.

  02-02-1994
  Sun, 02 Sep 93

- ❑ **Expiration Dates on Trial Software or Site Installations:** Specific date formats must not be used to determine product expiration dates.

Times

- ❑ **12/24 and AM/PM:** 12- or 24-hour time formats should be supported. It must be possible to translate, position, and show or suppress the AM/PM indicator.

  6:00 PM
  1800

- ❑ **Time Separator:** The hour, minute, second, and hundredth separators must be user-definable.

  18:00:00

8.30.00.000

8'30"

- ❑ **Time Strings:** An optional or required text string may accompany the time.

  12 o'clock

  18:00 Uhr

  14h15m

- ❑ **Leading Zero:** Display or omit.

  08:00

  0830

  8:00

Calendars

- ❑ **Internal = Julian Day Count, External = Gregorian Calendar:** All date functions should be based internally on the Julian Day Count. Calendars should display and compute all elements of the Gregorian calendar—days, weeks, months, and years.

  Products should support functions for:

day-of-year	(1-366)
week-of-year	(1-52)
day-of-week	(1-7)
month-of-year	(1-12)

- ❑ **Start Day of Week:** Defining the week start as Sunday or Monday should have no effect on date computations.
- ❑ **Written Dates:** Written dates may consist of textual, as well as numeric, data (July 4th, Year of the Rat, etc.).
- ❑ **Capitalizing Day and Month Names:** Not all countries capitalize day and month names. Make sure the software does not perform a TOUPPER on the initial character of the day or month name.
- ❑ **Abbreviating Day and Month Names:** Not all countries permit day and month abbreviations, and where abbrevi-

ation is allowed, it can't always be done in 3 characters or by selecting the first 3 characters of the full month. Make sure the software doesn't require abbreviations to exist, or place any limits on the abbreviation string length.

- ❑ **Alternate and Multiple Calendars:** Some countries support more than one calendar. For example, Japan uses a calendar system very similar to the Gregorian calendar, but the year count is restarted whenever a new Emperor ascends the throne. Users may wish to refer to both Gregorian and local dates in an application.

Other Format Checks

- ❑ **Measurement:** Systems and symbols for all measurements should be configurable:

rulers	(inches/centimeters)
distance	(miles/kilometers)
weight	(pounds/kilograms)
volume	(gallons/liters)
speed	(mph/kph)

- ❑ **Paper and Label Sizes:** The software should allow default paper and label sizes to be redefinable. Most of Europe uses A4 paper, which is longer and narrower than the letter-sized paper used in the U.S. Therefore, it's important that fixed-width printouts (samples and readme files, for example) be formatted to 65 characters or less to allow international users to print these effectively.
- ❑ **Address Formats:** U.S. addresses include ZIP codes and other elements not found in international addresses. If the product includes a default address format, for mail merge for example, it should have a generic default.

Name1	*Order of last/first*
Name2	*name can differ.*
Address1	*"Street," "city,"*

	"state" are not
Address2	*international.*
Address3	
Country	
Postcode	*Replaces ZIPCODE.*
Phone1	*Allow 15+ places for*
Phone2	*country, city, or local*
Phone3	*phone codes*

- ❑ **Printer Drivers:** These may need to be changed to support local standards in page and label dimensions, lines per page, characters per line, or accepted escape sequences.
- ❑ **Telecommunications Standards:** Different telecomm standards may need to be supported:
- ✦ Minitel and Prestel are used throughout Europe and require 8-bit mapping to 7-bit.
- ✦ Telecomm drivers must be adaptable. For example, in some countries, 75 baud support may still be needed.
- ✦ Synchronous modems (X.25) are very common in Europe.
- ✦ ISO Standard 007 needs to be supported for telecomm with older mainframes, many of which do not support 8-bit characters.

Character Sets & Code Pages

Character Sets

- ✦ **7-bit ASCII:** Unlike most other alphabets, the English alphabet requires only 26 characters, and these are available in uppercase and lowercase form at ASCII code points 0-127.
- ✦ **8-bit, Extended ASCII:** European alphabets require the characters available at code points 128-255. These are referred to as "extended characters" in the IFRD. Each US and European character glyph can be supported with an 8-bit char.

- **16-bit, ISO 10646 and Unicode:** Unicode and ISO 10646 are 16-bit character sets designed to manage all alphabets currently used on computers. Developing products that support Unicode allows us to build and test one code-base from which multiple language versions of our products are derived. 16-bit and other multi-byte character support requires implementation of wide-character processing, as described in the *International Programming Reference.*

Windows and DOS Character Sets

- **Windows/ANSI Character Set:** Windows uses the ANSI character set, which is fairly standard across Latin-based languages. ANSI code pages 1004 (for Win 3.0) and 1252 (for Win 3.1) are typically used by our products and support most European countries. Alternate ANSI pages are needed for some Eastern European alphabets.
- **DOS/OEM Code Pages:** DOS products use 256-glyph character sets called code pages. Many DOS products use code page 437, which supports few of the extended characters needed in European alphabets. Code page 850, used frequently in Europe, supports most, but not all extended characters, so specific code pages are needed in many countries. Products that manage DOS/OEM characters must be designed to support alternate code pages.

Proprietary Character Sets

Some companies use proprietary characters sets as in-house or open standards. LICS and LIMBICS are examples.

Most proprietary character sets were created to solve cross-platform character set issues. WordPerfect, for example, uses the same character set in their DOS, UNIX, and Windows products.

Interoperable and import/export code needs to access proprietary mapping tables if they exist.

Requirements

- **Character Set Independence:** The software must not expect any specific glyph or symbol to exist at any given code point.
- **Extended Character Support:** You should be able to enter extended characters for the given locale with Alt-Numkey or by connecting a local keyboard.
- **Valid Ranges:** In DOS products, review the resource files to ensure that it's possible to define valid alphabetic, numeric, and punctuation ranges of code points.
- **Named Objects:** You must be able to save and load all objects supported in the software with names that include extended characters. This includes file, field, form, query, or link names, for example.

  Also test that extended characters can be distinguished from one another. For example, save an object as CëÃ, and ensure that it can be distinguished from CèÀ or C followed by any two extended characters.
- **Mapping and Conversions:** Not all characters are mappable between different character sets.

  For example, extended characters input under CP850 or ANSI will display as graphic characters when run under CP437. Indexes based on extended characters may not operate under CP437, since the index character may not exist.

  In some cases, the software can manage this problem with a mapping table, which allows an alternate character to be used if the extended character can't be found. In other cases, mapping can't be performed, and the user should be able to view, but typically not edit, the data. Any operation that could result in data loss needs to provide a user-confirmation prompt.
- **Locale IDs for Data Files:** Data created in one character set may not be able to be effectively used by another language if the character sets are not equivalent.

For example, Dutch dBASE IV 1.1 DOS could not correctly index a German database file, because the German alphabet contains characters not included in Dutch. In a case such as this, the German characters should have been able to be mapped to characters or character pairs available in the Dutch character set. For example, the German "ß" should have mapped to "ss," and "ä" to "æ."

The application should track the character set of the data file by assigning a locale flag, and should warn the user of inconsistencies between the default and data file locales. It's up to the application to eliminate the possibility of file corruption, either by locale mapping, or by issuing the appropriate warning messages.

❑ **Commands, Functions, and Reserved Words:** Programming languages should not be translated. Their commands should be composed of letters in the English alphabet, which can be found in all character sets.

❑ **Language Properties:** In new products, the user should be able to select an object (a block of text, a page, field, cell, or other definable property), and assign a Language Property.

For example, in a German product, the user may want to mark a section of text as English, and automatically associate English language tools such as spell check dictionary, hyphenation, thesaurus, punctuation rules, and so on.

❑ **Word Delimiters and Punctuation:** The application must not require that specific characters be used as word delimiters, or expect any particular characters to be punctuation marks.

For example, French and Italian frequently use single quotation marks—often considered word delimiters in English— as components of words:

L'isle

L'escargot

n'est pas

Word parsing routines should also account for contractions:

can't

Don't assume that punctuation characters are available at specific code points, or that U.S. punctuation will fill international needs. For example, in Europe, common punctuation marks include:

« » (Alt-174 and Alt-175 in CP437 and 850) for open and close quotation marks

The inverted question-mark (Alt-168 in CP437) precedes a question in Spanish, and the inverted exclamation mark (Alt-173) precedes an exclamation.

- ❑ **Uppercase/Lowercase:** Verify that the upper/lower pairings change with changes in the code page or language.

  Verify that the product uses a resourced mapping table to determine uppercase/lowercase pairs. The program must not simply add or subtract 32 to determine case.

- ❑ **Line Drawing Characters:** Graphic characters in CP437 often map to alphabetic characters under an alternate code page. Verify that line drawing characters are not mapped to text characters when the code page or language changes.

- ❑ **CR, LF, or EOL Characters:** Verify that the CR, LF, or EOL characters don't conflict with characters in an alternate alphabet.

  For example, dBASE IV 1.0 used ASCII 141 (decimal) to delimit soft carriage returns in memo fields. In some code pages, ASCII 141 is an ì (i acute). Therefore, whenever international users entered ì in a memo field, dBASE IV 1.0 inserted a soft carriage return.

- ❑ **Screen Drivers and Defaults:** No product should depend on screen size, lines per screen, or any particular screen resolution. Lines per screen should be user-definable.

- ❑ **Keyboard Input:** If possible, test the software with an alternate keyboard to ensure that keyboard scan codes are not tied to specific character codes.

- **Multikey input:** Some keyboards use 2- or 3-key combinations to access specific characters. For example, on French keyboards, the numeric characters are accessed by pressing SHIFT and CAPS LOCK, then the desired key.
- **Unavailable keys:** Some characters that are available on U.S. keyboards are not available on other keyboards. For example, the tilde character ~ (126) is not present on the Danish keyboard.
- **CTRL and ALT:** All CONTROL-key and ALT-key combinations should be redefinable.

Collation (Sort) Sequences

Definition

A collation sequence is the ranking of characters in a sort. This section introduces some of the factors and rules involved in defining a collation sequence.

Collation sequences, like all customs, are somewhat subjective. They differ from product to product, and there is no absolute standard. This creates compatibility and interoperability issues that need to be addressed by all our products.

Borland has addressed most of these issues with drivers and technologies that we should use in-house, and make available to our OEM/co-developers.

ASCII and Dictionary Sorts

There are two basic types of collation:

- **ASCII sort** is based on the sequence of code points, and places all uppercase characters first, then lowercase characters, then extended characters, as shown in the following table. ASCII sorts are inappropriate for international products, because they support only the standard ASCII characters, 0-127, and omit the extended characters needed in languages other than English.

- **Dictionary sort** is based on the customs of the local language, and represents what you'd see in a local dictionary or phone book. Uppercase/lowercase sequence and grouping is based on the customs of the locale, not on ASCII code points.

ASCII	**Dictionary**
ABC	ABC
Destefano	ÅBC
Young	de Souza
XYZ	Destefano
de Souza	Young
ÅBC	XYZ

Collation Tables

A collation table is an external resource file that defines the sort elements for the locale. The collation table lists the valid characters for that language, and supplies information to determine the order in which characters appear in a sort.

Borland Language Drivers

The Borland Language Drivers (BLD) are a collection of functions that manage language and locale operations in Borland products. The language drivers work with collation tables used by Borland products and other ANSI and OEM standards.

BDE and the Borland Locales

BDE, Borland's Database Engine API, supports the language drivers. Borland's Windows products support BDE. DOS products should emulate BDE functionality and support the language drivers.

BDE will evolve to support:

- **Borland Locales,** which encompass and improve upon language driver functionality.

✦ **Competitive product collation sequences,** for interoperability with Oracle, Sybase, Access, Informix and so on.

If ODAPI/BLD support can't be attained, the product will be difficult to localize. Minimally, it should be providing a resourced, editable table that defines the collation sequences as described in the Requirements section.

Requirements

- ❑ **Valid Characters:** The collation table should identify what characters to include in the sort, and which to ignore.

  Some languages don't include all alphabetic characters in their sort. For example, vowels are ignored in Arabic sorting.

  The software should provide a flag to use an external sort algorithm, so, for example, the sorting routine can be rewritten to include an alternate parsing routine.
- ❑ **Folding (2-to-1 and 1-to-2):** In some languages, character pairs, such as "ch," are viewed a single character. are two characters must be treated as one in the sort. For example, in Spanish, CH and ch are sorted after Ç (ASCII 128), and before D. In other cases, one character sorts as two, such as the German ß, which sorts as double-s.
- ❑ **Uppercase/Lowercase Pairings (Monocasing):** The collation table should determine the uppercase and lowercase for each valid character. In some languages, when an accented character is uppercased, it loses its accent; in other languages, the accent is maintained.

  Make sure the collation table permits these casing rules to be applied:

✦ Uppercase and lowercase letters are of the same value: aAbBCc = AaBbCc.

✦ Uppercase always precedes lowercase: AaBbCc.

✦ Lowercase always precedes uppercase: aAbBcC.

✦ Accented and unaccented characters are the same value: a, ã, à have equal weight.

- ✦ Unaccented character precedes accented: a, ã, à.
- ✦ The order of accented characters is set.
- ❑ **Group Equivalent Characters:** For example, if the characters A, a, Å, and ã were grouped, a search for *A* should find any occurrence of the other characters in that group.
- ❑ **Alternate Mapping:** If the display or output device doesn't support the needed characters, a mapping table can be used to determine the closest equivalent alternatives. For example, if the current printer can support only ASCII, and the file contains extended characters, the mapping table might permit the letter "a" to replace "á" at the user's discretion. Note that in many cases, mapping may be impossible, so the user must have the option to omit characters that can't be accurately mapped.

UI, Graphics, & Bitmaps

Definition

The UI is the graphical presentation of the product, and the user's first learning tool: If the layout of the UI is clear and readable, and the design and icons make sense, the user will have a positive experience and quickly learn the product; if the UI is crowded and icons meaningless, the product will be harder to learn and use.

Requirements

- ❑ **Text Expansion:** Translated strings require 30-100% more space to display than strings of similar meaning in English. The UI must be designed with text expansion in mind, so that the general UI layout is not disrupted by translation.
- ❑ **International Graphic Images:** Graphics should be free from culture-bound images. The following items differ from country to country, and make poor choices for UI/graphic subject matter:
- ✦ automobiles and street signs

- ✦ mailboxes
- ✦ addresses
- ✦ telephones
- ❑ **Text-Free Graphics:** The icons, bitmaps, etc., must not contain *any* text. All text should be in a separate, localizable file.
- ❑ **International and Subsidiary Review:** Any graphic element that displays in the software should be evaluated by International and the Subsidiaries for appropriateness to worldwide markets.

Samples and Examples

Definition

Example files are often difficult to localize because:

- ✦ coding standards might be poor
- ✦ the business scenario might be meaningless outside the U.S.
- ✦ the data might be culturally insensitive
- ✦ the application might rely on specific menu or option names that are not in translated versions
- ✦ the application might not operate correctly under local versions of DOS or Windows

Requirements

- ❑ **Global Business Examples:** It's best to base examples on simple business applications like inventory. Business and accounting methods differ from country to country, so the example must be very generic.
- ❑ **International Data:** Create data files that are multi-cultural; this will enable the localizing countries to use the same data and examples as the U.S. Avoid humor, sports, and political references; they don't translate well!

- ❑ **Work with all Data Formats:** Make sure sample applications function when the data formats or OS settings change.
- ❑ **Don't Hardcode:** Make sure the sample meets the IFRD criteria for international software. It must be resourced externally or in the header file, support alternate numeric, monetary, date, time, and other formats, use locale/language driver collation, and so on.

Help, Tutors, and Print Docs

Definition

Help systems, tutors, and print documentation—all instructional components of the product—become worldwide marketing tools, and can minimize the technical support for a product. To work in all countries, they should avoid reflecting American values and ideas.

Requirements

- ❑ **Vocabulary and Writing Style** Well written documentation will be useful and translatable worldwide—the same rules apply:
- ✦ Keep sentence structures simple, short, and to the point.
- ✦ Avoid using the passive voice in the instructions. Clarify which words are subjects, actions and objects.
- ✦ Avoid jargon. It may be insulting or incomprehensible—even to people in English-speaking countries.
- ✦ Avoid verbalized nouns if possible, such as "to dialog".
- ✦ Avoid words that have multiple and potentially unclear meanings.
- ✦ Use the list format instead of the paragraph format for listing items.
- ❑ **Maintaining investment:** Instructional materials should only be rewritten if a compelling business reason exists. For example, if the precious documentation set or help

system was poorly received, or resulted in technical support problems, those sections should be rewritten.

Typically, in multigenerational products, only technical and UI related changes should be made.

If the product will depend on any existing chapters or Help topics or entire RTFs, these need to be clearly defined, isolated, and saved. New features should be developed in new files where possible. This alone could reduce support costs and enhance sales.

- ✦ Each product team should investigate the cost tradeoffs, including translation costs, then determine file sizes and page count appropriate to the complexity and sales price of the product.
- ✦ Preferably, writers can determine the best single location (help, CBT, or print doc) for each type of instructional material, so costs are not duplicated.

- ❑ **Style Sheets and Glossaries:** Establish technical words and use them consistently in all instructional material and the product.

  If the product must use verbalized nouns, such as "access," include these, and include the definitions of any acronyms or abbreviations that will be used, even if these are defined at their first occurrence in the text.

- ❑ **Tools:** Any tool used to develop print, online, or tutorial information must be made available worldwide.

- ✦ Before purchasing a new tool, contact the international project manager for the product, and plan some simple testing to verify that the tool will be appropriate for translation teams.
- ✦ Borland-developed conversion tools need to work with extended chars.
- ✦ Make sure adequate copies of the product are purchased early enough to be received by subsidiaries and their translation teams.

- ❑ **Graphics:** Use wordless instructions and text-free conceptual art where possible.

- ❑ **Font and Page Design:** Use the smallest number of fonts possible, and the most commonly available, to ensure that the translation teams can easily emulate Borland standard documentation formats.
- ❑ **Technical Change Tracking:** After handoff to international writer need to track TECHNICAL changes for each component in a log file. The log should list the filename, the section or topic title, and a solid description of the technical change. Translators are typically technical people with product knowledge, and it's always helpful to include the reason for the change, or information on how globally this will affect the files.

Integration & Configuration

Definition

Sometimes, the way in which files are managed in development or integration can be problematic for international.

Requirements

- ❑ **Reuse Existing Translations:** Design product upgrades to salvage all existing translation work and maintain Borland's localization investment. If the product depends on any existing software, be sure to consider how previous localizations of that module can be used in the new design.
- ❑ **Isolate Localizable Files:** Set up the PAK or ZIP files so localized files are separated from nonlocalizable files. Do not zip the localized resources, for example, with the non-localizable EXE. Separating localizable files has these advantages:
- ✦ It simplifies manufacturing. Operations can create a single set of disks for most of the product, with interchangeable localization disks for UI, helps, online, spell

checkers, etc. Major competitors who are successful in localization use this technique.

- ✦ It simplifies the integration debugging process, and helps us verify that all files in the localized PAK file are being pulled from the correct directories.
- ✦ It allows QA to easily distinguish localizable files.
- ✦ It simplifies the translation kit, in that only the localizable files have to be delivered with each kit upgrade.

- ❑ **Allow for File Expansion:** Translated components may require 20% to 50% more disk space than the corresponding US files. Additional space should be left on the localization disk to maintain the same disk configuration across languages.

APPENDIX E

Sample Locale

```
##
## fr_ca.lc
##
## French Canadian Locale fr_CA
##
## LC version: 1.0
##

<locale_name> "fr_CA"
<locale_desc> "French_Canadian"

#########
LC_CTYPE
#########

lower   <LATIN_SMALL_LETTER_A>;\
        <LATIN_SMALL_LETTER_B>;\
        <LATIN_SMALL_LETTER_C>;\
        <LATIN_SMALL_LETTER_D>;\
        <LATIN_SMALL_LETTER_E>;\
        <LATIN_SMALL_LETTER_F>;\
        <LATIN_SMALL_LETTER_G>;\
        <LATIN_SMALL_LETTER_H>;\
        <LATIN_SMALL_LETTER_I>;\
        <LATIN_SMALL_LETTER_J>;\
        <LATIN_SMALL_LETTER_K>;\
        <LATIN_SMALL_LETTER_L>;\
        <LATIN_SMALL_LETTER_M>;\
        <LATIN_SMALL_LETTER_N>;\
        <LATIN_SMALL_LETTER_O>;\
        <LATIN_SMALL_LETTER_P>;\
        <LATIN_SMALL_LETTER_Q>;\
        <LATIN_SMALL_LETTER_R>;\
        <LATIN_SMALL_LETTER_S>;\
```

```
        <LATIN_SMALL_LETTER_T>;\
        <LATIN_SMALL_LETTER_U>;\
        <LATIN_SMALL_LETTER_V>;\
        <LATIN_SMALL_LETTER_W>;\
        <LATIN_SMALL_LETTER_X>;\
        <LATIN_SMALL_LETTER_Y>;\
        <LATIN_SMALL_LETTER_Z>;\
        <LATIN_SMALL_LETTER_U_WITH_DIAERESIS>;\
        <LATIN_SMALL_LETTER_E_WITH_ACUTE>;\
        <LATIN_SMALL_LETTER_A_WITH_CIRCUMFLEX>;\
        <LATIN_SMALL_LETTER_A_WITH_DIAERESIS>;\
        <LATIN_SMALL_LETTER_A_WITH_GRAVE>;\
        <LATIN_SMALL_LETTER_A_WITH_RING_ABOVE>;\
        <LATIN_SMALL_LETTER_C_WITH_CEDILLA>;\
        <LATIN_SMALL_LETTER_E_WITH_CIRCUMFLEX>;\
        <LATIN_SMALL_LETTER_E_WITH_DIAERESIS>;\
        <LATIN_SMALL_LETTER_E_WITH_GRAVE>;\
        <LATIN_SMALL_LETTER_I_WITH_DIAERESIS>;\
        <LATIN_SMALL_LETTER_I_WITH_CIRCUMFLEX>;\
        <LATIN_SMALL_LETTER_I_WITH_GRAVE>;\
        <LATIN_SMALL_LIGATURE_AE>;\
        <LATIN_SMALL_LETTER_O_WITH_CIRCUMFLEX>;\
        <LATIN_SMALL_LETTER_O_WITH_DIAERESIS>;\
        <LATIN_SMALL_LETTER_O_WITH_GRAVE>;\
        <LATIN_SMALL_LETTER_U_WITH_CIRCUMFLEX>;\
        <LATIN_SMALL_LETTER_U_WITH_GRAVE>;\
        <LATIN_SMALL_LETTER_Y_WITH_DIAERESIS>;\
        <LATIN_SMALL_LETTER_O_WITH_STROKE>;\
        <LATIN_SMALL_LETTER_A_WITH_ACUTE>;\
        <LATIN_SMALL_LETTER_I_WITH_ACUTE>;\
        <LATIN_SMALL_LETTER_O_WITH_ACUTE>;\
        <LATIN_SMALL_LETTER_U_WITH_ACUTE>;\
        <LATIN_SMALL_LETTER_N_WITH_TILDE>;\
        <LATIN_SMALL_LETTER_A_WITH_TILDE>;\
        <LATIN_SMALL_LETTER_ETH_>;\
        <LATIN_SMALL_LETTER_SHARP_S_>;\
        <LATIN_SMALL_LETTER_O_WITH_TILDE>;\
        <LATIN_SMALL_LETTER_THORN_>;\
        <LATIN_SMALL_LETTER_Y_WITH_ACUTE>

upper   <LATIN_CAPITAL_LETTER_A>;\
        <LATIN_CAPITAL_LETTER_B>;\
        <LATIN_CAPITAL_LETTER_C>;\
        <LATIN_CAPITAL_LETTER_D>;\
        <LATIN_CAPITAL_LETTER_E>;\
        <LATIN_CAPITAL_LETTER_F>;\
        <LATIN_CAPITAL_LETTER_G>;\
        <LATIN_CAPITAL_LETTER_H>;\
        <LATIN_CAPITAL_LETTER_I>;\
        <LATIN_CAPITAL_LETTER_J>;\
```

```
        <LATIN_CAPITAL_LETTER_K>;\
        <LATIN_CAPITAL_LETTER_L>;\
        <LATIN_CAPITAL_LETTER_M>;\
        <LATIN_CAPITAL_LETTER_N>;\
        <LATIN_CAPITAL_LETTER_O>;\
        <LATIN_CAPITAL_LETTER_P>;\
        <LATIN_CAPITAL_LETTER_Q>;\
        <LATIN_CAPITAL_LETTER_R>;\
        <LATIN_CAPITAL_LETTER_S>;\
        <LATIN_CAPITAL_LETTER_T>;\
        <LATIN_CAPITAL_LETTER_U>;\
        <LATIN_CAPITAL_LETTER_V>;\
        <LATIN_CAPITAL_LETTER_W>;\
        <LATIN_CAPITAL_LETTER_X>;\
        <LATIN_CAPITAL_LETTER_Y>;\
        <LATIN_CAPITAL_LETTER_Z>;\
        <LATIN_CAPITAL_LETTER_C_WITH_CEDILLA>;\
        <LATIN_CAPITAL_LETTER_A_WITH_DIAERESIS>;\
        <LATIN_CAPITAL_LETTER_A_WITH_RING_ABOVE>;\
        <LATIN_CAPITAL_LETTER_E_WITH_ACUTE>;\
        <LATIN_CAPITAL_LIGATURE_AE>;\
        <LATIN_CAPITAL_LETTER_O_WITH_DIAERESIS>;\
        <LATIN_CAPITAL_LETTER_U_WITH_DIAERESIS>;\
        <LATIN_CAPITAL_LETTER_O_WITH_STROKE>;\
        <LATIN_CAPITAL_LETTER_N_WITH_TILDE>;\
        <LATIN_CAPITAL_LETTER_A_WITH_ACUTE>;\
        <LATIN_CAPITAL_LETTER_A_WITH_CIRCUMFLEX>;\
        <LATIN_CAPITAL_LETTER_A_WITH_GRAVE>;\
        <LATIN_CAPITAL_LETTER_A_WITH_TILDE>;\
        <LATIN_CAPITAL_LETTER_ETH_>;\
        <LATIN_CAPITAL_LETTER_E_WITH_CIRCUMFLEX>;\
        <LATIN_CAPITAL_LETTER_E_WITH_DIAERESIS>;\
        <LATIN_CAPITAL_LETTER_E_WITH_GRAVE>;\
        <LATIN_CAPITAL_LETTER_I_WITH_ACUTE>;\
        <LATIN_CAPITAL_LETTER_I_WITH_CIRCUMFLEX>;\
        <LATIN_CAPITAL_LETTER_I_WITH_DIAERESIS>;\
        <LATIN_CAPITAL_LETTER_I_WITH_GRAVE>;\
        <LATIN_CAPITAL_LETTER_O_WITH_ACUTE>;\
        <LATIN_CAPITAL_LETTER_O_WITH_CIRCUMFLEX>;\
        <LATIN_CAPITAL_LETTER_O_WITH_GRAVE>;\
        <LATIN_CAPITAL_LETTER_O_WITH_TILDE>;\
        <LATIN_CAPITAL_LETTER_THORN_>;\
        <LATIN_CAPITAL_LETTER_U_WITH_ACUTE>;\
        <LATIN_CAPITAL_LETTER_U_WITH_CIRCUMFLEX>;\
        <LATIN_CAPITAL_LETTER_U_WITH_GRAVE>;\
        <LATIN_CAPITAL_LETTER_Y_WITH_ACUTE>

cntrl   <SOH>;<STX>;<ETX>;<EOT>;<ENQ>;<ACK>;<BEL>;<BS>;<HT>;<LF>;<VT>;\
        <FF>;<CR>;<SO>;<SI>;<DLE>;<DC1>;<DC2>;<DC3>;<DC4>;<NAK>;<SYN>;\
        <ETB>;<CAN>;<EM>;<SUB>;<ESC>;<FS>;<GS>;<RS>;<US>;<DEL>
```

```
space   <BS>;<HT>;<LF>;<VT>;<FF>;<CR>;<SPACE>

blank   <HT>;<SPACE>

digit   <DIGIT_ZERO>;\
        <DIGIT_ONE>;\
        <DIGIT_TWO>;\
        <DIGIT_THREE>;\
        <DIGIT_FOUR>;\
        <DIGIT_FIVE>;\
        <DIGIT_SIX>;\
        <DIGIT_SEVEN>;\
        <DIGIT_EIGHT>;\
        <DIGIT_NINE>

xdigit  <DIGIT_ZERO>;\
        <DIGIT_ONE>;\
        <DIGIT_TWO>;\
        <DIGIT_THREE>;\
        <DIGIT_FOUR>;\
        <DIGIT_FIVE>;\
        <DIGIT_SIX>;\
        <DIGIT_SEVEN>;\
        <DIGIT_EIGHT>;\
        <DIGIT_NINE>;\
        <LATIN_CAPITAL_LETTER_A>;\
        <LATIN_CAPITAL_LETTER_B>;\
        <LATIN_CAPITAL_LETTER_C>;\
        <LATIN_CAPITAL_LETTER_D>;\
        <LATIN_CAPITAL_LETTER_E>;\
        <LATIN_CAPITAL_LETTER_F>;\
        <LATIN_SMALL_LETTER_A>;\
        <LATIN_SMALL_LETTER_B>;\
        <LATIN_SMALL_LETTER_C>;\
        <LATIN_SMALL_LETTER_D>;\
        <LATIN_SMALL_LETTER_E>;\
        <LATIN_SMALL_LETTER_F>

toupper (<LATIN_SMALL_LETTER_A>,        <LATIN_CAPITAL_LETTER_A>);\
        (<LATIN_SMALL_LETTER_B>,        <LATIN_CAPITAL_LETTER_B>);\
        (<LATIN_SMALL_LETTER_C>,        <LATIN_CAPITAL_LETTER_C>);\
        (<LATIN_SMALL_LETTER_D>,        <LATIN_CAPITAL_LETTER_D>);\
        (<LATIN_SMALL_LETTER_E>,        <LATIN_CAPITAL_LETTER_E>);\
        (<LATIN_SMALL_LETTER_F>,        <LATIN_CAPITAL_LETTER_F>);\
        (<LATIN_SMALL_LETTER_G>,        <LATIN_CAPITAL_LETTER_G>);\
        (<LATIN_SMALL_LETTER_H>,        <LATIN_CAPITAL_LETTER_H>);\
        (<LATIN_SMALL_LETTER_I>,        <LATIN_CAPITAL_LETTER_I>);\
        (<LATIN_SMALL_LETTER_J>,        <LATIN_CAPITAL_LETTER_J>);\
        (<LATIN_SMALL_LETTER_K>,        <LATIN_CAPITAL_LETTER_K>);\
```

```
(<LATIN_SMALL_LETTER_L>,                <LATIN_CAPITAL_LETTER_L>);\
(<LATIN_SMALL_LETTER_M>,                <LATIN_CAPITAL_LETTER_M>);\
(<LATIN_SMALL_LETTER_N>,                <LATIN_CAPITAL_LETTER_N>);\
(<LATIN_SMALL_LETTER_O>,                <LATIN_CAPITAL_LETTER_O>);\
(<LATIN_SMALL_LETTER_P>,                <LATIN_CAPITAL_LETTER_P>);\
(<LATIN_SMALL_LETTER_Q>,                <LATIN_CAPITAL_LETTER_Q>);\
(<LATIN_SMALL_LETTER_R>,                <LATIN_CAPITAL_LETTER_R>);\
(<LATIN_SMALL_LETTER_S>,                <LATIN_CAPITAL_LETTER_S>);\
(<LATIN_SMALL_LETTER_T>,                <LATIN_CAPITAL_LETTER_T>);\
(<LATIN_SMALL_LETTER_U>,                <LATIN_CAPITAL_LETTER_U>);\
(<LATIN_SMALL_LETTER_V>,                <LATIN_CAPITAL_LETTER_V>);\
(<LATIN_SMALL_LETTER_W>,                <LATIN_CAPITAL_LETTER_W>);\
(<LATIN_SMALL_LETTER_X>,                <LATIN_CAPITAL_LETTER_X>);\
(<LATIN_SMALL_LETTER_Y>,                <LATIN_CAPITAL_LETTER_Y>);\
(<LATIN_SMALL_LETTER_Z>,                <LATIN_CAPITAL_LETTER_Z>);\
(<LATIN_SMALL_LETTER_A_WITH_ACUTE>,      \
        <LATIN_CAPITAL_LETTER_A_WITH_ACUTE>);\
(<LATIN_SMALL_LETTER_A_WITH_RING_ABOVE>, \
        <LATIN_CAPITAL_LETTER_A_WITH_RING_ABOVE>);\
(<LATIN_SMALL_LETTER_A_WITH_CIRCUMFLEX>, \
        <LATIN_CAPITAL_LETTER_A_WITH_CIRCUMFLEX>);\
(<LATIN_SMALL_LETTER_A_WITH_DIAERESIS>,  \
        <LATIN_CAPITAL_LETTER_A_WITH_DIAERESIS>);\
(<LATIN_SMALL_LETTER_A_WITH_GRAVE>,      \
        <LATIN_CAPITAL_LETTER_A_WITH_GRAVE>);\
(<LATIN_SMALL_LETTER_A_WITH_TILDE>,      \
        <LATIN_CAPITAL_LETTER_A_WITH_TILDE>);\
(<LATIN_SMALL_LIGATURE_AE>,              \
        <LATIN_CAPITAL_LIGATURE_AE>);\
(<LATIN_SMALL_LETTER_C_WITH_CEDILLA>,    \
        <LATIN_CAPITAL_LETTER_C_WITH_CEDILLA>);\
(<LATIN_SMALL_LETTER_E_WITH_ACUTE>,      \
        <LATIN_CAPITAL_LETTER_E_WITH_ACUTE>);\
(<LATIN_SMALL_LETTER_E_WITH_CIRCUMFLEX>, \
        <LATIN_CAPITAL_LETTER_E_WITH_CIRCUMFLEX>);\
(<LATIN_SMALL_LETTER_E_WITH_DIAERESIS>,  \
        <LATIN_CAPITAL_LETTER_E_WITH_DIAERESIS>);\
(<LATIN_SMALL_LETTER_E_WITH_GRAVE>,      \
        <LATIN_CAPITAL_LETTER_E_WITH_GRAVE>);\
(<LATIN_SMALL_LETTER_ETH_>,              \
        <LATIN_CAPITAL_LETTER_ETH_>);\
(<LATIN_SMALL_LETTER_I_WITH_ACUTE>,      \
        <LATIN_CAPITAL_LETTER_I_WITH_ACUTE>);\
(<LATIN_SMALL_LETTER_I_WITH_CIRCUMFLEX>, \
        <LATIN_CAPITAL_LETTER_I_WITH_CIRCUMFLEX>);\
(<LATIN_SMALL_LETTER_I_WITH_DIAERESIS>,  \
        <LATIN_CAPITAL_LETTER_I_WITH_DIAERESIS>);\
(<LATIN_SMALL_LETTER_I_WITH_GRAVE>,      \
        <LATIN_CAPITAL_LETTER_I_WITH_GRAVE>);\
```

```
        (<LATIN_SMALL_LETTER_N_WITH_TILDE>,       \
                <LATIN_CAPITAL_LETTER_N_WITH_TILDE>);\
        (<LATIN_SMALL_LETTER_O_WITH_ACUTE>,       \
                <LATIN_CAPITAL_LETTER_O_WITH_ACUTE>);\
        (<LATIN_SMALL_LETTER_O_WITH_CIRCUMFLEX>, \
                <LATIN_CAPITAL_LETTER_O_WITH_CIRCUMFLEX>);\
        (<LATIN_SMALL_LETTER_O_WITH_DIAERESIS>,  \
                <LATIN_CAPITAL_LETTER_O_WITH_DIAERESIS>);\
        (<LATIN_SMALL_LETTER_O_WITH_GRAVE>,       \
                <LATIN_CAPITAL_LETTER_O_WITH_GRAVE>);\
        (<LATIN_SMALL_LETTER_O_WITH_STROKE>,      \
                <LATIN_CAPITAL_LETTER_O_WITH_STROKE>);\
        (<LATIN_SMALL_LETTER_O_WITH_TILDE>,       \
                <LATIN_CAPITAL_LETTER_O_WITH_TILDE>);\
        (<LATIN_SMALL_LETTER_THORN_>,             \
                <LATIN_CAPITAL_LETTER_THORN_>);\
        (<LATIN_SMALL_LETTER_U_WITH_ACUTE>,       \
                <LATIN_CAPITAL_LETTER_U_WITH_ACUTE>);\
        (<LATIN_SMALL_LETTER_U_WITH_CIRCUMFLEX>, \
                <LATIN_CAPITAL_LETTER_U_WITH_CIRCUMFLEX>);\
        (<LATIN_SMALL_LETTER_U_WITH_DIAERESIS>,  \
                <LATIN_CAPITAL_LETTER_U_WITH_DIAERESIS>);\
        (<LATIN_SMALL_LETTER_U_WITH_GRAVE>,       \
                <LATIN_CAPITAL_LETTER_U_WITH_GRAVE>);\
        (<LATIN_SMALL_LETTER_Y_WITH_ACUTE>,       \
                <LATIN_CAPITAL_LETTER_Y_WITH_ACUTE>);\
        (<LATIN_SMALL_LETTER_Y_WITH_DIAERESIS>,  \
                <LATIN_SMALL_LETTER_Y_WITH_DIAERESIS>)

tolower (<LATIN_CAPITAL_LETTER_A>,              <LATIN_SMALL_LETTER_A>);\
        (<LATIN_CAPITAL_LETTER_B>,              <LATIN_SMALL_LETTER_B>);\
        (<LATIN_CAPITAL_LETTER_C>,              <LATIN_SMALL_LETTER_C>);\
        (<LATIN_CAPITAL_LETTER_D>,              <LATIN_SMALL_LETTER_D>);\
        (<LATIN_CAPITAL_LETTER_E>,              <LATIN_SMALL_LETTER_E>);\
        (<LATIN_CAPITAL_LETTER_F>,              <LATIN_SMALL_LETTER_F>);\
        (<LATIN_CAPITAL_LETTER_G>,              <LATIN_SMALL_LETTER_G>);\
        (<LATIN_CAPITAL_LETTER_H>,              <LATIN_SMALL_LETTER_H>);\
        (<LATIN_CAPITAL_LETTER_I>,              <LATIN_SMALL_LETTER_I>);\
        (<LATIN_CAPITAL_LETTER_J>,              <LATIN_SMALL_LETTER_J>);\
        (<LATIN_CAPITAL_LETTER_K>,              <LATIN_SMALL_LETTER_K>);\
        (<LATIN_CAPITAL_LETTER_L>,              <LATIN_SMALL_LETTER_L>);\
        (<LATIN_CAPITAL_LETTER_M>,              <LATIN_SMALL_LETTER_M>);\
        (<LATIN_CAPITAL_LETTER_N>,              <LATIN_SMALL_LETTER_N>);\
        (<LATIN_CAPITAL_LETTER_O>,              <LATIN_SMALL_LETTER_O>);\
        (<LATIN_CAPITAL_LETTER_P>,              <LATIN_SMALL_LETTER_P>);\
        (<LATIN_CAPITAL_LETTER_Q>,              <LATIN_SMALL_LETTER_Q>);\
        (<LATIN_CAPITAL_LETTER_R>,              <LATIN_SMALL_LETTER_R>);\
        (<LATIN_CAPITAL_LETTER_S>,              <LATIN_SMALL_LETTER_S>);\
        (<LATIN_CAPITAL_LETTER_T>,              <LATIN_SMALL_LETTER_T>);\
```

```
(<LATIN_CAPITAL_LETTER_U>,                <LATIN_SMALL_LETTER_U>);\
(<LATIN_CAPITAL_LETTER_V>,                <LATIN_SMALL_LETTER_V>);\
(<LATIN_CAPITAL_LETTER_W>,                <LATIN_SMALL_LETTER_W>);\
(<LATIN_CAPITAL_LETTER_X>,                <LATIN_SMALL_LETTER_X>);\
(<LATIN_CAPITAL_LETTER_Y>,                <LATIN_SMALL_LETTER_Y>);\
(<LATIN_CAPITAL_LETTER_Z>,                <LATIN_SMALL_LETTER_Z>);\
(<LATIN_CAPITAL_LETTER_A_WITH_RING_ABOVE>, \
        <LATIN_SMALL_LETTER_A_WITH_RING_ABOVE>);\
(<LATIN_CAPITAL_LETTER_A_WITH_CIRCUMFLEX>, \
        <LATIN_SMALL_LETTER_A_WITH_CIRCUMFLEX>);\
(<LATIN_CAPITAL_LETTER_A_WITH_DIAERESIS>,  \
        <LATIN_SMALL_LETTER_A_WITH_DIAERESIS>);\
(<LATIN_CAPITAL_LETTER_A_WITH_GRAVE>,      \
        <LATIN_SMALL_LETTER_A_WITH_GRAVE>);\
(<LATIN_CAPITAL_LETTER_A_WITH_TILDE>,      \
        <LATIN_SMALL_LETTER_A_WITH_TILDE>);\
(<LATIN_CAPITAL_LETTER_A_WITH_ACUTE>,      \
        <LATIN_SMALL_LETTER_A_WITH_ACUTE>);\
(<LATIN_CAPITAL_LIGATURE_AE>,              \
        <LATIN_SMALL_LIGATURE_AE>);\
(<LATIN_CAPITAL_LETTER_C_WITH_CEDILLA>,    \
        <LATIN_SMALL_LETTER_C_WITH_CEDILLA>);\
(<LATIN_CAPITAL_LETTER_E_WITH_ACUTE>,      \
        <LATIN_SMALL_LETTER_E_WITH_ACUTE>);\
(<LATIN_CAPITAL_LETTER_E_WITH_CIRCUMFLEX>, \
        <LATIN_SMALL_LETTER_E_WITH_CIRCUMFLEX>);\
(<LATIN_CAPITAL_LETTER_E_WITH_DIAERESIS>,  \
        <LATIN_SMALL_LETTER_E_WITH_DIAERESIS>);\
(<LATIN_CAPITAL_LETTER_E_WITH_GRAVE>,      \
        <LATIN_SMALL_LETTER_E_WITH_GRAVE>);\
(<LATIN_CAPITAL_LETTER_ETH_>,              \
        <LATIN_SMALL_LETTER_ETH_>);\
(<LATIN_CAPITAL_LETTER_I_WITH_ACUTE>,      \
        <LATIN_SMALL_LETTER_I_WITH_ACUTE>);\
(<LATIN_CAPITAL_LETTER_I_WITH_CIRCUMFLEX>, \
        <LATIN_SMALL_LETTER_I_WITH_CIRCUMFLEX>);\
(<LATIN_CAPITAL_LETTER_I_WITH_DIAERESIS>,  \
        <LATIN_SMALL_LETTER_I_WITH_DIAERESIS>);\
(<LATIN_CAPITAL_LETTER_I_WITH_GRAVE>,      \
        <LATIN_SMALL_LETTER_I_WITH_GRAVE>);\
(<LATIN_CAPITAL_LETTER_N_WITH_TILDE>,      \
        <LATIN_SMALL_LETTER_N_WITH_TILDE>);\
(<LATIN_CAPITAL_LETTER_O_WITH_CIRCUMFLEX>, \
        <LATIN_SMALL_LETTER_O_WITH_CIRCUMFLEX>);\
(<LATIN_CAPITAL_LETTER_O_WITH_ACUTE>,      \
        <LATIN_SMALL_LETTER_O_WITH_ACUTE>);\
(<LATIN_CAPITAL_LETTER_O_WITH_DIAERESIS>,  \
        <LATIN_SMALL_LETTER_O_WITH_DIAERESIS>);\
(<LATIN_CAPITAL_LETTER_O_WITH_GRAVE>,      \
```

```
                <LATIN_SMALL_LETTER_O_WITH_GRAVE>);\
        (<LATIN_CAPITAL_LETTER_O_WITH_STROKE>,      \
                <LATIN_SMALL_LETTER_O_WITH_STROKE>);\
        (<LATIN_CAPITAL_LETTER_THORN_>,             \
                <LATIN_SMALL_LETTER_THORN_>);\
        (<LATIN_CAPITAL_LETTER_U_WITH_ACUTE>,       \
                <LATIN_SMALL_LETTER_U_WITH_ACUTE>);\
        (<LATIN_CAPITAL_LETTER_U_WITH_CIRCUMFLEX>, \
                <LATIN_SMALL_LETTER_U_WITH_CIRCUMFLEX>);\
        (<LATIN_CAPITAL_LETTER_U_WITH_DIAERESIS>,  \
                <LATIN_SMALL_LETTER_U_WITH_DIAERESIS>);\
        (<LATIN_CAPITAL_LETTER_U_WITH_GRAVE>,       \
                <LATIN_SMALL_LETTER_U_WITH_GRAVE>);\
        (<LATIN_CAPITAL_LETTER_Y_WITH_ACUTE>,       \
                <LATIN_SMALL_LETTER_Y_WITH_ACUTE> )

END LC_CTYPE

#######
LC_TIME
#######

# %a
abday   "<LATIN_SMALL_LETTER_D><LATIN_SMALL_LETTER_I><LATIN_SMALL_LETTER_M>\
                <FULL_STOP>";\
        "<LATIN_SMALL_LETTER_L><LATIN_SMALL_LETTER_U><LATIN_SMALL_LETTER_N>\
                <LATIN_SMALL_LETTER_D><LATIN_SMALL_LETTER_I>";\
        "<LATIN_SMALL_LETTER_M><LATIN_SMALL_LETTER_A><LATIN_SMALL_LETTER_R>\
                <LATIN_SMALL_LETTER_D><LATIN_SMALL_LETTER_I>";\
        "<LATIN_SMALL_LETTER_M><LATIN_SMALL_LETTER_E><LATIN_SMALL_LETTER_R>\
                <LATIN_SMALL_LETTER_C><LATIN_SMALL_LETTER_R><FULL_STOP>";\
        "<LATIN_SMALL_LETTER_J><LATIN_SMALL_LETTER_E><LATIN_SMALL_LETTER_U>\
                <LATIN_SMALL_LETTER_D><LATIN_SMALL_LETTER_I>";\
        "<LATIN_SMALL_LETTER_V><LATIN_SMALL_LETTER_E><LATIN_SMALL_LETTER_N>\
                <LATIN_SMALL_LETTER_D><LATIN_SMALL_LETTER_R><FULL_STOP>";\
        "<LATIN_SMALL_LETTER_S><LATIN_SMALL_LETTER_A><LATIN_SMALL_LETTER_M>\
                <FULL_STOP>"

# %A
day     "<LATIN_SMALL_LETTER_D><LATIN_SMALL_LETTER_I><LATIN_SMALL_LETTER_M>\
                <LATIN_SMALL_LETTER_A><LATIN_SMALL_LETTER_N>\
                <LATIN_SMALL_LETTER_C><LATIN_SMALL_LETTER_H>\
                <LATIN_SMALL_LETTER_E>";\
        "<LATIN_SMALL_LETTER_L><LATIN_SMALL_LETTER_U><LATIN_SMALL_LETTER_N>\
                <LATIN_SMALL_LETTER_D><LATIN_SMALL_LETTER_I>";\
        "<LATIN_SMALL_LETTER_M><LATIN_SMALL_LETTER_A><LATIN_SMALL_LETTER_R>\
                <LATIN_SMALL_LETTER_D><LATIN_SMALL_LETTER_I>";\
        "<LATIN_SMALL_LETTER_M><LATIN_SMALL_LETTER_E><LATIN_SMALL_LETTER_R>\
                <LATIN_SMALL_LETTER_C><LATIN_SMALL_LETTER_R>\
```

```
                <LATIN_SMALL_LETTER_E><LATIN_SMALL_LETTER_D>\
                <LATIN_SMALL_LETTER_I>";\
        "<LATIN_SMALL_LETTER_J><LATIN_SMALL_LETTER_E><LATIN_SMALL_LETTER_U>\
                <LATIN_SMALL_LETTER_D><LATIN_SMALL_LETTER_I>";\
        "<LATIN_SMALL_LETTER_V><LATIN_SMALL_LETTER_E><LATIN_SMALL_LETTER_N>\
                <LATIN_SMALL_LETTER_D><LATIN_SMALL_LETTER_R>\
                <LATIN_SMALL_LETTER_E><LATIN_SMALL_LETTER_D>\
                <LATIN_SMALL_LETTER_I>";\
        "<LATIN_SMALL_LETTER_S><LATIN_SMALL_LETTER_A><LATIN_SMALL_LETTER_M>\
                <LATIN_SMALL_LETTER_E><LATIN_SMALL_LETTER_D>\
                <LATIN_SMALL_LETTER_I>"

# %b
abmon   "<LATIN_SMALL_LETTER_J><LATIN_SMALL_LETTER_A><LATIN_SMALL_LETTER_N>\
                <LATIN_SMALL_LETTER_V><FULL_STOP>";\
        "<LATIN_SMALL_LETTER_F><LATIN_SMALL_LETTER_E_WITH_ACUTE>\
                <LATIN_SMALL_LETTER_V><LATIN_SMALL_LETTER_R><FULL_STOP>";\
        "<LATIN_SMALL_LETTER_M><LATIN_SMALL_LETTER_A><LATIN_SMALL_LETTER_R>\
                <LATIN_SMALL_LETTER_S>";\
        "<LATIN_SMALL_LETTER_A><LATIN_SMALL_LETTER_V><LATIN_SMALL_LETTER_R>\
                <FULL_STOP>";\
        "<LATIN_SMALL_LETTER_M><LATIN_SMALL_LETTER_A><LATIN_SMALL_LETTER_I>";\
        "<LATIN_SMALL_LETTER_J><LATIN_SMALL_LETTER_U><LATIN_SMALL_LETTER_I>\
                <LATIN_SMALL_LETTER_N>";\
        "<LATIN_SMALL_LETTER_J><LATIN_SMALL_LETTER_U><LATIN_SMALL_LETTER_I>\
                <LATIN_SMALL_LETTER_L><FULL_STOP>";\
        "<LATIN_SMALL_LETTER_A><LATIN_SMALL_LETTER_O>\
                <LATIN_SMALL_LETTER_U_WITH_CIRCUMFLEX>\
                <LATIN_SMALL_LETTER_T>";\
        "<LATIN_SMALL_LETTER_S><LATIN_SMALL_LETTER_E><LATIN_SMALL_LETTER_P>\
                <LATIN_SMALL_LETTER_T><FULL_STOP>";\
        "<LATIN_SMALL_LETTER_O><LATIN_SMALL_LETTER_C><LATIN_SMALL_LETTER_T>\
                <FULL_STOP>";\
        "<LATIN_SMALL_LETTER_N><LATIN_SMALL_LETTER_O><LATIN_SMALL_LETTER_V>\
                <FULL_STOP>";\
        "<LATIN_SMALL_LETTER_D><LATIN_SMALL_LETTER_E_WITH_ACUTE>\
                <LATIN_SMALL_LETTER_C><FULL_STOP>"

# %B
mon     "<LATIN_SMALL_LETTER_J><LATIN_SMALL_LETTER_A><LATIN_SMALL_LETTER_N>\
                <LATIN_SMALL_LETTER_V><LATIN_SMALL_LETTER_I>\
                <LATIN_SMALL_LETTER_E><LATIN_SMALL_LETTER_R>";\
        "<LATIN_SMALL_LETTER_F><LATIN_SMALL_LETTER_E_WITH_ACUTE>\
                <LATIN_SMALL_LETTER_V><LATIN_SMALL_LETTER_R>\
                <LATIN_SMALL_LETTER_I><LATIN_SMALL_LETTER_E>\
                <LATIN_SMALL_LETTER_R>";\
        "<LATIN_SMALL_LETTER_M><LATIN_SMALL_LETTER_A><LATIN_SMALL_LETTER_R>\
                <LATIN_SMALL_LETTER_S>";\
        "<LATIN_SMALL_LETTER_A><LATIN_SMALL_LETTER_V><LATIN_SMALL_LETTER_R>\
```

```
                <LATIN_SMALL_LETTER_I><LATIN_SMALL_LETTER_L>";\
         "<LATIN_SMALL_LETTER_M><LATIN_SMALL_LETTER_A><LATIN_SMALL_LETTER_I>";\
         "<LATIN_SMALL_LETTER_J><LATIN_SMALL_LETTER_U><LATIN_SMALL_LETTER_I>\
                <LATIN_SMALL_LETTER_N>";\
         "<LATIN_SMALL_LETTER_J><LATIN_SMALL_LETTER_U><LATIN_SMALL_LETTER_I>\
                <LATIN_SMALL_LETTER_L><LATIN_SMALL_LETTER_L>\
                <LATIN_SMALL_LETTER_E><LATIN_SMALL_LETTER_T>";\
         "<LATIN_SMALL_LETTER_A><LATIN_SMALL_LETTER_O>\
                <LATIN_SMALL_LETTER_U_WITH_CIRCUMFLEX>\
                <LATIN_SMALL_LETTER_T>";\
         "<LATIN_SMALL_LETTER_S><LATIN_SMALL_LETTER_E><LATIN_SMALL_LETTER_P>\
                <LATIN_SMALL_LETTER_T><LATIN_SMALL_LETTER_E>\
                <LATIN_SMALL_LETTER_M><LATIN_SMALL_LETTER_B>\
                <LATIN_SMALL_LETTER_R><LATIN_SMALL_LETTER_E>";\
         "<LATIN_SMALL_LETTER_O><LATIN_SMALL_LETTER_C><LATIN_SMALL_LETTER_T>\
                <LATIN_SMALL_LETTER_O><LATIN_SMALL_LETTER_B>\
                <LATIN_SMALL_LETTER_R><LATIN_SMALL_LETTER_E>";\
         "<LATIN_SMALL_LETTER_N><LATIN_SMALL_LETTER_O><LATIN_SMALL_LETTER_V>\
                <LATIN_SMALL_LETTER_E><LATIN_SMALL_LETTER_M>\
                <LATIN_SMALL_LETTER_B><LATIN_SMALL_LETTER_R>\
                <LATIN_SMALL_LETTER_E>";\
         "<LATIN_SMALL_LETTER_D><LATIN_SMALL_LETTER_E_WITH_ACUTE>\
                <LATIN_SMALL_LETTER_C><LATIN_SMALL_LETTER_E>\
                <LATIN_SMALL_LETTER_M><LATIN_SMALL_LETTER_B>\
                <LATIN_SMALL_LETTER_R><LATIN_SMALL_LETTER_E>"

# %p
am_pm    "<LATIN_SMALL_LETTER_A><LATIN_SMALL_LETTER_M>";\
         "<LATIN_SMALL_LETTER_P><LATIN_SMALL_LETTER_M>"

# %c
# consists of: %a %b %d %X %Z %Y
d_t_fmt "<PERCENT_SIGN><LATIN_SMALL_LETTER_A><SPACE><PERCENT_SIGN>\
                <LATIN_SMALL_LETTER_B><SPACE><PERCENT_SIGN>\
                <LATIN_SMALL_LETTER_D><SPACE><PERCENT_SIGN>\
                <LATIN_CAPITAL_LETTER_X><SPACE><PERCENT_SIGN>\
                <LATIN_CAPITAL_LETTER_Z><SPACE><PERCENT_SIGN>\
                <LATIN_CAPITAL_LETTER_Y>"

# %x
# consists of: %a %b %d
d_fmt    "<PERCENT_SIGN><LATIN_SMALL_LETTER_A><SPACE><PERCENT_SIGN>\
                <LATIN_SMALL_LETTER_B><SPACE><PERCENT_SIGN>\
                <LATIN_SMALL_LETTER_D>"

# %X
# consists of: %I:%M:%S
t_fmt    "<PERCENT_SIGN><LATIN_CAPITAL_LETTER_I><COLON><PERCENT_SIGN>\
                <LATIN_CAPITAL_LETTER_M><COLON><PERCENT_SIGN>\
                <LATIN_CAPITAL_LETTER_S>"
```

```
# %r
# consists of: %I:%M:%S %p
t_fmt_ampm "<PERCENT_SIGN><LATIN_CAPITAL_LETTER_I><COLON><PERCENT_SIGN>\
                <LATIN_CAPITAL_LETTER_M><COLON><PERCENT_SIGN>\
                <LATIN_CAPITAL_LETTER_S><SPACE><PERCENT_SIGN>\
                <LATIN_SMALL_LETTER_P>"

alt_digits  "<DIGIT_ZERO>";\
            "<DIGIT_ONE>";\
            "<DIGIT_TWO>";\
            "<DIGIT_THREE>";\
            "<DIGIT_FOUR>";\
            "<DIGIT_FIVE>";\
            "<DIGIT_SIX>";\
            "<DIGIT_SEVEN>";\
            "<DIGIT_EIGHT>";\
            "<DIGIT_NINE>";\
            "<DIGIT_ONE><DIGIT_ZERO>";\
            "<DIGIT_ONE><DIGIT_ONE>";\
            "<DIGIT_ONE><DIGIT_TWO>";\
            "<DIGIT_ONE><DIGIT_THREE>";\
            "<DIGIT_ONE><DIGIT_FOUR>";\
            "<DIGIT_ONE><DIGIT_FIVE>";\
            "<DIGIT_ONE><DIGIT_SIX>";\
            "<DIGIT_ONE><DIGIT_SEVEN>";\
            "<DIGIT_ONE><DIGIT_EIGHT>";\
            "<DIGIT_ONE><DIGIT_NINE>";\
            "<DIGIT_TWO><DIGIT_ZERO>";\
            "<DIGIT_TWO><DIGIT_ONE>";\
            "<DIGIT_TWO><DIGIT_TWO>";\
            "<DIGIT_TWO><DIGIT_THREE>";\
            "<DIGIT_TWO><DIGIT_FOUR>";\
            "<DIGIT_TWO><DIGIT_FIVE>";\
            "<DIGIT_TWO><DIGIT_SIX>";\
            "<DIGIT_TWO><DIGIT_SEVEN>";\
            "<DIGIT_TWO><DIGIT_EIGHT>";\
            "<DIGIT_TWO><DIGIT_NINE>";\
            "<DIGIT_THREE><DIGIT_ZERO>";\
            "<DIGIT_THREE><DIGIT_ONE>";\
            "<DIGIT_THREE><DIGIT_TWO>";\
            "<DIGIT_THREE><DIGIT_THREE>";\
            "<DIGIT_THREE><DIGIT_FOUR>";\
            "<DIGIT_THREE><DIGIT_FIVE>";\
            "<DIGIT_THREE><DIGIT_SIX>";\
            "<DIGIT_THREE><DIGIT_SEVEN>";\
            "<DIGIT_THREE><DIGIT_EIGHT>";\
            "<DIGIT_THREE><DIGIT_NINE>";\
            "<DIGIT_FOUR><DIGIT_ZERO>";\
            "<DIGIT_FOUR><DIGIT_ONE>";\
            "<DIGIT_FOUR><DIGIT_TWO>";\
```

```
"<DIGIT_FOUR><DIGIT_THREE>";\
"<DIGIT_FOUR><DIGIT_FOUR>";\
"<DIGIT_FOUR><DIGIT_FIVE>";\
"<DIGIT_FOUR><DIGIT_SIX>";\
"<DIGIT_FOUR><DIGIT_SEVEN>";\
"<DIGIT_FOUR><DIGIT_EIGHT>";\
"<DIGIT_FOUR><DIGIT_NINE>";\
"<DIGIT_FIVE><DIGIT_ZERO>";\
"<DIGIT_FIVE><DIGIT_ONE>";\
"<DIGIT_FIVE><DIGIT_TWO>";\
"<DIGIT_FIVE><DIGIT_THREE>";\
"<DIGIT_FIVE><DIGIT_FOUR>";\
"<DIGIT_FIVE><DIGIT_FIVE>";\
"<DIGIT_FIVE><DIGIT_SIX>";\
"<DIGIT_FIVE><DIGIT_SEVEN>";\
"<DIGIT_FIVE><DIGIT_EIGHT>";\
"<DIGIT_FIVE><DIGIT_NINE>";\
"<DIGIT_SIX><DIGIT_ZERO>";\
"<DIGIT_SIX><DIGIT_ONE>";\
"<DIGIT_SIX><DIGIT_TWO>";\
"<DIGIT_SIX><DIGIT_THREE>";\
"<DIGIT_SIX><DIGIT_FOUR>";\
"<DIGIT_SIX><DIGIT_FIVE>";\
"<DIGIT_SIX><DIGIT_SIX>";\
"<DIGIT_SIX><DIGIT_SEVEN>";\
"<DIGIT_SIX><DIGIT_EIGHT>";\
"<DIGIT_SIX><DIGIT_NINE>";\
"<DIGIT_SEVEN><DIGIT_ZERO>";\
"<DIGIT_SEVEN><DIGIT_ONE>";\
"<DIGIT_SEVEN><DIGIT_TWO>";\
"<DIGIT_SEVEN><DIGIT_THREE>";\
"<DIGIT_SEVEN><DIGIT_FOUR>";\
"<DIGIT_SEVEN><DIGIT_FIVE>";\
"<DIGIT_SEVEN><DIGIT_SIX>";\
"<DIGIT_SEVEN><DIGIT_SEVEN>";\
"<DIGIT_SEVEN><DIGIT_EIGHT>";\
"<DIGIT_SEVEN><DIGIT_NINE>";\
"<DIGIT_EIGHT><DIGIT_ZERO>";\
"<DIGIT_EIGHT><DIGIT_ONE>";\
"<DIGIT_EIGHT><DIGIT_TWO>";\
"<DIGIT_EIGHT><DIGIT_THREE>";\
"<DIGIT_EIGHT><DIGIT_FOUR>";\
"<DIGIT_EIGHT><DIGIT_FIVE>";\
"<DIGIT_EIGHT><DIGIT_SIX>";\
"<DIGIT_EIGHT><DIGIT_SEVEN>";\
"<DIGIT_EIGHT><DIGIT_EIGHT>";\
"<DIGIT_EIGHT><DIGIT_NINE>";\
"<DIGIT_NINE><DIGIT_ZERO>";\
"<DIGIT_NINE><DIGIT_ONE>";\
```

```
            "<DIGIT_NINE><DIGIT_TWO>";\
            "<DIGIT_NINE><DIGIT_THREE>";\
            "<DIGIT_NINE><DIGIT_FOUR>";\
            "<DIGIT_NINE><DIGIT_FIVE>";\
            "<DIGIT_NINE><DIGIT_SIX>";\
            "<DIGIT_NINE><DIGIT_SEVEN>";\
            "<DIGIT_NINE><DIGIT_EIGHT>";\
            "<DIGIT_NINE><DIGIT_NINE>"

END LC_TIME

##########
LC_NUMERIC
##########

decimal_point       <COMMA>

thousands_sep       <FULL_STOP>

grouping            3;0

exponential_sign    "<LATIN_SMALL_LETTER_E>"

END LC_NUMERIC

###########
LC_MONETARY
###########

int_curr_symbol        "<LATIN_CAPITAL_LETTER_C><LATIN_CAPITAL_LETTER_A>\
                 <LATIN_CAPITAL_LETTER_D> "

currency_symbol        "<DOLLAR_SIGN>"

mon_decimal_point   <COMMA>

mon_thousands_sep   <SPACE>

mon_grouping        3 ; 0

positive_sign       "<NULL>"

negative_sign       "<HYPHEN-MINUS>"

int_frac_digits     2

frac_digits         2

p_cs_precedes       0
```

```
p_sep_by_space      1

n_cs_precedes       0

n_sep_by_space      1

p_sign_posn         1

n_sign_posn         0

END LC_MONETARY

############
LC_MESSAGES
############

yesexpr "<LATIN_SMALL_LETTER_O>"

noexpr "<LATIN_SMALL_LETTER_N>"

END LC_MESSAGES

###########
LC_COLLATE
###########

collating-symbol <LOWER>
collating-symbol <SUB_LOWERCASE>
collating-symbol <SUPER_LOWERCASE>
collating-symbol <CK_RESERVED>
collating-symbol <UPPER>
collating-symbol <SUB_UPPERCASE>
collating-symbol <SUPER_UPPERCASE>
collating-symbol <NORMAL_ARABIC_DIGIT>
collating-symbol <SUBSCRIPT_ARABIC_DIGIT>
collating-symbol <SUPERSCRIPT_ARABIC_DIGIT>
collating-symbol <QUARTER>
collating-symbol <HALF>
collating-symbol <THREEQUARTER>

collating-symbol <NO_DIACRITIC_MARK>
collating-symbol <SPECIAL_MARK>
collating-symbol <LIGATURE_MARK>
collating-symbol <ACUTE_MARK>
collating-symbol <GRAVE_MARK>
collating-symbol <BREVE_MARK>
collating-symbol <CIRCUMFLEX_MARK>
collating-symbol <CARON_MARK>
collating-symbol <OVERCIRCLE_MARK>
```

```
collating-symbol <DIAERESIS_UMLAUT_MARK>
collating-symbol <DIAERESIS_ACUTE_MARK>
collating-symbol <DOUBLE_ACUTE_MARK>
collating-symbol <TILDE_MARK>
collating-symbol <OVERDOT_MARK>
collating-symbol <MACRON_MARK>
collating-symbol <DK_RESERVED>
collating-symbol <MIDDLE_DOT_MARK>
collating-symbol <STROKE_MARK>
collating-symbol <CEDILLA_MARK>
collating-symbol <OGONEK_MARK>
collating-symbol <UNDERDOT_MARK>
collating-symbol <UNDERLINE_MARK>

order_start forward;backward;forward;forward,position

<LOWER>
<SUB_LOWERCASE>
<SUPER_LOWERCASE>
<CK_RESERVED>
<UPPER>
<SUB_UPPERCASE>
<SUPER_UPPERCASE>
<NORMAL_ARABIC_DIGIT>
<SUBSCRIPT_ARABIC_DIGIT>
<SUPERSCRIPT_ARABIC_DIGIT>
<QUARTER>
<HALF>

<NO_DIACRITIC_MARK>
<SPECIAL_MARK>
<LIGATURE_MARK>
<ACUTE_MARK>
<GRAVE_MARK>
<BREVE_MARK>
<CIRCUMFLEX_MARK>
<CARON_MARK>
<OVERCIRCLE_MARK>
<DIAERESIS_UMLAUT_MARK>
<DIAERESIS_ACUTE_MARK>
<DOUBLE_ACUTE_MARK>
<TILDE_MARK>
<OVERDOT_MARK>
<MACRON_MARK>
<DK_RESERVED>
<MIDDLE_DOT_MARK>
<STROKE_MARK>
<CEDILLA_MARK>
<OGONEK_MARK>
```

```
<UNDERDOT_MARK>
<UNDERLINE_MARK>

<DIGIT_ZERO>  <DIGIT_ZERO>; <NO_DIACRITIC_MARK>; <NORMAL_ARABIC_DIGIT>; IGNORE
<DIGIT_ONE>   <DIGIT_ONE>;  <NO_DIACRITIC_MARK>; <NORMAL_ARABIC_DIGIT>; IGNORE
<DIGIT_TWO>   <DIGIT_TWO>;  <NO_DIACRITIC_MARK>; <NORMAL_ARABIC_DIGIT>; IGNORE
<DIGIT_THREE> <DIGIT_THREE>;<NO_DIACRITIC_MARK>; <NORMAL_ARABIC_DIGIT>; IGNORE
<DIGIT_FOUR>  <DIGIT_FOUR>; <NO_DIACRITIC_MARK>; <NORMAL_ARABIC_DIGIT>; IGNORE
<DIGIT_FIVE>  <DIGIT_FIVE>; <NO_DIACRITIC_MARK>; <NORMAL_ARABIC_DIGIT>; IGNORE
<DIGIT_SIX>   <DIGIT_SIX>;  <NO_DIACRITIC_MARK>; <NORMAL_ARABIC_DIGIT>; IGNORE
<DIGIT_SEVEN> <DIGIT_SEVEN>;<NO_DIACRITIC_MARK>; <NORMAL_ARABIC_DIGIT>; IGNORE
<DIGIT_EIGHT> <DIGIT_EIGHT>;<NO_DIACRITIC_MARK>; <NORMAL_ARABIC_DIGIT>; IGNORE
<DIGIT_NINE>  <DIGIT_NINE>; <NO_DIACRITIC_MARK>; <NORMAL_ARABIC_DIGIT>; IGNORE

<VULGAR_FRACTION_ONE_QUARTER>    DIGIT_ZERO; <NO_DIACRITIC_MARK>;\
        <QUARTER>;      IGNORE
<VULGAR_FRACTION_ONE_HALF>  DIGIT_ZERO; <NO_DIACRITIC_MARK>;\
        <HALF>;         IGNORE
<VULGAR_FRACTION_THREE_QUARTERS> DIGIT_ZERO; <NO_DIACRITIC_MARK>;\
        <THREEQUARTER>; IGNORE

<SOH> IGNORE; IGNORE; IGNORE; <SOH>
<STX> IGNORE; IGNORE; IGNORE; <STX>
<ETX> IGNORE; IGNORE; IGNORE; <ETX>
<EOT> IGNORE; IGNORE; IGNORE; <EOT>
<ENQ> IGNORE; IGNORE; IGNORE; <ENQ>
<ACK> IGNORE; IGNORE; IGNORE; <ACK>
<BEL> IGNORE; IGNORE; IGNORE; <BEL>
<BS>  IGNORE; IGNORE; IGNORE; <BS>
<HT>  IGNORE; IGNORE; IGNORE; <HT>
<LF>  IGNORE; IGNORE; IGNORE; <LF>
<VT>  IGNORE; IGNORE; IGNORE; <VT>
<FF>  IGNORE; IGNORE; IGNORE; <FF>
<CR>  IGNORE; IGNORE; IGNORE; <CR>
<SO>  IGNORE; IGNORE; IGNORE; <SO>
<SI>  IGNORE; IGNORE; IGNORE; <SI>
<DLE> IGNORE; IGNORE; IGNORE; <DLE>
<DC1> IGNORE; IGNORE; IGNORE; <DC1>
<DC2> IGNORE; IGNORE; IGNORE; <DC2>
<DC3> IGNORE; IGNORE; IGNORE; <DC3>
<DC4> IGNORE; IGNORE; IGNORE; <DC4>
<NAK> IGNORE; IGNORE; IGNORE; <NAK>
<SYN> IGNORE; IGNORE; IGNORE; <SYN>
<ETB> IGNORE; IGNORE; IGNORE; <ETB>
<CAN> IGNORE; IGNORE; IGNORE; <CAN>
<EM>  IGNORE; IGNORE; IGNORE; <EM>
<SUB> IGNORE; IGNORE; IGNORE; <SUB>
<ESC> IGNORE; IGNORE; IGNORE; <ESC>
```

```
<FS>  IGNORE; IGNORE; IGNORE; <FS>
<GS>  IGNORE; IGNORE; IGNORE; <GS>
<RS>  IGNORE; IGNORE; IGNORE; <RS>
<US>  IGNORE; IGNORE; IGNORE; <US>

<SPACE>         IGNORE; IGNORE; IGNORE; <SPACE>
<COMMA>         IGNORE; IGNORE; IGNORE; <COMMA>
<FULL_STOP>     IGNORE; IGNORE; IGNORE; <FULL_STOP>
<HYPHEN-MINUS> IGNORE; IGNORE; IGNORE; <HYPHEN-MINUS>
<APOSTROPHE>    IGNORE; IGNORE; IGNORE; <APOSTROPHE>

<LATIN_SMALL_LETTER_A>   <LATIN_SMALL_LETTER_A>; <NO_DIACRITIC_MARK>;\
        <LOWER>; IGNORE
<LATIN_CAPITAL_LETTER_A> <LATIN_SMALL_LETTER_A>; <NO_DIACRITIC_MARK>;\
        <UPPER>; IGNORE

<FEMININE_ORDINAL_INDICATOR>        <LATIN_SMALL_LETTER_A>; <SPECIAL_MARK>;\
        <SUPER_LOWERCASE>; IGNORE

<LATIN_SMALL_LETTER_A_WITH_ACUTE>   <LATIN_SMALL_LETTER_A>; <ACUTE_MARK>;\
        <LOWER>; IGNORE
<LATIN_CAPITAL_LETTER_A_WITH_ACUTE> <LATIN_SMALL_LETTER_A>; <ACUTE_MARK>;\
        <UPPER>; IGNORE

<LATIN_SMALL_LETTER_A_WITH_GRAVE>   <LATIN_SMALL_LETTER_A>; <GRAVE_MARK>;\
        <LOWER>; IGNORE
<LATIN_CAPITAL_LETTER_A_WITH_GRAVE> <LATIN_SMALL_LETTER_A>; <GRAVE_MARK>;\
        <UPPER>; IGNORE

<LATIN_SMALL_LETTER_A_WITH_CIRCUMFLEX>   <LATIN_SMALL_LETTER_A>;\
        <CIRCUMFLEX_MARK>; <LOWER>; IGNORE
<LATIN_CAPITAL_LETTER_A_WITH_CIRCUMFLEX> <LATIN_SMALL_LETTER_A>;\
        <CIRCUMFLEX_MARK>; <UPPER>; IGNORE

<LATIN_SMALL_LETTER_A_WITH_TILDE>   <LATIN_SMALL_LETTER_A>; <TILDE_MARK>;\
        <LOWER>; IGNORE
<LATIN_CAPITAL_LETTER_A_WITH_TILDE> <LATIN_SMALL_LETTER_A>; <TILDE_MARK>;\
        <UPPER>; IGNORE

<LATIN_SMALL_LETTER_A_WITH_DIAERESIS>   <LATIN_SMALL_LETTER_A>;\
        <DIAERESIS_UMLAUT_MARK>; <LOWER>; IGNORE
<LATIN_CAPITAL_LETTER_A_WITH_DIAERESIS> <LATIN_SMALL_LETTER_A>;\
        <DIAERESIS_UMLAUT_MARK>; <UPPER>; IGNORE

<LATIN_SMALL_LETTER_A_WITH_RING_ABOVE>   <LATIN_SMALL_LETTER_A>;\
        <OVERCIRCLE_MARK>; <LOWER>; IGNORE
<LATIN_CAPITAL_LETTER_A_WITH_RING_ABOVE> <LATIN_SMALL_LETTER_A>;\
        <OVERCIRCLE_MARK>; <UPPER>; IGNORE
```

```
<LATIN_SMALL_LIGATURE_AE>   <LATIN_SMALL_LETTER_A><LATIN_SMALL_LETTER_E>;\
        <LIGATURE_MARK><LIGATURE_MARK>; <LOWER><LOWER>; IGNORE IGNORE
<LATIN_CAPITAL_LIGATURE_AE> <LATIN_SMALL_LETTER_A><LATIN_SMALL_LETTER_E>;\
        <LIGATURE_MARK><LIGATURE_MARK>; <UPPER><UPPER>; IGNORE IGNORE

<LATIN_SMALL_LETTER_B>   <LATIN_SMALL_LETTER_B>; <NO_DIACRITIC_MARK>;\
        <LOWER>; IGNORE
<LATIN_CAPITAL_LETTER_B> <LATIN_SMALL_LETTER_B>; <NO_DIACRITIC_MARK>;\
        <UPPER>; IGNORE

<LATIN_SMALL_LETTER_C>   <LATIN_SMALL_LETTER_C>; <NO_DIACRITIC_MARK>;\
        <LOWER>; IGNORE
<LATIN_CAPITAL_LETTER_C> <LATIN_SMALL_LETTER_C>; <NO_DIACRITIC_MARK>;\
        <UPPER>; IGNORE

<LATIN_SMALL_LETTER_C_WITH_CEDILLA>   <LATIN_SMALL_LETTER_C>;\
        <CEDILLA_MARK>; <LOWER>; IGNORE
<LATIN_CAPITAL_LETTER_C_WITH_CEDILLA> <LATIN_SMALL_LETTER_C>;\
        <CEDILLA_MARK>; <UPPER>; IGNORE

<LATIN_SMALL_LETTER_D>   <LATIN_SMALL_LETTER_D>; <NO_DIACRITIC_MARK>;\
        <LOWER>; IGNORE
<LATIN_CAPITAL_LETTER_D> <LATIN_SMALL_LETTER_D>; <NO_DIACRITIC_MARK>;\
        <UPPER>; IGNORE

<LATIN_SMALL_LETTER_ETH_>   <LATIN_SMALL_LETTER_D>; <SPECIAL_MARK>;\
        <LOWER>; IGNORE
<LATIN_CAPITAL_LETTER_ETH_> <LATIN_SMALL_LETTER_D>; <SPECIAL_MARK>;\
        <UPPER>; IGNORE

<LATIN_SMALL_LETTER_E>   <LATIN_SMALL_LETTER_E>; <NO_DIACRITIC_MARK>;\
        <LOWER>; IGNORE
<LATIN_CAPITAL_LETTER_E> <LATIN_SMALL_LETTER_E>; <NO_DIACRITIC_MARK>;\
        <UPPER>; IGNORE

<LATIN_SMALL_LETTER_E_WITH_ACUTE>   <LATIN_SMALL_LETTER_E>; <ACUTE_MARK>;\
        <LOWER>; IGNORE
<LATIN_CAPITAL_LETTER_E_WITH_ACUTE> <LATIN_SMALL_LETTER_E>; <ACUTE_MARK>;\
        <UPPER>; IGNORE

<LATIN_SMALL_LETTER_E_WITH_GRAVE>   <LATIN_SMALL_LETTER_E>; <GRAVE_MARK>;\
        <LOWER>; IGNORE
<LATIN_CAPITAL_LETTER_E_WITH_GRAVE> <LATIN_SMALL_LETTER_E>; <GRAVE_MARK>;\
        <UPPER>; IGNORE

<LATIN_SMALL_LETTER_E_WITH_CIRCUMFLEX>   <LATIN_SMALL_LETTER_E>;\
        <CIRCUMFLEX_MARK>; <LOWER>; IGNORE
<LATIN_CAPITAL_LETTER_E_WITH_CIRCUMFLEX> <LATIN_SMALL_LETTER_E>;\
        <CIRCUMFLEX_MARK>; <UPPER>; IGNORE
```

```
<LATIN_SMALL_LETTER_E_WITH_DIAERESIS>   <LATIN_SMALL_LETTER_E>;\
        <DIAERESIS_UMLAUT_MARK>; <LOWER>; IGNORE
<LATIN_CAPITAL_LETTER_E_WITH_DIAERESIS> <LATIN_SMALL_LETTER_E>;\
        <DIAERESIS_UMLAUT_MARK>; <UPPER>; IGNORE

<LATIN_SMALL_LETTER_F>   <LATIN_SMALL_LETTER_F>; <NO_DIACRITIC_MARK>;\
        <LOWER>; IGNORE
<LATIN_CAPITAL_LETTER_F> <LATIN_SMALL_LETTER_F>; <NO_DIACRITIC_MARK>;\
        <UPPER>; IGNORE

<LATIN_SMALL_LETTER_G>   <LATIN_SMALL_LETTER_G>; <NO_DIACRITIC_MARK>;\
        <LOWER>; IGNORE
<LATIN_CAPITAL_LETTER_G> <LATIN_SMALL_LETTER_G>; <NO_DIACRITIC_MARK>;\
        <UPPER>; IGNORE

<LATIN_SMALL_LETTER_H>   <LATIN_SMALL_LETTER_H>; <NO_DIACRITIC_MARK>;\
        <LOWER>; IGNORE
<LATIN_CAPITAL_LETTER_H> <LATIN_SMALL_LETTER_H>; <NO_DIACRITIC_MARK>;\
        <UPPER>; IGNORE

<LATIN_SMALL_LETTER_I>   <LATIN_SMALL_LETTER_I>; <NO_DIACRITIC_MARK>;\
        <LOWER>; IGNORE
<LATIN_CAPITAL_LETTER_I> <LATIN_SMALL_LETTER_I>; <NO_DIACRITIC_MARK>;\
        <UPPER>; IGNORE

<LATIN_SMALL_LETTER_I_WITH_ACUTE>   <LATIN_SMALL_LETTER_I>; <ACUTE_MARK>;\
        <LOWER>; IGNORE
<LATIN_CAPITAL_LETTER_I_WITH_ACUTE> <LATIN_SMALL_LETTER_I>; <ACUTE_MARK>;\
        <UPPER>; IGNORE

<LATIN_SMALL_LETTER_I_WITH_GRAVE>   <LATIN_SMALL_LETTER_I>; <GRAVE_MARK>;\
        <LOWER>; IGNORE
<LATIN_CAPITAL_LETTER_I_WITH_GRAVE> <LATIN_SMALL_LETTER_I>; <GRAVE_MARK>;\
        <UPPER>; IGNORE

<LATIN_SMALL_LETTER_I_WITH_CIRCUMFLEX>   <LATIN_SMALL_LETTER_I>;\
        <CIRCUMFLEX_MARK>; <LOWER>; IGNORE
<LATIN_CAPITAL_LETTER_I_WITH_CIRCUMFLEX> <LATIN_SMALL_LETTER_I>;\
        <CIRCUMFLEX_MARK>; <UPPER>; IGNORE

<LATIN_SMALL_LETTER_I_WITH_DIAERESIS>   <LATIN_SMALL_LETTER_I>;\
        <DIAERESIS_UMLAUT_MARK>; <LOWER>; IGNORE
<LATIN_CAPITAL_LETTER_I_WITH_DIAERESIS> <LATIN_SMALL_LETTER_I>;\
        <DIAERESIS_UMLAUT_MARK>; <UPPER>; IGNORE

<LATIN_SMALL_LETTER_J>   <LATIN_SMALL_LETTER_J>; <NO_DIACRITIC_MARK>;\
        <LOWER>; IGNORE
<LATIN_CAPITAL_LETTER_J> <LATIN_SMALL_LETTER_J>; <NO_DIACRITIC_MARK>;\
        <UPPER>; IGNORE
```

```
<LATIN_SMALL_LETTER_K>   <LATIN_SMALL_LETTER_K>; <NO_DIACRITIC_MARK>;\
        <LOWER>; IGNORE
<LATIN_CAPITAL_LETTER_K> <LATIN_SMALL_LETTER_K>; <NO_DIACRITIC_MARK>;\
        <UPPER>; IGNORE

<LATIN_SMALL_LETTER_L>   <LATIN_SMALL_LETTER_L>; <NO_DIACRITIC_MARK>;\
        <LOWER>; IGNORE
<LATIN_CAPITAL_LETTER_L> <LATIN_SMALL_LETTER_L>; <NO_DIACRITIC_MARK>;\
        <UPPER>; IGNORE

<LATIN_SMALL_LETTER_M>   <LATIN_SMALL_LETTER_M>; <NO_DIACRITIC_MARK>;\
        <LOWER>; IGNORE
<LATIN_CAPITAL_LETTER_M> <LATIN_SMALL_LETTER_M>; <NO_DIACRITIC_MARK>;\
        <UPPER>; IGNORE

<LATIN_SMALL_LETTER_N>   <LATIN_SMALL_LETTER_N>; <NO_DIACRITIC_MARK>;\
        <LOWER>; IGNORE
<LATIN_CAPITAL_LETTER_N> <LATIN_SMALL_LETTER_N>; <NO_DIACRITIC_MARK>;\
        <UPPER>; IGNORE

<LATIN_SMALL_LETTER_N_WITH_TILDE>   <LATIN_SMALL_LETTER_N>; <TILDE_MARK>;\
        <LOWER>; IGNORE
<LATIN_CAPITAL_LETTER_N_WITH_TILDE> <LATIN_SMALL_LETTER_N>; <TILDE_MARK>;\
        <UPPER>; IGNORE

<LATIN_SMALL_LETTER_O>   <LATIN_SMALL_LETTER_O>; <NO_DIACRITIC_MARK>;\
        <LOWER>; IGNORE
<LATIN_CAPITAL_LETTER_O> <LATIN_SMALL_LETTER_O>; <NO_DIACRITIC_MARK>;\
        <UPPER>; IGNORE

<MASCULINE_ORDINAL_INDICATOR> <LATIN_SMALL_LETTER_O>; <SPECIAL_MARK>;\
        <SUPER_LOWERCASE>; IGNORE

<LATIN_SMALL_LETTER_O_WITH_ACUTE>   <LATIN_SMALL_LETTER_O>; <ACUTE_MARK>;\
        <LOWER>; IGNORE
<LATIN_CAPITAL_LETTER_O_WITH_ACUTE> <LATIN_SMALL_LETTER_O>; <ACUTE_MARK>;\
        <UPPER>; IGNORE

<LATIN_SMALL_LETTER_O_WITH_GRAVE>   <LATIN_SMALL_LETTER_O>; <GRAVE_MARK>;\
        <LOWER>; IGNORE
<LATIN_CAPITAL_LETTER_O_WITH_GRAVE> <LATIN_SMALL_LETTER_O>; <GRAVE_MARK>;\
        <UPPER>; IGNORE

<LATIN_SMALL_LETTER_O_WITH_CIRCUMFLEX>   <LATIN_SMALL_LETTER_O>;\
        <CIRCUMFLEX_MARK>; <LOWER>; IGNORE
<LATIN_CAPITAL_LETTER_O_WITH_CIRCUMFLEX> <LATIN_SMALL_LETTER_O>;\
        <CIRCUMFLEX_MARK>; <UPPER>; IGNORE

<LATIN_SMALL_LETTER_O_WITH_TILDE>   <LATIN_SMALL_LETTER_O>; <TILDE_MARK>;\
```

```
        <LOWER>; IGNORE
<LATIN_CAPITAL_LETTER_O_WITH_TILDE> <LATIN_SMALL_LETTER_O>; <TILDE_MARK>;\
        <UPPER>; IGNORE

<LATIN_SMALL_LETTER_O_WITH_DIAERESIS>   <LATIN_SMALL_LETTER_O>;\
        <DIAERESIS_UMLAUT_MARK>; <LOWER>; IGNORE
<LATIN_CAPITAL_LETTER_O_WITH_DIAERESIS> <LATIN_SMALL_LETTER_O>;\
        <DIAERESIS_UMLAUT_MARK>; <UPPER>; IGNORE

<LATIN_SMALL_LETTER_O_WITH_STROKE>   <LATIN_SMALL_LETTER_O>; <STROKE_MARK>;\
        <LOWER>; IGNORE
<LATIN_CAPITAL_LETTER_O_WITH_STROKE> <LATIN_SMALL_LETTER_O>; <STROKE_MARK>;\
        <UPPER>; IGNORE

<LATIN_SMALL_LETTER_P>   <LATIN_SMALL_LETTER_P>; <NO_DIACRITIC_MARK>;\
        <LOWER>; IGNORE
<LATIN_CAPITAL_LETTER_P> <LATIN_SMALL_LETTER_P>; <NO_DIACRITIC_MARK>;\
        <UPPER>; IGNORE

<LATIN_SMALL_LETTER_Q>   <LATIN_SMALL_LETTER_Q>; <NO_DIACRITIC_MARK>;\
        <LOWER>; IGNORE
<LATIN_CAPITAL_LETTER_Q> <LATIN_SMALL_LETTER_Q>; <NO_DIACRITIC_MARK>;\
        <UPPER>; IGNORE

<LATIN_SMALL_LETTER_R>   <LATIN_SMALL_LETTER_R>; <NO_DIACRITIC_MARK>;\
        <LOWER>; IGNORE
<LATIN_CAPITAL_LETTER_R> <LATIN_SMALL_LETTER_R>; <NO_DIACRITIC_MARK>;\
        <UPPER>; IGNORE

<LATIN_SMALL_LETTER_S>   <LATIN_SMALL_LETTER_S>; <NO_DIACRITIC_MARK>;\
        <LOWER>; IGNORE
<LATIN_CAPITAL_LETTER_S> <LATIN_SMALL_LETTER_S>; <NO_DIACRITIC_MARK>;\
        <UPPER>; IGNORE

<LATIN_SMALL_LETTER_SHARP_S_> <LATIN_SMALL_LETTER_S><LATIN_SMALL_LETTER_S>;\
        <LIGATURE_MARK><LIGATURE_MARK>; <LOWER><LOWER>; IGNORE IGNORE

<LATIN_SMALL_LETTER_T>   <LATIN_SMALL_LETTER_T>; <NO_DIACRITIC_MARK>;\
        <LOWER>; IGNORE
<LATIN_CAPITAL_LETTER_T> <LATIN_SMALL_LETTER_T>; <NO_DIACRITIC_MARK>;\
        <UPPER>; IGNORE

<LATIN_SMALL_LETTER_THORN_>   <LATIN_SMALL_LETTER_T><LATIN_SMALL_LETTER_H>;\
        <SPECIAL_MARK><SPECIAL_MARK>; <LOWER><LOWER>; IGNORE IGNORE
<LATIN_CAPITAL_LETTER_THORN_> <LATIN_SMALL_LETTER_T><LATIN_SMALL_LETTER_H>;\
        <SPECIAL_MARK><SPECIAL_MARK>; <UPPER><UPPER>; IGNORE IGNORE

<LATIN_SMALL_LETTER_U>   <LATIN_SMALL_LETTER_U>; <NO_DIACRITIC_MARK>;\
        <LOWER>; IGNORE
```

```
<LATIN_CAPITAL_LETTER_U> <LATIN_SMALL_LETTER_U>; <NO_DIACRITIC_MARK>;\
        <UPPER>; IGNORE

<LATIN_SMALL_LETTER_V>   <LATIN_SMALL_LETTER_V>; <NO_DIACRITIC_MARK>;\
        <LOWER>; IGNORE
<LATIN_CAPITAL_LETTER_V> <LATIN_SMALL_LETTER_V>; <NO_DIACRITIC_MARK>;\
        <UPPER>; IGNORE

<LATIN_SMALL_LETTER_W>   <LATIN_SMALL_LETTER_W>; <NO_DIACRITIC_MARK>;\
        <LOWER>; IGNORE
<LATIN_CAPITAL_LETTER_W> <LATIN_SMALL_LETTER_W>; <NO_DIACRITIC_MARK>;\
        <UPPER>; IGNORE

<LATIN_SMALL_LETTER_X>   <LATIN_SMALL_LETTER_X>; <NO_DIACRITIC_MARK>;\
        <LOWER>; IGNORE
<LATIN_CAPITAL_LETTER_X> <LATIN_SMALL_LETTER_X>; <NO_DIACRITIC_MARK>;\
        <UPPER>; IGNORE

<LATIN_SMALL_LETTER_Y>   <LATIN_SMALL_LETTER_Y>; <NO_DIACRITIC_MARK>;\
        <LOWER>; IGNORE
<LATIN_CAPITAL_LETTER_Y> <LATIN_SMALL_LETTER_Y>; <NO_DIACRITIC_MARK>;\
        <UPPER>; IGNORE

<LATIN_SMALL_LETTER_Y_WITH_ACUTE>   <LATIN_SMALL_LETTER_Y>; <ACUTE_MARK>;\
        <LOWER>; IGNORE
<LATIN_CAPITAL_LETTER_Y_WITH_ACUTE> <LATIN_SMALL_LETTER_Y>; <ACUTE_MARK>;\
        <UPPER>; IGNORE

<LATIN_SMALL_LETTER_Y_WITH_DIAERESIS> <LATIN_SMALL_LETTER_Y>;\
        <DIAERESIS_UMLAUT_MARK>; <LOWER>; IGNORE

<LATIN_SMALL_LETTER_Z>   <LATIN_SMALL_LETTER_Z>; <NO_DIACRITIC_MARK>;\
        <LOWER>; IGNORE
<LATIN_CAPITAL_LETTER_Z> <LATIN_SMALL_LETTER_Z>; <NO_DIACRITIC_MARK>;\
        <UPPER>; IGNORE

<LEFT_PARENTHESIS>  IGNORE ; IGNORE ; IGNORE; <LEFT_PARENTHESIS>
<RIGHT_PARENTHESIS> IGNORE ; IGNORE ; IGNORE; <RIGHT_PARENTHESIS>

order_end

END LC_COLLATE
```

APPENDIX F

Sample Character Map

```
##
##    File: ibm863.cm
##
## CharSet: MS-DOS code page 863
##
## Created: 1994.07.29
##

<code_set_name> "DOS863"

<mb_cur_max> 1
<mb_cur_min> 1

CHARMAP

<NULL> \d0
<WHITE_SMILING_FACE> \d1
<BLACK_SMILING_FACE> \d2
<BLACK_HEART_SUIT> \d3
<BLACK_DIAMOND_SUIT> \d4
<BLACK_CLUB_SUIT> \d5
<BLACK_SPADE_SUIT> \d6
<BULLET> \d7
<INVERSE_BULLET> \d8
<WHITE_CIRCLE> \d9
<INVERSE_WHITE_CIRCLE> \d10
<MALE_SIGN> \d11
<FEMALE_SIGN> \d12
<EIGHTH_NOTE> \d13
<BEAMED_EIGHTH_NOTES> \d14
<WHITE_SUN_WITH_RAYS> \d15
<BLACK_RIGHT-POINTING_POINTER> \d16
<BLACK_LEFT-POINTING_POINTER> \d17
<UP_DOWN_ARROW> \d18
<DOUBLE_EXCLAMATION_MARK> \d19
```

```
<PILCROW_SIGN> \d20
<SECTION_SIGN> \d21
<BLACK_RECTANGLE> \d22
<UP_DOWN_ARROW_WITH_BASE> \d23
<UPWARDS_ARROW> \d24
<DOWNWARDS_ARROW> \d25
<RIGHTWARDS_ARROW> \d26
<LEFTWARDS_ARROW> \d27
<RIGHT_ANGLE> \d28
<LEFT_RIGHT_ARROW> \d29
<BLACK_UP-POINTING_TRIANGLE> \d30
<BLACK_DOWN-POINTING_TRIANGLE> \d31
<SPACE> \d32
<EXCLAMATION_MARK> \d33
<QUOTATION_MARK> \d34
<NUMBER_SIGN> \d35
<DOLLAR_SIGN> \d36
<PERCENT_SIGN> \d37
<AMPERSAND> \d38
<APOSTROPHE> \d39
<LEFT_PARENTHESIS> \d40
<RIGHT_PARENTHESIS> \d41
<ASTERISK> \d42
<PLUS_SIGN> \d43
<COMMA> \d44
<HYPHEN-MINUS> \d45
<FULL_STOP> \d46
<SOLIDUS> \d47
<DIGIT_ZERO> \d48
<DIGIT_ONE> \d49
<DIGIT_TWO> \d50
<DIGIT_THREE> \d51
<DIGIT_FOUR> \d52
<DIGIT_FIVE> \d53
<DIGIT_SIX> \d54
<DIGIT_SEVEN> \d55
<DIGIT_EIGHT> \d56
<DIGIT_NINE> \d57
<COLON> \d58
<SEMICOLON> \d59
<LESS-THAN_SIGN> \d60
<EQUALS_SIGN> \d61
<GREATER-THAN_SIGN> \d62
<QUESTION_MARK> \d63
<COMMERCIAL_AT> \d64
<LATIN_CAPITAL_LETTER_A> \d65
<LATIN_CAPITAL_LETTER_B> \d66
<LATIN_CAPITAL_LETTER_C> \d67
<LATIN_CAPITAL_LETTER_D> \d68
```

```
<LATIN_CAPITAL_LETTER_E> \d69
<LATIN_CAPITAL_LETTER_F> \d70
<LATIN_CAPITAL_LETTER_G> \d71
<LATIN_CAPITAL_LETTER_H> \d72
<LATIN_CAPITAL_LETTER_I> \d73
<LATIN_CAPITAL_LETTER_J> \d74
<LATIN_CAPITAL_LETTER_K> \d75
<LATIN_CAPITAL_LETTER_L> \d76
<LATIN_CAPITAL_LETTER_M> \d77
<LATIN_CAPITAL_LETTER_N> \d78
<LATIN_CAPITAL_LETTER_O> \d79
<LATIN_CAPITAL_LETTER_P> \d80
<LATIN_CAPITAL_LETTER_Q> \d81
<LATIN_CAPITAL_LETTER_R> \d82
<LATIN_CAPITAL_LETTER_S> \d83
<LATIN_CAPITAL_LETTER_T> \d84
<LATIN_CAPITAL_LETTER_U> \d85
<LATIN_CAPITAL_LETTER_V> \d86
<LATIN_CAPITAL_LETTER_W> \d87
<LATIN_CAPITAL_LETTER_X> \d88
<LATIN_CAPITAL_LETTER_Y> \d89
<LATIN_CAPITAL_LETTER_Z> \d90
<LEFT_SQUARE_BRACKET> \d91
<REVERSE_SOLIDUS> \d92
<RIGHT_SQUARE_BRACKET> \d93
<CIRCUMFLEX_ACCENT> \d94
<LOW_LINE> \d95
<GRAVE_ACCENT> \d96
<LATIN_SMALL_LETTER_A> \d97
<LATIN_SMALL_LETTER_B> \d98
<LATIN_SMALL_LETTER_C> \d99
<LATIN_SMALL_LETTER_D> \d100
<LATIN_SMALL_LETTER_E> \d101
<LATIN_SMALL_LETTER_F> \d102
<LATIN_SMALL_LETTER_G> \d103
<LATIN_SMALL_LETTER_H> \d104
<LATIN_SMALL_LETTER_I> \d105
<LATIN_SMALL_LETTER_J> \d106
<LATIN_SMALL_LETTER_K> \d107
<LATIN_SMALL_LETTER_L> \d108
<LATIN_SMALL_LETTER_M> \d109
<LATIN_SMALL_LETTER_N> \d110
<LATIN_SMALL_LETTER_O> \d111
<LATIN_SMALL_LETTER_P> \d112
<LATIN_SMALL_LETTER_Q> \d113
<LATIN_SMALL_LETTER_R> \d114
<LATIN_SMALL_LETTER_S> \d115
<LATIN_SMALL_LETTER_T> \d116
<LATIN_SMALL_LETTER_U> \d117
```

```
<LATIN_SMALL_LETTER_V> \d118
<LATIN_SMALL_LETTER_W> \d119
<LATIN_SMALL_LETTER_X> \d120
<LATIN_SMALL_LETTER_Y> \d121
<LATIN_SMALL_LETTER_Z> \d122
<LEFT_CURLY_BRACKET> \d123
<VERTICAL_LINE> \d124
<RIGHT_CURLY_BRACKET> \d125
<TILDE> \d126
<HOUSE> \d127
<LATIN_CAPITAL_LETTER_C_WITH_CEDILLA> \d128
<LATIN_SMALL_LETTER_U_WITH_DIAERESIS> \d129
<LATIN_SMALL_LETTER_E_WITH_ACUTE> \d130
<LATIN_SMALL_LETTER_A_WITH_CIRCUMFLEX> \d131
<LATIN_CAPITAL_LETTER_A_WITH_CIRCUMFLEX> \d132
<LATIN_SMALL_LETTER_A_WITH_GRAVE> \d133
<PILCROW_SIGN> \d134
<LATIN_SMALL_LETTER_C_WITH_CEDILLA> \d135
<LATIN_SMALL_LETTER_E_WITH_CIRCUMFLEX> \d136
<LATIN_SMALL_LETTER_E_WITH_DIAERESIS> \d137
<LATIN_SMALL_LETTER_E_WITH_GRAVE> \d138
<LATIN_SMALL_LETTER_I_WITH_DIAERESIS> \d139
<LATIN_SMALL_LETTER_I_WITH_CIRCUMFLEX> \d140
<DOUBLE_LOW_LINE> \d141
<LATIN_CAPITAL_LETTER_A_WITH_GRAVE> \d142
<SECTION_SIGN> \d143
<LATIN_CAPITAL_LETTER_E_WITH_ACUTE> \d144
<LATIN_CAPITAL_LETTER_E_WITH_GRAVE> \d145
<LATIN_CAPITAL_LETTER_E_WITH_CIRCUMFLEX> \d146
<LATIN_SMALL_LETTER_O_WITH_CIRCUMFLEX> \d147
<LATIN_CAPITAL_LETTER_E_WITH_DIAERESIS> \d148
<LATIN_CAPITAL_LETTER_I_WITH_DIAERESIS> \d149
<LATIN_SMALL_LETTER_U_WITH_CIRCUMFLEX> \d150
<LATIN_SMALL_LETTER_U_WITH_GRAVE> \d151
<CURRENCY_SIGN> \d152
<LATIN_CAPITAL_LETTER_O_WITH_CIRCUMFLEX> \d153
<LATIN_CAPITAL_LETTER_U_WITH_DIAERESIS> \d154
<CENT_SIGN> \d155
<POUND_SIGN> \d156
<LATIN_CAPITAL_LETTER_U_WITH_GRAVE> \d157
<LATIN_CAPITAL_LETTER_U_WITH_CIRCUMFLEX> \d158
<LATIN_SMALL_LETTER_F_WITH_HOOK> \d159
<BROKEN_BAR> \d160
<ACUTE_ACCENT> \d161
<LATIN_SMALL_LETTER_O_WITH_ACUTE> \d162
<LATIN_SMALL_LETTER_U_WITH_ACUTE> \d163
<DIAERESIS> \d164
<CEDILLA> \d165
<SUPERSCRIPT_THREE> \d166
```

```
<MACRON> \d167
<LATIN_CAPITAL_LETTER_I_WITH_CIRCUMFLEX> \d168
<REVERSED_NOT_SIGN> \d169
<NOT_SIGN> \d170
<VULGAR_FRACTION_ONE_HALF> \d171
<VULGAR_FRACTION_ONE_QUARTER> \d172
<VULGAR_FRACTION_THREE_QUARTERS> \d173
<LEFT-POINTING_DOUBLE_ANGLE_QUOTATION_MARK> \d174
<RIGHT-POINTING_DOUBLE_ANGLE_QUOTATION_MARK> \d175
<LIGHT_SHADE> \d176
<MEDIUM_SHADE> \d177
<DARK_SHADE> \d178
<BOX_DRAWINGS_LIGHT_VERTICAL> \d179
<BOX_DRAWINGS_LIGHT_VERTICAL_AND_LEFT> \d180
<BOX_DRAWINGS_VERTICAL_SINGLE_AND_LEFT_DOUBLE> \d181
<BOX_DRAWINGS_VERTICAL_DOUBLE_AND_LEFT_SINGLE> \d182
<BOX_DRAWINGS_DOWN_DOUBLE_AND_LEFT_SINGLE> \d183
<BOX_DRAWINGS_DOWN_SINGLE_AND_LEFT_DOUBLE> \d184
<BOX_DRAWINGS_DOUBLE_VERTICAL_AND_LEFT> \d185
<BOX_DRAWINGS_DOUBLE_VERTICAL> \d186
<BOX_DRAWINGS_DOUBLE_DOWN_AND_LEFT> \d187
<BOX_DRAWINGS_DOUBLE_UP_AND_LEFT> \d188
<BOX_DRAWINGS_UP_DOUBLE_AND_LEFT_SINGLE> \d189
<BOX_DRAWINGS_UP_SINGLE_AND_LEFT_DOUBLE> \d190
<BOX_DRAWINGS_LIGHT_DOWN_AND_LEFT> \d191
<BOX_DRAWINGS_LIGHT_UP_AND_RIGHT> \d192
<BOX_DRAWINGS_LIGHT_UP_AND_HORIZONTAL> \d193
<BOX_DRAWINGS_LIGHT_DOWN_AND_HORIZONTAL> \d194
<BOX_DRAWINGS_LIGHT_VERTICAL_AND_RIGHT> \d195
<BOX_DRAWINGS_LIGHT_HORIZONTAL> \d196
<BOX_DRAWINGS_LIGHT_VERTICAL_AND_HORIZONTAL> \d197
<BOX_DRAWINGS_VERTICAL_SINGLE_AND_RIGHT_DOUBLE> \d198
<BOX_DRAWINGS_VERTICAL_DOUBLE_AND_RIGHT_SINGLE> \d199
<BOX_DRAWINGS_DOUBLE_UP_AND_RIGHT> \d200
<BOX_DRAWINGS_DOUBLE_DOWN_AND_RIGHT> \d201
<BOX_DRAWINGS_DOUBLE_UP_AND_HORIZONTAL> \d202
<BOX_DRAWINGS_DOUBLE_DOWN_AND_HORIZONTAL> \d203
<BOX_DRAWINGS_DOUBLE_VERTICAL_AND_RIGHT> \d204
<BOX_DRAWINGS_DOUBLE_HORIZONTAL> \d205
<BOX_DRAWINGS_DOUBLE_VERTICAL_AND_HORIZONTAL> \d206
<BOX_DRAWINGS_UP_SINGLE_AND_HORIZONTAL_DOUBLE> \d207
<BOX_DRAWINGS_UP_DOUBLE_AND_HORIZONTAL_SINGLE> \d208
<BOX_DRAWINGS_DOWN_SINGLE_AND_HORIZONTAL_DOUBLE> \d209
<BOX_DRAWINGS_DOWN_DOUBLE_AND_HORIZONTAL_SINGLE> \d210
<BOX_DRAWINGS_UP_DOUBLE_AND_RIGHT_SINGLE> \d211
<BOX_DRAWINGS_UP_SINGLE_AND_RIGHT_DOUBLE> \d212
<BOX_DRAWINGS_DOWN_SINGLE_AND_RIGHT_DOUBLE> \d213
<BOX_DRAWINGS_DOWN_DOUBLE_AND_RIGHT_SINGLE> \d214
<BOX_DRAWINGS_VERTICAL_DOUBLE_AND_HORIZONTAL_SINGLE> \d215
```

```
<BOX_DRAWINGS_VERTICAL_SINGLE_AND_HORIZONTAL_DOUBLE> \d216
<BOX_DRAWINGS_LIGHT_UP_AND_LEFT> \d217
<BOX_DRAWINGS_LIGHT_DOWN_AND_RIGHT> \d218
<FULL_BLOCK> \d219
<LOWER_HALF_BLOCK> \d220
<LEFT_HALF_BLOCK> \d221
<RIGHT_HALF_BLOCK> \d222
<UPPER_HALF_BLOCK> \d223
<GREEK_SMALL_LETTER_ALPHA> \d224
<LATIN_SMALL_LETTER_SHARP_S> \d225
<GREEK_CAPITAL_LETTER_GAMMA> \d226
<GREEK_SMALL_LETTER_PI> \d227
<GREEK_CAPITAL_LETTER_SIGMA> \d228
<GREEK_SMALL_LETTER_SIGMA> \d229
<MICRO_SIGN> \d230
<GREEK_SMALL_LETTER_TAU> \d231
<GREEK_CAPITAL_LETTER_PHI> \d232
<GREEK_CAPITAL_LETTER_THETA> \d233
<GREEK_CAPITAL_LETTER_OMEGA> \d234
<GREEK_SMALL_LETTER_DELTA> \d235
<INFINITY> \d236
<GREEK_SMALL_LETTER_PHI> \d237
<GREEK_SMALL_LETTER_EPSILON> \d238
<INTERSECTION> \d239
<IDENTICAL_TO> \d240
<PLUS-MINUS_SIGN> \d241
<GREATER-THAN_OR_EQUAL_TO> \d242
<LESS-THAN_OR_EQUAL_TO> \d243
<TOP_HALF_INTEGRAL> \d244
<BOTTOM_HALF_INTEGRAL> \d245
<DIVISION_SIGN> \d246
<ALMOST_EQUAL_TO> \d247
<DEGREE_SIGN> \d248
<BULLET_OPERATOR> \d249
<MIDDLE_DOT> \d250
<SQUARE_ROOT> \d251
<SUPERSCRIPT_LATIN_SMALL_LETTER_N> \d252
<SUPERSCRIPT_TWO> \d253
<BLACK_SQUARE> \d254
<NO-BREAK_SPACE> \d255

END CHARMAP
```

Bibliography

Bach, James. *The Persistence of Ad Hoc Testing,* presented at 10th International Conference on Software Testing, Washington D.C., 1993.

Lunde, Ken, *Understanding Japanese Information Processing,* O'Reilly & Associates, Inc., 1993.

Code for the Representation of Names of Countries, International Standard ISO 3166, International Organization for Standardization, 1988.

Code for the Representation of Names of Languages, International Standard ISO 639, International Organization for Standardization, 1988.

Information Technology—Portable Operating System Interface (POSIX)—Part 1: System Application Program Interface (API) [C Language], ISO/IEC 9945-1, IEEE Std 1003.1, 1st edition, 1990-12-07, Institute of Electrical and Electronics Engineers, Inc.

Information Technology—Portable Operating System Interface (POSIX), Part 2: Shell and Utilities, ISO/IEC 9945-2, ANSI/IEEE Std 1003.2, 1st edition, 1993-12-22, volumes I and II.

International Handbook for Software Design, Microsoft Corporation, 1993.

National Language Support Reference Manual, International Business Machines Corporation, 2nd edition, March 1990.

The Unicode Standard: Worldwide Character Encoding, Version 1.0, Volume 1, The Unicode Consortium, Addison-Wesley, 1991, Unicode Inc.

The Unicode Standard: Worldwide Character Encoding, Version 1.0, Volume 2, The Unicode Consortium, Addison-Wesley, 1992, Unicode Inc.

Index

Index

Index